The Order of Forms

The Order of Forms

Realism, Formalism, and Social Space

ANNA KORNBLUH

The University of Chicago Press
Chicago and London

The University of Chicago Press, Chicago 60637
The University of Chicago Press, Ltd., London

Published 2019
Printed in the United States of America

28 27 26 25 24 23 22 21 20 19   1 2 3 4 5

ISBN-13: 978-0-226-65320-4 (cloth)
ISBN-13: 978-0-226-65334-1 (paper)
ISBN-13: 978-0-226-65348-8 (e-book)
DOI: https://doi.org/10.7208/chicago/9780226653488.001.0001

The University of Chicago Press gratefully acknowledges the generous support of the University of Illinois at Chicago toward publication of this book.

Library of Congress Cataloging-in-Publication Data

Names: Kornbluh, Anna, author.
Title: The order of forms : realism, formalism, and social space / Anna Kornbluh.
Description: Chicago ; London : The University of Chicago Press, 2019.| Includes bibliographical references and index.
Identifiers: LCCN 20190191131 | ISBN 9780226653204 (cloth : alk. paper) | ISBN 9780226653341 (pbk. : alk. paper) | ISBN 9780226653488 (ebook)
Subjects: LCSH: Formalism (Literary analysis) | Criticism.
Classification: LCC PN98.F6 K675 2019 | DDC 801/.95—dc23
LC record available at https://lccn.loc.gov/2019019113

♾ This paper meets the requirements of ANSI/NISO Z39.48-1992 (Permanence of Paper).

to the collective of my brilliant friends

Contents

Figures

Acknowledgments

Forms make relations possible. And relations in turn enable other forms. The form of this book is owing to the institution of the university, that standing formation for the universal, which even amid its irrevocable structural adjustment still provided me with one of the last tenure-track jobs, with eager students, with stimulating programming, with sabbatical leave, with research funding, with a Dean's Award for publication support, and with devoted colleagues. At the University of Illinois at Chicago, I thank the United Faculty Union, the professors serving intensely to run the institution, such as my talented department heads Lisa Freeman and Walter Benn Michaels, the dazzling conversationalists Nasser Mufti, Peter Coviello, Helen Jun, Nicholas Brown, Sunil Agnani, Mark Canuel, Jennifer Ashton, Rachel Havrelock, Stephen Engelmann, Elise Archias, and Blake Stimson, and the inspiring students Rithika Ramamurthy, Mary Hale, Davis Smith Brecheisen, Robert Ryan, Justin Raden, Heidi Smith, and Corbin Hiday (and Corbin, again, for indispensable research assistance and manuscript preparation).

Brittany Amoroso, Rithika Ramamurthy, and Sarah Marie Coogan, along with Mr. Mike and Ms. Dylan of Jewish Community Youth Services, took loving care of my tiny child for thousands of hours while I eked out these pages. Chicago Public Schools are supporting her wonderfully in kindergarten as I type this.

At home, the Inter Chicago Circle for Experimental Critical Theory (InterCcECT), especially Adam Kotsko and Christopher Breu, promotes all the best speculative abstraction, while nearby comrades Julie Orlemanski, Benjamin Morgan, Ariel Kalil, Sianne Ngai, Jude Stewart, Seth Brodsky, Liesl Olson, Kate Marshall, Zach Samalin, Eric Santner, Kasia Bartoszynska, Andrew Cutrofello, and Lauren Berlant make every day sparkle. Outside

Chicago, the friendship and mentorship of Caroline Levine, Jodi Dean, Julia Reinhard Lupton, Todd McGowan, Emily Steinlight, Steven Miller, Audrey Wasser, Rob Lehman, Elizabeth Anker, Nathan Hensley, Russ Sbriglia, Leigh Claire La Berge, Janet Neary, Tim Bewes, and Eleanor Courtemanche sustain it all. The V21 Collective has provided constant impetus for bolder ideas and bigger parties. Journals, presses, and the collaborative labor behind them expansively host our work; I thank *The Henry James Review, Novel: A Forum on Fiction*, and *Theory & Event* for permission to reprint portions of work they originally platformed, and the manuscript reviewers, editors, and the rest of the staff of the University of Chicago Press for producing this book.

Engaging audiences, sharp students, and warm hosts at Brown University, Cornell University, Harvard University, the University of Notre Dame, Stanford University, the University of Pennsylvania, Yale University, Humboldt University of Berlin, the University of Bern, Concordia University of Montreal, the University of Southern Denmark, and the fabulous publics of the University at Buffalo (SUNY), Illinois State University, Indiana University, the University of Washington, the University of Arizona, and the University of California, Berkeley, built the arguments outward and upward.

The generosity of my instituted family renews me daily. I am grateful to my giving grandparents, my architect dad, my constructive mom, my brilliant brother, my kind in-laws, my Ezra, and my Mira Blue.

I thank my city, my house, my libraries, my trains, and my parks, and so very many beautiful novels, for marvelous models of what forms do. Make new collectives!

*

Chapter 1 appeared as "The Realist Blueprint" in *The Henry James Review*, 36, no. 3 (2015): 199–211, © 2015 The Johns Hopkins University Press; chapter 5 appeared as "Obscure Forms," in *Novel: A Forum on Fiction* 48, no. 1 (2015): 1–17; and chapter 6 appeared as "States of Psychoanalysis," in *Theory & Event* 19, no. 3 (July 2016), muse.jhu.edu/article/623989.

Introduction

The Order of Forms: Mathematic, Aesthetic, and Political Formalisms

> It is evident that the polis belongs to the class of things that exist by nature, and that man is by nature a political animal.
>
> —ARISTOTLE, *Politics*

> One day humanity will play with law just as children play with disused objects, not in order to restore them to their canonical use but to free them from it for good.
>
> —AGAMBEN, *State of Exception*

Literary critics do not generally think of their work as building. We prize particularities, revere sublimities, linger with the singular; or we document discourses, quantify patterns, and accumulate information about the past; or we break down popular pleasures, dismantle generalizations, and anatomize domination. Easy as it might be to name the tensions among these principles—between, say, a certain deconstructive regard for the unique turning of tropes and a certain scientistic regard for indexing "semantic units"—there remains uniform in so many literary critical practices a code of particularizing and concretizing, of destabilizing norms, disassembling systems, undoing universals—of taking things apart. This particulate ethos coincides with predominant contemporary logics in fields beyond literary criticism (in philosophy and political theory and history) working against abstraction: ending metaphysics, impugning grand narratives, spurning institutions. Prominent theoretical traditions like Nietzschean genealogy, Benjaminian materialism, Foucauldian historicism, feminism, and deconstruction—and, more immediately, the literary critical reflexes shaped by these traditions—exalt unmaking and unbuilding, rejecting in building such dubious forays as constitution, synthesis, form itself.

Recent debates in literary study strike clumsily at this consensus without fully discerning it, positing a methodological hegemony of "critique" and "symptomatic reading" that results in too much distance from literature.[1] For detractors, critique aggrandizes the critic, implementing a spatial orientation of vertical distance and detachment from cultural production, while the alternatives of postcritique, attachment, description, and surface reading promote instead a horizontal flat ontology, a planarity of distributed agency in which, as its premier exponent, Bruno Latour, puts it, "nothing is, by itself, either reducible or irreducible to anything else."[2] Yet, even as these innovations proclaim their intention to break with a theoretical, methodological, and political status quo, they preserve those very mores of molar disassembling that stand as anathema to building. Even, that is, as postcritique has endeavored to articulate literary study's insufficient affirmations, its terms of engagement and entailed spatial logics have maintained the truly dominant underlying orientation of taking things apart, immanentizing interactivity of singular individualities, resisting constructivist projects.

There is no better encapsulation of the extent of this attitude than the spectacularly influential philosopher Giorgio Agamben's summation of his best-selling *Homo Sacer* trilogy:

> Life is not in itself political. . . . If to constituent power there correspond revolutions, revolts, and new constitutions, namely, a violence that puts in place and constitutes a new law, for *destituent potential* it is necessary to think entirely different strategies.[3]

"Destituent potential" (from the Latin *destituens*: "forsaking," "abandoning") opposes constituent power: building things up, making life in collectivities through revolution, constitution, and law. Conflating constituting with violence, Agamben conjures an alternative in destituent chaos, the flow of vitality without constitution, structure, order, or form. For Agamben and the critical matrix he epitomizes, "one day humanity will . . . be free from (law) for good"; freedom means nothing more than destituent play, deforming and unforming, ceaseless tearing down. Formlessness becomes the ideal uniting a variety of theories, from the mosh of the multitude to the localization of microstruggle and microaggression, from the voluntarist assembly of actors and networks to the flow of affects untethered from constructs, from the deification of irony and incompletion to the culminating conviction that life springs forth without form and thrives in form's absence. Noting its characteristic horizon of *an-arche*, the "without of order," we might deem this beatific fantasy of formless life "anarcho-vitalism."

This pervasive political lament of form's order has profoundly shaped the study of aesthetic form and the tradition of articulating aesthetics and politics. Since the middle of the twentieth century, when human beings dramatically escalated the means, technologies, and purviews of political conflict through worldwide war, nuclear fission, and the Final Solution, the domains of philosophical and artistic inquiry termed "critical theory" have addressed the interactions of politics and aesthetics. Thinkers such as Theodor Adorno, Walter Benjamin, and Slavoj Žižek have asked what happens when the inevitability of political strife is represented in, dispelled through, or fueled by aesthetic media such as slogans, propaganda, graphic design, photography, dance, and literature. In its earliest incarnations, this discourse warned that one of the very most insidious tendencies of human association—fascism—could be dubbed "the aestheticization of politics": treating the unending antagonisms and deliberations and improvisations of political existence as if soluble by the imposition of the ideal unities emblematized in the hermeticism of art for art's sake.[4] Aesthetics become incriminated for their boundedness—to give form is to oppressively contain—with the upshot that the study of art favors fragmentation, unmaking, decomposition. Privileging modernism over realism, openness over closure, transgression over synthesis, irony over telos, methodological protocols and theoretical truisms in the study of art have celebrated forms that undo their own formedness and have imagined politics as demolition. The value of what forms build recedes.

Notably, the very latest theories of aesthetics and politics invert many of the Frankfurt School's precepts, while nonetheless continuing to elevate disruption and unsettling above forming and building. Jacques Rancière and Caroline Levine have both markedly revalorized the aestheticization of politics by arguing that far from being an epiphenomenon dispelling politics, aesthetics amount to the core of politics: arrangement, patterning, and ordering of the socialities and indeed of the sensory bodily experience of everyday life. For Rancière, politics signals the designed configuration of social relations, including who counts as a subject, who can be heard or recognized by political institutions, what counts as a collective, and the corresponding constitution of the sensorium.[5] When kinetic design arrests in an order, that order equates to "the police." Hence, disruption shimmers as a means that is its own end. Such centralization of the aesthetics proper to politics gives rise to a vision of politics as finally about disruption itself. What is more, the exuberant energies of distributing sensation appear to exceed the determining forces that prevent aesthetic play from fully transforming political relations—namely, the domination of political assignations by the contradictions of the capitalist mode of production. Excising determination of this type is an explicit principle for Caroline Levine, whose theses on form depart from "too strong an analytic emphasis on deep structures" like "causality" to explore alternatives of "social *dis*organization."[6] In her groundbreaking *Forms: Whole, Rhythm, Hierarchy, Network* Levine defines "form" as "all shapes and configurations, all ordering principles, all patterns of repetition and difference"[7] and reconstructs formalism as a crucial tool for social analysis, since it has "the potential to unsettle conventional, rigid social and conceptual forms";[8] she similarly concludes the book by according the savvy formalist the emancipatory political agency of "refusing to join hierarchies and escaping from enclosing shapes."[9]

Against this ubiquity of unsettling and unmaking, *The Order of Forms* embraces projects of building. As its title suggests, the book principally affirms the order made by forms and the forms made by order. Form is composed relationality. Little precedes this composed relationality, yet the lure of formlessness is powerful and distorting. Against this lure, I argue that forming is a value unto itself: a value that animates literature, and a value that formalist literary critics can embrace as an alternative to destituent theory. Formalism should study how to compose and to direct—rather than ceaselessly oppose—form, formalization, and forms of sociability. A formalism that professes such constituency might be deemed "political formalism" on account of its willingness to entertain the political imagining that can issue from studying forms, and even more so because its elementary affirmation addresses the formed quality of the political as such. Contrary to the destituent paradigm's ideal of formlessness, a formalism of the political avouches the constitution and agency of forms, underscoring that life itself essentially depends upon composed relations, institutions, states. If such a formalism were to animate critical appraisals, we might find new opportunities for engaging with aesthetic productions as sites for and modalities of thinking about this essentiality, for mediating social building, for building in criticism projects for social composition.

Political formalism evaluates form's composedness and form's agency—the contingent and emergent quality of form's relationality, the dispensation of interrelation and what relations make possible—and thereby approaches politics and aesthetics from the purview of the constitution of social form, not just destituent dismantling. Where anarcho-vitalism refuses form and deplores standing formations of the sort epitomized by the state, instead elevating hybridity, evanescence, and particularity, political formalism ratifies form itself. It admits the fundamentality of formal collectivities and formalized sociability; it avows structuration in general, thus chartering improvisation and contestation. In a context in which scholars rallying under the banners of surface reading, postcritique, the descriptive turn, cognitive studies, and some strains of affect theory have arguably resigned criticism's political aims, and in the now permanent emergency imperiling university study of literature, I contend that formalism not only comprises the central proficiency of literary critics, but also funds their unique worldly purchase: ideas about making, about making relations, about making spaces and orders deliberately and justly.

The study of literary form is at root the analysis of how language furnishes a medium for composing sustained repetitions, delimited contours, performative conjurings, and synthetic abstractions. Experts in these constructions are equipped, I contend, to understand and even engineer parallel formations in the phenomenal realm of everyday life, in everyday spaces in everyday institutions, as these too emerge in the medium of language. What norms ought be supported by such constructions is a question for collective answering; but I do propose that a constructive commitment—a formalist commitment to the essentiality of form, to its ontological dimension, to the marvels of building—amounts to its own norm, since its aims differ so dramatically from the destituent paradigm. Embracing form serves as the foundation for projects to constitute and institute collective values; regarding form as essential for living serves as the foundation for other normative claims to justice, such as the equitable benefit from form's provisions.

To confirm in this way the substratum of constructed justice is admittedly a utopian gesture, in the strict sense of utopia defined by Ernst Bloch as the endeavor to build "a space adequate for human beings."[10] One intuition of this book is that such utopianism remains a strength of Marxian materialism, the study of human social existence that distinguishes itself from the idealist study of human intellectual capacity while sustaining its own ideal: a normative pursuit of better collectivities. Revolutionary reconfiguration of social relations must be guided by a commitment to relationality as such, and by the attendant work for alternate forms for interdependence, material thriving, and distribution of goods and powers. Marxism does not constitute a technical manual for how to design such forms—that we cannot prescribe in advance is a complement of revolution's relentlessness, the unending "real movement to abolish the present state of things."[11] Yet this social process of ongoing instituting should not be confused for permanent unmaking. As I develop more below, Marxism imparts a formalist commitment to the ontological dimension of form, alongside the communist formula "from each according to his ability, to each according to his needs."[12] Drawing on this materialist legacy, *The Order of Forms* holds axiomatically that humans cannot exist without forms that scaffold sociability, even though the particular forms that human sociality takes are not fixed. Laws for the making of life are foundational, but no foundational law lives. This ontological claim provides a unique ground for rethinking aesthetics and politics: human beings make—emergently, unwittingly, spontaneously—the forms on which their lives depend. Politics, in this materialist view, becomes more than the venture for formlessness; it is the struggle to create a just collective amidst desperate interdependence, the struggle to infrastructuralize flourishing above immiseration, the struggle to contrive spaces adequate for human beings even as we recognize the ungroundedness of every space. The work of building—not just resisting but reconstituting; not just breaking forms but making new ones; not just performative disruption but scaled construction—founds affirmative orders. Pursuant to this materialist affirmative politics follow revised theses on aesthetics. Neither the false resolution of contradiction nor the perpetual displacement of order, aesthetics would then be the rendering sensuous of forms and formalization, rendering their produced quality, their madeness, so as to stir thinking about contour and about making and about flourishing. Architecture or photography or the novel might each in their own ways invite reflection on social composition, lavishing their mediations beyond the bounds of immediate phenomenal experience. The forms in art may themselves theorize the forms in life, and questions of social configuration may be abstractly posed in art in ways that the concretude of experience blocks.

In granting aesthetics this agency for thinking, I appeal to Kantian motifs, as I discuss in more detail to come, and I diverge significantly from the political aesthetics of Rancière and Levine by invoking the Marxian notion of "mediation."[13] Mediation marks the dialectic proper to aesthetics. Just as materialist dialectics considers the history of social relations in the interest of their future, it appraises cultural productions in their relative autonomy. From origins in Aristotle's esteem for the virtues of the intermediate, to articulations in Hegel's project for self-reflective epistemology, mediation names for Marx the materialist critique of immediacy in Hegel, and ultimately synonymizes labor itself, that social activity of reciprocal transformation between nature and humans.[14] Raymond Williams usefully posits mediation as "a positive process in social reality," stressing the varieties of agency in the "interaction between separate forces" that is the "relationship of society and art."[15] In strict concurrence with Marxism's conception of the communist future as an outgrowth of the capitalist present, dialectics allow that aesthetic representations do more than reflect the conditions and context of their production; art acts upon extant relations, even and especially when it projects inexistent relations. In *Realizing Capital* I referred to this mediating faculty as "aesthetic thinking," and *The Order of Forms* pursues this thinking to its abstract and synthetic culminations, finding in aesthetic production inspiration for new figuring, projecting, building.

This Marxist emphasis on the aesthetic capacity for thinking runs counter to routine literary criticism. Although we often cherish literature's concretization—its texturizing of lived experience, its sensualization of language, its specification of social constructs—in this book I advocate for its unique abstractions. I argue throughout for recognizing those abstractions in the plastic syntheses by which novels suspensively integrate multiple ideas, and in the projective models of relations through which literary realism discloses the ungroundedness of all socialities while building them up anyway. Attending to these literary abstractions opens up the power of literary form to reveal and revalue the abstractions at work in social life, including ideology and institutions, laws and calculations, and our foundationless socius itself.

Projects of Mathematical Formalism

Political formalism takes inspiration from recent, disparate efforts to reinvent formalism in literary criticism.[16] But an odder source sparked it first: math. The specific understanding of formalism from which I launch this study hails from the nineteenth-century moment of Marx, of the first uses of "formalism" in English, of the aestheticism that has long been associated with formalism—and of the less studied revolutionary advent of *mathematical* formalism. Mathematical formalism radically redefines the scope and methods of math, elevating abstractions and their internal consistency above phenomena and their experiential measure. Prior to such redefinition, the conventional mathematical realism yoked mathematical signs to real things. Afterward, mathematical formalism valued the power of signs to exceed experiential reality and even to project rigorously consistent hypothetical realities.[17] Formalist mathematics therefore crystallizes what forms do: provide structure for new possibles. *The Order of Forms* wields this crystal to refract the form-thinking in the better-known discourses of the same moment, Marxian materialism and literary realism. Common to math, Marxism, and the novel in the nineteenth century is an extraordinary promotion of form as the construction of possible relations; this commonality can and should inspire a more constructive theoretical criticism in the twenty-first.

Originative Victorian mathematicians like George Boole, Augustus De Morgan, and William Stanley Jevons established formalist math as the prizing of logic, interrelation, and the integrity of rigorous representations above and beyond the correspondence that anchored classical mathematics. Where for a classicist, the formula for the area of a triangle corresponds to triangles in nature and reality, for a formalist the value of a formula depends upon its integral coherence and therefore upon what in excess of nature or present reality it renders thinkable. Take infinity. One way to think of it is as something available to perception but requiring a long time to count it up. In this view, experience remains a portal to reality, if only we could overcome finite bodies to go on counting forever. Formalism poses an alternative way to think about infinity, as unavailable to perception but nonetheless thinkable or writable. Instead of privileging the immediacy of experience (counting it up), formalism favors the mediacy of signification (algebraic letters and symbols). We cannot count infinity, but we can write it. Valuing in this way the mathematical symbol and the system in which it functions over and above the meaning that might be attributed to it, formalist mathematics also values the coherence of axioms and formulas over their correlation to or description of real objects, and values the perfection of abstraction over, and through, its ungroundedness; it values the force of structural interrelationships over any putative outside of structure. Such valuing makes formalist math at once a cardinal precursor to formalist aesthetics, as Andrea Henderson has ably explored, and also a framework for theorizing political formalism.[18] In mathematics, form itself affords liberation from the bounds of the actual. Conceiving politics as the flight toward formlessness overlooks the practical marvel of politics as the fight for forming; building up and writing down institute new socialities.

Mathematical formalism thus powerfully recognizes what forms *do*: forms inscribe, thereby making relations among abstractions fathomable and reconfigurable. Rather than describing already extant entities, formalist math imagines possible relations among possible entities. As the historian Morris Kline describes the non-Euclidean break, it "forced the realization that mathematics is not portraying laws inherent in the design of the universe but is merely providing man-made schemes or models which we can use."[19] Although axiomatically imposed and fabricated by human minds, these laws usefully inscribe schemas of relationships and introduce ways of organizing thought that then in turn put new schemas and new organizations within grasp. In this enabling modeling mathematical formalism emphatically forecasts political formalism. Mathematical formalism involves the acknowledgment and affirmation of the madeness and therefore ungroundedness of laws and states of relationality, an approach that could mightily revise political theorizing.

The utopian prospects of formalist mathematics grow from its approach to inscription and form, to make-ability and malleability and untold horizons. They lodge as well in its main content, the radicalization of *space*. Spaces beyond the immediately perceptible orientate formalization, which inquires into the foreign laws that might govern hyperspace, the drastically different configurations of space coextensive with familiar arrangements on a Hegelian plane, the necessity that infinitely extending space abut its own others, and the heterotopic volume of completely alteritous infinity. These commitments to the fathoming and projection of nowheres and elsewheres and anywheres comprise the utopian inclination of mathematical formalism, and suggest that spatial dispensations like art and politics work intrinsically with the utopian imperative to multiply space.

The imaginative projection of other spaces powerfully links formalist mathematics with literature. The two share as well a distinctive relationship to the *letter*, to inscription in excess of signification. Mathematics formalizes the dimension of the literary that escapes conventional aesthetics, since it embraces the graphic letter as the only object of mathematical inquiry. One of the earliest histories of formalist math, by Clarence Lewis in 1918, defined formalism as "a mathematical system . . . [of] operations performed according to rules which are independent of any meaning assigned to the marks.[20] This sidestepping of meaning was an explicit and reiterated principle, elevated to an almost axiomatic status. As Felix Hausdorff had it in 1904 in his manuscript "Formalism," "Mathematics totally disregards the actual significance conveyed to its concepts, the actual validity that one can accord to its theorems. Its indefinable concepts are arbitrarily chosen objects of thought and its axioms are arbitrarily, albeit consistently, chosen relations among these objects."[21] The historian of mathematics Catarina Dutilh Novaes describes this estrangement engendered by the letter as "de-semantification": writing the letters in mathematical inscription as "purely formal amounts to viewing symbols as blueprints (inscriptions) with no meaning at all—as pure mathematical objects and thus no longer as signs properly speaking."[22]

Blueprints with no meaning, projections without signification, the letter-strewn formulae of formalist mathematics attend to the letter of language in what Jacques Lacan refers to as its "material substrate," its performative nonsense, its sheer inscription that produces without referring.[23] The letter is here not the sign of an absent thing, but rather a mark of something that cannot be read, that cannot be assimilated to intuition, experience, phenomenality. An act, not a revelation. *The Order of Forms* finds its animating drive in these fortuitous acts. How does the letter generate the constituting of new spaces? The readings in these pages wager that form itself, in its very contentlessness, operates freedom: that every form is open to deployment, debate, and deformation; that every form is open to the promise of building differently; that every form performs elementary construction in the spirit of collective life.

The mathematical motifs of affirming the letter, radicalizing space, and lauding abstraction prompt many of this book's questions and figure many of its answers. Formalist mathematics serves this enabling function for my arguments somewhat abstractly—as a guiding style of thought rather than as a topic for my analysis. Therefore, readers in search of a discursive history of the formalist revolution will need to look elsewhere.[24] Correspondingly, I do not chart the ways literary creations adopted mathematical protocols.[25]

In lieu of such an accounting *about* math, I try to *think with* mathematical formalism, zeroing in on the theory of representation and theory of human projections at the center of the revolution. I take mathematical formalism as a model, a model of, as it were, *modeling.* Non-Euclidean geometry, set theory, symbolic logic, and advanced calculus each open domains of mathematical grasping of the infinite, the beyond of empiricism and experience, the horizon of possible spaces. These developments in math sanctify the letter as the minimal-est unit of signification, the material substrate of representation, and they practice what the signifier offers. They formulate human thought as a modeling of the possible rather than a describing of the extant, a modeling made from minimalist writing.

Indeed, it is this notion of *model*, etymologically rooted in the Latin *modulus*, a unit of measure, and indicating in the first instance "the representation of structure" (*OED*)—a notion of model as a representation abstracted from, scaled away from, distilling, or synthesizing that which it models—that provides the book with a way of thinking about both aesthetics and politics.[26] The mathematical practice of constructing models has been taken by the mathematician-philosopher Alain Badiou to perform a kind of knowledge-formation that is "primary and productive" with regard to all other sciences; mathematical models are the fundamental form that human knowing takes.[27] The semiotician Jean Baudrillard similarly sees models as the ultimate abstraction, the generation of "a real without origin."[28] In this productive faculty, "model" evokes the manifold projective enterprises so dominant in the nineteenth century, from the panoramic installation to the adoption of the prime meridian to the phantasmagoria—on up to empire itself.[29] Yet it also evokes the projections as yet unrealized, and the pressure exerted upon constituted reality by the construction of other visions. I thus use the term "model" to encompass both of the functions typed by the anthropologist Clifford Geertz: "model of," a heuristic for apprehending a system, such as a scale diorama of a city, and "model for," a heuristic for producing a system, such as the architectural blueprint.[30] In my analysis, these two functions fuse: we build models in order to learn, criticize, build, and rebuild; we build works of worldly art, such as the novel, in order to push the bounds of possibility; we build social relations "without origin." Every project *of* is a project *for.* Instituted social relations remain models insofar as they will never overcome their own ungroundedness and will never ground their projective dimension. Literarily instituted social relations, of which the novel is the paradigmatic form, intrinsically model worlds, mediating both what is and what could be.

With mathematical formalism as its inspiration, an extrapolation braces the central ideas of the book: the modeling of possible space in mathematics guides my vision of the modeling of possible space in social form and in literature. I make this extrapolation in part via the inventive notion of "social space" elaborated by the Marxist philosopher Henri Lefebvre. The "social" in "social space" names the always constituted, always modeled quality of space; the "space" names the medium of social formalization. For Lefebvre, "social space" is first of all a corrective to the presumption that space is merely metaphysical; it indicates for him the opposite of an recondite object of knowledge or a "passive locus" of relations. Social space is "irreducible to a form imposed upon phenomena, upon things, upon physical materiality"[31] and rather denominates "the active role of space—the operational or instrumental—role of space as knowledge and action, in the existing mode of production."[32] "Mode of production" is the Marxist name for the configuration of social relations; the concept serves to accent the contingency of any given configuration. Lefebvre's imbrication of space with the mode of production encompasses "logico-epistemological space, the space of social practice, the space occupied by sensory phenomena, including products of the imagination such as projects and projections, symbols and utopias."[33] Social space can ultimately name that which is produced by a mode of production: "Social space . . . infiltrates, even invades, the concept of production, becoming part—perhaps the essential part—of its content."[34]

Social space consists in a matrix of practices and representations that precondition physical materiality. These practices include production and reproduction in the economic sense, *and* the representations in and of those practices, whether administrative "knowledge, signs, codes" that attend the "order" of practical relations, or relatively autonomous, such as art.[35] Crucially, Lefebvre accords these representations agency in the production of space: "Representations of space must therefore have a substantial role and a specific influence in the production of space. Their intervention occurs by way of construction—in other words, by way of architecture, conceived of not as the building of a particular structure, palace, or monument, but rather as a project embedded in a spatial context and a texture which call for 'representations' that will not vanish into the symbolic or imaginary realms."[36]

Although, then, social space solicits the aid of different precepts than mathematical space, Lefebvre's emphasis that "social space is a social product" reads analogously to the formalist mathematical opening of new domains of space via new produced formulae. A logically consistent formula *projects* space; a systemic mode of production similarly results in the projection of social space. This core sense of constituting projections unites mathematical formalism and political formalism. Like the imaginary space probed by the integral formula, social space is ultimately "not a thing but rather a set of relations between things";[37] "social spaces interpenetrate one another and/or superimpose themselves upon one another. They are not things, which have mutually limiting boundaries."[38] This non-thingness points to the figurality and multiplicity of social spaces—as much as Lefebvre is describing a "real" phenomenon, one cannot go inside social space as one would go inside a house, even though one is always in social spaces. On account of this multiplicity and non-thingness of space, methods for spatial analysis must not presume reified relations so much as attend to the principles of intercalation and combination, to the metonymic and metaphoric axes of composition.

Vignettes of Aesthetic Formalism

Although some of the connections I have begun to sketch between formalist mathematics and literary projects apply to literature generally, my arguments in this book focus on the novel, which I think about in these pages as a blend of abstraction, performative language, and world-building. Describing the novel as a model implies that scale, consistency, and integrality of the work of art are leading issues for consideration. Just such concerns have long anchored aesthetic formalism in literary study, even as those formalisms have tended to ignore the novel in favor of poetry. My methods of reading thus draw upon formalist traditions while plotting them along new axes. The formalist reading method I pursue has deep affinities with both the first projects of "intrinsic" criticism in the Anglo-American context in the 1930s and 1940s and the Russian formalists of the 1910s and 1920s, with which New Criticism had some shared sympathies, but little direct bridge.[39] In reading closely, attending to the inner logic of texts—their syntax and grammar, their tropes and rhetoric, their cantilevering of reference and allegory—studying the principles of interrelation of literary elements, tracking how literary ideas work, my method resembles these older schools. Moreover, I follow the Russian emphasis on "literariness" and on dialectical inquiry, and the New Critical emphasis on objectivity, to claim the disciplinary specificity of literary criticism. Not poor-man's philology, not amateur history, not psychology of the dead, literary criticism as early formalists defined it was meant to emerge in almost scientific clarity as a set of questions about the essence of the object, about the grounds of objectivity in literary study, about the boundaries between literary and nonliterary language, about how literature thinks. These remain important goals, providing an intellectual backbone for the institutional and indeed political scramble over the distinction of the literary from informatics and of the humanities from STEM.

Influenced as I am then by the Russian formalists and the New Critics, I still depart from those traditions by beholding the logic internal to, and the special conceptuality issuant from, the novel. Literary formalists regularly prefer poetry, and literary theory since the rise of the novel usually presumes poetry a worthier, more interlocutive subject, while often pronouncing the novel untheorizable. Shifting that pole, I read for the systematic interrelation of multiple components of novelistic discourse, and for the conceptual dynamism produced in that reverberation. How does plot relate to setting, and in turn relate to narration, to imagery, to temporality, to characterization? In trying to always ask after all of these elements, I aspire to a synthetic comprehensiveness; my formalism of the novel is not a formalism of one or two factors, but of all the factors in integral connection. Mapping these connections, grasping the unique fusion of literary elements, the suspensive admixture of different arcs of thought simultaneously, this formalism attends to the novel's in-dwelling abstraction. The coalesced interrelationality of the novel form performs the integrity of worlds; the novel theorizes what infrastructures of relation support a world, abstracting from concrete content to produce and limn wholes. If, as Jonathan Culler helpfully argues, the novel "does not presume a reality already given and to be represented, but posits its own truth, it inscribes its own context, institutes its own scene, and gives us to experience that instituting," then we might consider the kind of thinking that the form of the novel uniquely achieves to be a thinking of felicitous instituting, a thinking of context coherency, a thinking of world-making—in the abstract.[40]

In emphasizing literature's unique propensity for abstraction, I rub against the grain of one prominent and perennial strand of formalist theory that contrastingly advocates for literature's disruption of abstraction.[41] Victor Shklovsky's pathbreaking elaboration of defamiliarization aligns aesthetic experience with sensuousness and dilation that works against abstraction: "The device of art is the estrangement of things and the complication of the form, which increases the duration and complexity of perception, as the process of perception is, in art, an end in itself and must be prolonged."[42] Shklovsky's notion of defamiliarization radically anticipates Rancière's notion of the (re)distribution of the sensible (as evident in Shklovsky's specification of the defamiliarizing potential of poetic language, which "removes signs from their places," "always incites insurrection among things" which are "always in a state of revolt," "casting off their old names and adopting new names and new faces") and counterposes the politics of instrumentality:[43]

> Considering the laws of perception we see that routine actions become automatic. . . . This property of thinking suggests not only the path of algebra but even the particular choice of symbols (letters and especially initial letters).

> This algebraic way of thinking takes in things by counting and spatializing them; we do not see them but we recognize them by their initial features. . . . Perceived in this way, the thing dries up.[44]

Shklovsky here presents what Adorno and Horkheimer and others would come to cement as a critical theoretical suspicion of mathematical abstraction, and he derives his sense of the revolutionary power of art, and of literature in particular, from its countervalence to this abstraction. If abstraction strips out particularities and thus legitimates sovereignty, domination, automation, industrialization, and instrumentality, up to and including the horrors of empire and the atrocities of the Third Reich, then literature, this story would hold, aerates the resistance to abstraction, as an elongation and estrangement of thought.[45] This is a commanding and satisfying opposition, one that has ruled postwar literary study and fueled literary suspicions of formalism. Critics working against the political relations they associate with abstraction have championed the particular, the concrete, the body, the ineffable, the hybrid—all that which would seem nonexchangeable and thus outside of the exchange circuit—and adopted methodological protocols that are anathema to formalism. Yet this cannot be the only story of abstraction.

Other stories might issue from mathematical formalism more closely regarded, since it practices abstraction as the opening of new possibilities, rather than the cementing of old givens. Too, this promise of generative abstraction was embraced by the very first aesthetic formalist, Immanuel Kant. It is a particular guise of aesthetic formalism, but not its only face, to culminate in admiring the art object as a sublimity evading the clutches of the concept; some can catch the specific kind of conceptuality in the work of art in its difference from the reign of instrumental reason. Aesthetic theories of forms, aesthetic readings of forms, and aesthetic formalism attune us to the made form, the built form, the unexpected, uncontrolled effects of form, form's autonomy. Aesthetic formalism gives us to think the uses of form beyond intent, the power of form beyond its maker, the faculties of form in excess of iterative discourse or conceptual logic. Form works in Kant as a category between matter and idea, a category of agency that both thwarts and sublates the opposition between pure and practical reason. When I define form as composed interrelation with the capacity to mediate itself, I invoke this tradition of a thinking that is nevertheless not conceptual, since "concept" is for Kant a *form* of understanding (space and time are the preeminent pure forms of intuition; substance and cause also qualify), but the aesthetic makes use of some sub- or paraconcept—chiefly, as he describes it, the "sensus communis," a feeling of objectivity that preconditions collectivity. In the words of Robert Kaufman, "The aesthetic is *formal* because rather than being determined by, it provides the form for conceptual objective thought or cognition."[46] For Kant the marvelous thing about aesthetic judging is its surprising objectivity: aesthetic judgment exceeds subjective feelings like "I like this" and exceeds quasi-objective assessments like "This is beauty" because, in his strict definition, the judgment performs an objective universality like "Everyone agrees this is beauty." Even though the aesthetic's distance from pure and practical reason would seem to suggest its subjective status as against their objectivity, aesthetic thinking is for Kant a paradoxically objective, specially social process, a registering of qualities beyond subjective sensation that simultaneously conjures an extensive social field of others who share the same registering. Such objectivity consists in the palpability of sociality, a mental experience of our materially interdependent interconnectedness. As Sianne Ngai explains in her extraordinary work on categories beyond the beautiful, the aesthetic is a kind of "referring . . . to the social matrix of others with whom we are compelled to share these feelings in public," a referring that is both constative and performative, summoning the public that is the condition of possibility for the judgment.[47] Such compulsion is not a matter of ideologies of taste, but of the purely formal, mathematically deductive kind of thinking that the aesthetic occasions.

Ngai and other perspicacious readers of Kant help underscore that the aesthetic by definition mediates sociality. This social dimension of aesthetics becomes accentuated in the nineteenth century, when "formalism" first enters the English lexicon, and when, simultaneously, Kantian heirs from Schiller to Pater decisively politicized the aesthetic. It is also the era that installs our contemporary political order (finance capitalism, liberalism, imperialism, anthropogenic climate change), and that speculatively embarks on what remain the most commanding critiques of that order (Marxism, realism, utopianism, psychoanalysis). And so too this period incubates the aesthetic form that, I claim, most vividly unites mathematical formalism with political formalism: literary realism. Literary realism perennially centers debates about aesthetics and politics, with their frequent focus on art's truth-telling faculties and the quest for adequate representation of political subjectivity and political totality, but there remains much to be said about how realism mediates the real and how it theorizes the political. Encompassing broad points in realist form, from the middle of the nineteenth century to the end, the novels I read distinctly combine mathematical signifiers with inquiry into elementary social structuration. They model integral worlds and thus meditate on the infrastructures of sociability, the composed relations that build life.

Theorizing realism as a projective, formalist model requires overcoming several deeply held critical truisms. Even in the wake of deconstruction, the Auerbachian definition of realism as the serious representation of the actually existing world remains paradigmatic.[48] This conceit that realism essentially *represents* bolsters today's hegemonic consensus that literature is information, and that the task of the critic is to tabulate information, correlating work to cause, word to referent, with ever more granularity.[49] For an alternative theory that turns away from mimesis, thereby buttressing literary criticism against its reduction to science, I take inspiration from mathematical formalism's radical modeling, and from the tropes of modeling evoked by the repeated recurrence of "architecture" in the work of two of the most important theorists of realism, Henry James and Fredric Jameson. Theorizing realism as model dispenses with the problematic of mimetic fidelity to the single world, privileging realism's drafting and projecting of worlds: realism fundamentally designs and erects socialities, imagines the grounds of collectivities, probes the mystique of materialities, modulates institutions and productions beyond the scope of the given.[50]

A formalist theory of realism, in other words, opens onto realism's own formalism, its propensity to abstract social relations into their essential configurations, to fathom form as essential social infrastructure. I therefore work to read realism formalistically, and my readings work to stimulate insights into thinking the political formalistically. Just as mathematical formalism radicalizes space, pursuing the multiplicity of infinity and the manifold dimensions of the universe inaccessible to finite beings except in language, and just as political formalism affirms space as the medium in which social order is produced, aesthetic formalism prizes space as the means for mediating relationality as such. Formalist regard for realism pays attention to form as space: the volume produced by a work, the force field it generates, the integral fusion of its elements with one another that enables it to be perceived as a contoured whole. Approaching realism formalistically, as a model of social space (the produced relations that take space as their medium), we can think doubly spatially, about its concern with integrality of structuration—with social breadth and psychic depth, with connections among multiple centers, with ensuring that its world holds together—and about the integrality of its own composition. *The Order of Forms* strives to convey the isomorphism between this principle of integrity in the literary formalist view of the work of art as integral whole, the formalist mathematical principle of integral logic, and the political formalist affirmation of structuration.

Throughout this book, this isomorphism comes into relief via a specific trope: the built form. Architecture appears in these pages as metaphor for the modeling of social space, the production of realist aesthetics, and the building up of social forms. My readings attend to architectural and spatial tropes in a variety of works, and these tropes in turn open projects of building, drafting, sheltering, and structuring that found the constituent commitments of political formalism. Criticism responsive to these constructivist impulses and their interfiguration could more rigorously bolster building, and analysis of how forms work can furnish both tools and sites for putting new forms together.

Snapshots of Political Formalism

Let us enter into a pair of works that together activate the trope of the built form so central to *The Order of Forms*, from the spatiality common to mathematical and aesthetic formalism, to the architectural modeling of literary realism, through to political formalism's insights into the structuration of social space. I began with the proclivity of contemporary literary criticism to idealize formlessness as political virtue. And I suggested that there remains to be strongly formulated a Marxist schema of aesthetics and politics that asserts the ontological necessity and aestheticized aspect of social forms. As a step toward that formulation, I want to situate this in Marx's own formalism.

What do I mean by Marx's formalism? Both his method and his premises set important precedents for the special purchase of formalism, by elevating form to the object of rigorous analysis, and by attesting to the facticity of form in nature. Remark the indispensable importance of *form* to Marxism's own methods of analysis, and indeed the formalism of Marx's critical procedure, which commends formalism in our literary criticism too. *Capital*, Marx's culminating work, of course famously begins with the commodity form. This intense focus on form distinguishes Marx's *critique* of political economy from the erudite bourgeois discipline that was its target. Labor theory predates Marx; formalist analysis of value, of commodities, of capital does not. Empirical analysis of exploitation and contradiction predates Marx; formalist analysis of capitalism's drive to sublate the contradictions it precipitates does not. Quasi-philosophical discernment of the intellective paradoxes of credit predates Marx; the theory of capitalism as a specific metaphysic, engendering pervasive new topoi of belief, newly ungrounded rationality, and newly reversing cause-and-effect, does not. Each of these Marxian conceptual innovations is facilitated by thinking in terms of form: representation of, against, and in matter; of structure, agency, and interlocking composites; of ideations innate in arrangement and order; of Platonic registers and their lapsarian instantiation.

A closer study of a few momentous images in *The German Ideology*, the first systematic text of materialism, will help frame this formalism in Marx and the argument in the book as a whole, since they splice together a materialist account of human being and a formalist regard for the spaces of being. To get an idea of how form in its inevitability and variability textures Marx's thought, we can focus on just one paragraph in the first section of this very long and poliform text. In the beginning, taking distance from Hegelians, for whom consciousness is the first premise of any judgment of the world, Marx offers a counter starting point, which he notably pluralizes. He starts not with a single fact nor some single stratum of matter but with a plural "First Premises of a Materialist Method," and the premises directly concern plurality: "The first premise of all human history is, of course, the existence of living human individuals."[51] Marx's manifest materialism launches thought from actual living individuals, plural, in their definite social relations, plural. The difference between the singular and the plural is at least as important here as the conventional one between thinking and living, ideas and matter. The point is less that embodiment precedes consciousness than that *plurality* is prior; the field of relations precedes individuals. As if in performance of this irrepressible relationality, the first premise cannot be easily cordoned from another priority in the second sentence: "Thus the first fact of the case to be established is the physical organization of these individuals and their consequent relation to the rest of nature."[52] A premise is not self-identical but divisible into premise and fact, a premise is not an origin but a promontory to be "established," "stated," "verified"; "material" is not simply available to be registered, but must be carefully mediated into registry by representational processes. On this fulcrum of the fact and the representation rests none other than the question of "organization." Plurality is social, the first fact is aggregation, a quantity to which corresponds the quality of organization. "Organization" is the elementary, primal fact, the ratification of which distinguishes a materialist from an idealist.

Materialism, Marx asserts, starts not with "consciousness" but with laboring beings who "produce their means of subsistence, a step which is conditioned by their physical organization."[53] Making collective life is the free work paradoxically arising from physical necessity; our "organization" as interdependent causes but does not define the form of our living productions. Diverse forms result from historical contingencies of creative building, but the ontological fact of sociality remains the occasion for this production.

Throughout *The German Ideology* and across his other works, Marx invokes organization variously as "form," "structure," "state," "sociality," "association." In focusing on the ur-organizations as the first facts for materialism, *The German Ideology* breaks substantially with the social contract scenarios of idealist theory, sieving the generality of organization from its predicates or properties, and accentuating this generality by repeated employ of only one adjective attached to social organization: "spontaneous"/*naturwuchsig* (nature-grown/nature-made). Marx's social structuration as *nature-made* probes minimally inscribed sociality, provisionally formalized sociality at an ontological level: being is not tragically ensnared in organizations; *being is organization.* Where contemporary anarcho-vitalism (the neo-Deleuzianisms and neo-Spinozisms such as those of Hardt and Negri, messianisms such as Agamben's, antistatism in Foucauldian and Marxist flavors, antinomianism in queer theory, assemblage theory) opposes order to life, Marx, like Aristotle before him (whose axiom of plurality Marx directly repeats: "Man is *zoon politikon* in the most literal sense: he is not only a social animal, but an animal that can be individualized only within society"[54]), avows order as the condition of possibility of life as such, the very matter of life itself, the very matter to which materialism addresses itself. Crucially, the ordering done by Marx's proliferating forms is indeterminate, open, unpredicated—the organizational function of form, not its specific content, is the matter at issue. Often accused of pubescent humanism in these anthropological moments, Marx rather articulates a variety of formalism—of undetermined, unrooted, social organization. The fact of organization in the abstract is where materialism starts; even though its emphasis on the extant rather than the ideal might seem to suggest concretude, what materialism underscores is the material abstraction, the formalism in nature.

Materialism comes to be defined in *The German Ideology* as an approach to constructing knowledge not from the vantage point of the individually lived experience of consciousness, but instead from the vantage point of the collectively lived experience of social relations. Materialism differs from idealism in this premising of collective social life. Although this difference is sometimes framed as one between rationalism and empiricism, or the study of the abstract and the study of the concrete, it is crucial to underscore how lithely Marx's materialism thwarts these oppositions. As the premise of materialism, collective social life does not sit a sublunary solidity awaiting empirical attention; both the object "collective social life" and the subject "materialism" refer to processes. Wonderfully, Marx contrasts immediate uptake of the material with an exercise of interpretation he calls "the writing of history,"[55] which he practices as dynamically narrating, in hybrid genres, the contingencies determining social space. And similarly, what issues through this process is itself a process: collective social life not as empirical referent, but as ever-evolving, provisionally stable, improvised form. Even in its unassailable facticity, collectivity lacks given institutions. The fundamental ungivenness and openness of what shape collective life takes—this negativity at the heart of sociality—this dynamism centers "the first premise" of materialist method. Human life depends upon necessary collectivities of contingent form, and materialism is the study of these contingent formalizations that illuminates the dialectic of natural necessity and historical contingency, of human animality and aestheticized improvisation.

At the very center of *The German Ideology*, in the strongest synthetic statement the text makes about its subject, stands a paramount image that Marx uses to illustrate the ways in which the formalism in nature precipitates social contests over the contents of given forms: the image of the *camera obscura*. The "dark room" names early projective experiments in channeling rays of light through pinholes in the room's exterior walls and thereby producing inverted images on the walls inside the room of the setting outside the room. The inversions preserve perspective, dimension, and color, but reverse orientation. The projective technology of the *camera obscura* mimics the physiology of the human eye, which is itself a kind of dark space with a pupil pinhole. Marx uses this figure of preservative, inverted projection to define ideology. Ideology is the intellectual predicament of human life in all its physicality and collectivity; it is not false, because it preserves so much that is true; it is not unnatural, because its mechanism belongs to the laws of physics and of anatomy; it is not conquerable, because the setting in which perspective takes place cannot appear otherwise than inverted. "If in all ideology men and their relations appear upside-down as in a *camera obscura*, this phenomenon arises just as much from their historical life-process as the inversion of objects on the retina does from their physical life-process."[56] Ideology is image-production through physical processes of refracted light and enclosed space; its inversions and distortions arise naturally, socially, and physically. "It is not immediately evident," W. J. T. Mitchell observes, "how one is to circumvent the camera obscura and gain access to true versions or representations of the world, any more than it is clear how one can see without using one's own eyes."[57] Space does not appear to the eye except through processes of inversion; any mediation of space in the form of a representation, extract, projection, or model will invariably invert, less because humans are hopelessly inadequate to material reality, than because material reality itself is contingent, formed. There is no unideological appearance, unideological consciousness, unideological representation of men and their relations—in the words of Althusser, "*Ideology has no history*"—because the very installation of the form of relationality is always ungrounded, radically imposed, radically improvised, radically contrived formation.[58] The made world cannot but appear inverted; social forms are simultaneously indispensable infrastructure and arbitrary artifice.

Marx's use of the *camera obscura* as such an indispensable crux has, of course, a wide variety of implications for Marxian theories of technology, the body, media, and aesthetics. Beyond noting that the image prima facie asserts that social formalizations cannot be apprehended unideologically, I want to focus on how his explanation of ideology evokes multidimensional *spatiality*: ideology is defined as a *space*, a *camera obscura*, a space that projects a model of a broader space, whose configuration refracts the natural fact of human sociality. Marx folds sociality, the knowability and representability of sociality, and spatial technologies and spatial tropes into one another.

The socio-spatial trope of the camera at the center of Marx's materialism condenses his concept of ungrounded social organization—form without content—as the essence of human experience. That this trope could bear so much weight is partly owing, I want now to suggest, to Marx's mobilization of it at a decisive moment in the history of the camera: *The German Ideology* was written just one year after the publication of the first ever book of photographs, a book that wonderfully establishes the camera as mediation of social space. (This is the second of the two works I am using to frame political formalism.) Intended to introduce the medium to the public, *The Pencil of Nature* presented the work of one of photography's foremost inventors (William Henry Fox Talbot, who claimed to be *the* foremost), and arrayed twenty-four salt-paper plates that cover a range of possible uses for the new process—facsimiles of writing usable as legal documents, catalogues of art objects usable by collectors, studies of natural and technical objects usable by industrious minds. Amid all this diversity of purpose there is nonetheless a surprising singularity of focus: a superabundance of *architecture*. Thirteen of the twenty-four plates represent buildings. *The Pencil of Nature* rather unexpectedly—given its title, given Talbot's prioritization of flowers, leaves, hairs, in his earliest works, and given our scholarly impressions of early photography—put forth no nature-scapes and no portraits, but rather a series of highly defined built spaces.[59] In devising a silver nitrate process for adhering shadows to surfaces, Talbot develops the technology of photography from the *camera obscura*, a projection of external space internally via a room with walls—*image as architecture*—into lasting prints holding *architecture as image*. At the very moment at which Marx implies that spatial mediations compose social relations (the formalizing of collectivities for living) and equally compose the unmappability of those relations (the camera is the paradigm of ideology), the camera's faculty for mediating space underwent its own inversion. With Talbot's buildings, the medium of photography defined itself by incorporating its own technology, camera architecture, into its self-reflexive substance, architecture as such. Photography thus articulates itself as both an art of spatial construction and a trope of spatial arts. What is more, as I want to tease out, the rhetoric of *The Pencil of Nature* prefigures the tenets of materialism as Marx will articulate them: built collectivities are the writing that nature makes. Talbot's foundational fixation on architecture magnifies the inherently spatial quality of photography—its faculty for presenting a setting—into a politically insightful medium, anticipating Lefebvre's notion of social space, and exposing spatial formalization as the elementary art of the political.[60]

It is worth lingering over a few of these initial images to bring home the point about a materialist aesthetics of space and a mid-nineteenth-century practice of mediating social form. One could of course approach these images through available argumentative templates like media archaeology questions about their technological process, or sociopolitical contextual questions about Talbot's aristocratic position. The method I introduce here differs, by considering the rhetoric of the composed collection as a whole, and by look-

FIGURE 1. William Henry Fox Talbot, *Part of Queen's College, Oxford* (1844–1846). Salted paper print from paper negative, 15.2 x 20.3 cm. Gift of Jean Horblit, in memory of Harrison D. Horblit (1994.197.1-.6). The Metropolitan Museum of Art, New York.

FIGURE 2. William Henry Fox Talbot, *View of the Boulevards at Paris* (May–June 1843). Salted paper print from paper negative. 15.1 x 19.9 cm. Gilman Collection, Purchase, The Horace W. Goldsmith Foundation Gift, through Joyce and Robert Menschel (2005.100.609). The Metropolitan Museum of Art, New York.

ing at the images as imaginative productions that contemplatively conceptualize themselves and their subjects.

Talbot's book's very first plate, *Part of Queen's College, Oxford*, shows a cluster of buildings, decorative statuary, windows, a walkway, and scaffolding around a structure in the background. "Part" formidably defines the aesthetic: it is asymmetrically composed, the buildings all shown in partial (and under construction), the frame cutting off the top of the foreground building, the lopsided horizon, the cornered perspective and distorted scale—the photograph is but a shard of a broader extent, an extract or abstract of space. The camera is situated on the same horizontal plane as the subjects, but angles itself to concentrate on the corner where the horizontality and verticality meet the depth axis, presenting the main building in three rather than two dimensions. Photography first comes into relief as the deliberately abstract, highly composed, multiplanar, conspicuously framed, angular inquiry into interstices; an aestheticization of space, spatial organization, spatial overlap and underlap, foreground, background, middle ground, shifting ground.

And all of these formal qualities of the photograph complicate its subject: the college under construction, the institution undergoing installation, are fixed in their developing state. We might say, with Roland Barthes, that the *studium* here, the context that the photograph proffers for study, is the university, that institution of institutions, while the *punctum*, the riveting detail, is the scaffold, the unshakably emergent character of any institution.[61]

The second plate, *View of the Boulevards at Paris*, enlarges from the first's study of collegial, emergent space out to wider-scale urban and international space, replacing the imbalanced grounds of the first with imbalanced aerial abstraction, the planar equality of camera and subject traded for a relation more removed, gazing out at colonnades, street lamps, gate posts, shutters, and "a whole forest of chimneys" from a rooftop. Corners and three dimensionalities again anchor the image, with horizontal breadth pitched across proliferating verticalities, and the camera situated on neither axis so much as at their obscure convergence. The line of sight created by the camera directly diverges from the line of sight created by the boulevard, and the surprisingly curvilinear tree eerily blocks the latter, seeming to suggest that the built environment will not have done with raw material obstacles, that contrived perspectives will not achieve totalization. City space is vertical *and* horizontal *and* lateral, dense *and* sprawling, manifold *and* unrevealed. The plate's marked continuation of the asymmetrical, multiplanar rhetoric of "partiality" seems to say that even in its grander urban scale, even in its international frame, photography's meditation on space is no more total, the question of the configuration of space no more met. Even the conclusion of construction of the college in the first image would betoken less a finished whole than that whole's immersion in a new emergence, the blurry extent and obstructed expanse of concatenated, massed urbanism.

The investigation of partiality propelling these first two images still defines what has become the genre of architectural photography, which is animated by problems of perspective and the representability of space.[62] The plates that follow continue to study spatial construction (doors, gates, bridges, abbeys, cloisters, towers), pointedly exhibiting the camera as a study of collective *camera*—rooms, built forms, interstices, institutions. Buildings of course stand still, posing particularly amenable to long exposure times, but convenience alone cannot account for their overrepresentation in *The Pencil*, since indeed Talbot's great technological innovation was to reduce exposure times through new fixatives. Rather, the composition of the images bespeak Talbot's commitment to photography as a medium in which content autonomizes itself (as he put it, "This is the first instance, on record, of a house having painted its own portrait"[63]), and architecture thematically figures this medium-become-art, etymologically as the first art, *arche-tekne*, but also, as Hegel preeminently argues, as the very pivot into art as such, limning the boundary between function and symbolism, between necessity and freedom.[64] If shelter would seem so entirely functional as to preclude art, the perceptible contingencies of any given shelter—its materials, its location, its design—leap into art's realm. Buildings and photography both sculpt space; photography reflexively archives the chance craft of such sculpting. The medium "reflects" the social space that is its subject not as a mirror reciprocates phenomena, but rather, and only, in its own constitutive constructedness and partiality. Photography presents itself as artificially imposed, and equates its artifices with the edifices of social spaces that are its subject.

At first exposure, then, one finds a tension between this artifice and the title's invocation of *nature*. Even though Talbot's introductory essay differentiates from the engraver or painter or sketcher who makes with his own pencil the photographer who captures what nature makes, *only one* of the twenty-four plates could remotely be said to depict Nature: "The Leaf of a Plant," which is a leaf conspicuously removed from its habitat, laid flat on paper, presented for scale. Colloquial, earthly, scenic nature simply does not appear in *The Pencil of Nature*—there are no landscape photographs nor rose candids; the nature here is a different order of nature, the nature that is architecture, the built collectivity, the polis that exists by nature. What is natural in *The Pencil of Nature* are the cameras of collective life, the built forms of social space.

The title *The Pencil of Nature* laminates this natural building to tropes of graphic writing, since pencils are implements of both writing and architectural drafting. Indeed, numerous facets in Talbot's work tacitly theorize writing, from the collection's preponderance of text, its showcased facsimiles of text, its suggestion that photographs be not viewed but "read," and its status as one of the very first instances of the word "photography" in the English language. Photography emerges through this work as technologically continuous with writing, as a kind of light-writing and image-writing that inscribes and defines and relays and records.[65] The pencil of nature is the writing done in nature and the writing of sociation, the necessary interdependence of human animals that is nonetheless contingently inscribed in every socius, the writing that is the design of social space, bridging and dooring and roofing and framing the social terrain. Writing, nature, and architecture are composited together here, imaging the paradoxical essentiality of that which is constructed. *The Pencil of Nature* thus, in the course of inventing photography as the mediation of social fabrication, also shutters a snapshot of political formalism. Talbot's work theorizes that form is general—the writerly shaping of space, the inscriptive instituting of elemental socialities, the structuration of nature that can be built differently but not wished away—and that form is also, simultaneously, specific, the local contours of art that mediates that generality.

The figure of writing tightens the ties to *The German Ideology*, since as we have seen Marx keenly invents materialism not as empiricism and not as supra-ideological knowledge, but as situated *writing*. To return to the very same paragraph we were originally considering, take its final sentences: "Of course, we cannot here go either into the actual physical nature of man, or into the natural conditions in which man finds himself—geological, hydrographical, climatic and so on. The writing of history must always set out from these natural bases and their modification in the course of history through the action of men."[66] Materialism is not geology, not empiricism, not the fetish of concretude, but is rather, writing, *Geschichtschreibung*, the writing of history. And it is a writing that addresses itself to, endeavors to perform, the writing in nature—not the physical facticity of life, but the "definite form of expressing life."[67] Marx equates the spontaneous order of the social with language itself, which he defines as fundamentally *material*. The "material intercourse of men" he aligns with "the language of real life," and he then continues, "Language is as old as consciousness, language is practical consciousness that exists also for other men, and for that reason alone it really exists for me personally as well; language, like consciousness, only arises from the need, the necessity, of intercourse with other men."[68] Moreover, since this material language consistent with material sociality is the matter of materialism, materialism itself must be fundamentally distinguished by its concern with writing: at its moment of manifesto-like definition, materialism is asserted as the writing of form. What nature writes is the mutual concern that affiliates *The German Ideology* and *The Pencil of Nature*. The nature-writing that impels photography, the scaffolded, developing, variegated building of space, is the spontaneous organization that materialist philosophy takes as its first premise.

The Pencil of Nature and *The German Ideology* share a commitment to social form as the *writing that nature makes*, a commitment to an ontology of structuration as the very matter of our political nature. Together they give dimension to political formalism, and by their lights we can begin to apprehend this formalism entailing not only a lasting consideration of form's art—where art means artifice and made-ness, design and contingency—but another consideration as well, of form's essence—where essence means irreducible quiddity, ontological facticity. In the space between the two cameras, then, we can map out an aesthetically theorized fundamentality of forms.

By "political formalism," then, I want to designate the order of forms, the order made by forms and the forms made by order, and to designate as well the theory thereof, theory most often performed by art. Political formalism is the thought whose first premise is that the polis is a form, a making of collective order, which is irreducible and indispensable, but which is merely formal in the sense of lacking any inherent form, merely formal in the sense of belonging to something like a Platonic order of forms, every material instantiation of which is partial. The polis is ontological, it pertains to the constitutive condition of possibility for being, yet it has no ontology, no predication of being in advance. There is no life without form, yet form has many lives. Form is "spontaneous" in Marx's sense—the writing of nature, wholly necessary and wholly contingent. Any dispensation of the socius is simultaneously ungrounded/ideological/aestheticized, and, effectively, neutral. Even though political theory, literary critical methods, and the left fetishism of anarchy have relentlessly portrayed the nonimmanence of social installations as "violence," nonimmanence has no alternative. Mirages of Edenic identities, flowing energies, and deluging multitudes fantasize freedom in formlessness. Yet formed, mediated relations are the truth of our social being—a truth the mediations of art give us to think, in their ultimate aesthetic politics. Formalism's capacity for fathoming these mediations primes it to commend composition, organization, building; we must renounce our renunciation of form to build new spaces, new poleis, new orders of forms.

Ordering *The Order of Forms*

The title *The Order of Forms* cannot but evoke two intertexts about which I need to say a bit at the outset: Plato's theory of forms, and Michel Foucault's *The Order of Things*. In Plato's dialogues, most famously *The Republic*, forms have their own order: forms (both ideas and shapes) belong to an abstract realm of general essences that are only experienceable as materialized in specifically concrete situations. The realm encompasses quotidian inanimate objects like "table," every incarnation of which both expresses and falls short of the form, and transcendent evanescent objects like "justice," which take wider latitude in their emanation from contingent republics. Within the material world, we find no immanent form, only improvised, arbitrary, aleatory forms. These Platonic overtones, most especially my enthusiasm for abstraction, will likely aggrieve some readers, but I find them useful in illuminating why form has both ontological quiddity and political contestability. It is of course this contestability that informs Aristotle's departure from Plato, his assertion in the *Metaphysics* that form is in fact something materially available for engagement, and these Aristotelian poetics continue to resurface in my analysis as a complement to the Aristotelian politics sparking political formalism. Platonic motifs of the play between appearance and essence, discourse and being, operate throughout Foucault's *The Order of Things*, even considering that the English translation of the French title *Les mots et les choses* (literally, "words and things") exaggerates the cast. Yet Foucault's unique obliquity to the project of philosophy also involves subtracting the tensions between idealism and materialism, since both frameworks equally produce *discourse*, the representations and resemblances that administer life. *The Order of Things* is a formidable precondition of this study insofar as it archaeologizes "the nineteenth century's . . . advance toward formalism in thought."[69] At the same time, *The Order of Forms* assumes its mandate in countering many Foucauldianisms, especially the tendency to reduce all possible political relations to those of power's exercise.[70]

My contention that form is simultaneously indispensable and reformable countenances none of the denunciation of "institution as such," "law as such," "state as such," that has become so habitual after the genealogy of discipline.[71] Foucault sees power gratifying itself at the expense of life, and Agamben, the self-proclaimed completion of Foucault, sees every human institution as human domination. For Aristotle "it is evident that the polis is among the class of things that exist by nature, and that man is by nature a political animal," but such definition of the human as existing *not only in but because of* collective forms is explicitly repudiated in the antiformalisms of Foucault, Agamben, and their touchstone, Hannah Arendt. Arendt champions politics as an "essential" realm that comes after the "merely necessary" activities of community-making, elevating politics as the pursuit of the good life, but doing so at the expense of any acceptance of the necessity of politics for life.[72] Foucault resounds this epiphenomenal conception of politics as after life; he very starkly rewrites Aristotle: "Man is a living animal with the additional capacity for political existence."[73] And, of course, Agamben reads the history of humanity as the history of its domination by the polis. Quarantining life from the political, the vitalist signature in political theory and in "flat ontology," mistakes the specificity of the human animal, which is its need for a polis, its biological interdependency. As Jacques Derrida writes in his final seminars entitled "The Beast and the Sovereign," "Precisely, what Aristotle says—is that man is . . . a political living being . . . that's his essential definition, that's what is proper to him; what is proper to man is politics . . . and therefore man is immediately zoo-political, in his very life."[74] Politics, the concocting of paradigms for this interdependence, defines the human not against the animal but *as* animal; politics is the sphere of human animality, on which Marx too already insists: "Man is *zoon politikon* in the most literal sense: he is not only a social animal, but an animal that can be individualized only within society."[75]

In opposition to anarcho-vitalism, political formalism links Marxism, psychoanalysis, and structuralism, through their joint vision of the symbolic structuration of social life as real—meaning both insuperable and unimmanentizable, ungroundable. From Marx's writings to Sigmund Freud's, and on into the small contemporary field that merges the two, I find resources for a decisive affirmation of the structuration of social life, an affirmation unconquerably distant from the Foucauldian (and Arendtian-Agambenian-Negrian) repudiation of form in life.[76] This opposition involves the counterintuitive paradox that the materialist position, the one addressing itself to the real of sociality, admits of a certain transcendence, the universal incompletion in the social order, while the idealist position, the one hypostasizing a vital experience that could be unleashed from the constraints of law, language, and interdependence, refuses that transcendence, reducing both its enemy (form) and its hero (life) to a plane of immanence upon which life should simply flow and upon which every hitherto given society fully expresses the logic of sociality as such.

The overarching argument of this book is divided into two uneven parts. The first, larger part outlines political formalism, articulates a formalist theory of literary realism, and then practices close readings of four major Victorian novels by that light, attending to their surprising engagements with the tropes and logics pertaining to the formalization of math, and propounding the political formalism the texts magnify. The second part takes its inspiration from that nineteenth-century aesthetic formulation of political formalism to consider resources in the twentieth and twenty-first century that might yet buttress it, even amid regnant antiformalisms. These resources include psychoanalytic theory, with its abiding interest in the collective conditioning of the psyche and the symbolic configuration of the social, and varieties of Marxist aesthetic and political theory, with their speculative elaborations of form in politics. The combined effect of the two parts of the book, I hope, is to build new support for political formalism across field and disciplinary lines. Theorists are also makers. Formalist close readers, those among our ranks who embrace our core proficiency rather than appropriating the knowledge protocols of history or statistics, pay such careful attention to how things are composed that we realize lots of practical knowledge about how to make different and new things—new forms, new arrangements, new institutions, new relations.[77] More formalism rather than less is key to the future of our discipline, more political speculation and less romantic anarchism are keys to our ability to advocate and organize for the future of our profession, more projection and composition are the keys to building a better world.

Chapter 1, "The Realist Blueprint: For a Formalist Theory of Literary Realism" pursues an antimimetic theory of realism as production that emphasizes its faculty as social model and its affinity with the art of architecture. I argue that realism is best understood as a speculative projection of hypothetical social space, where "social space" signals the medium of collective life. Where literary criticism has insistently maintained that realism is the least figurative, "more highly referential" of the literary modes, and where formalist criticism has abrogated the question of the novel in general and realism specifically (with the very notable exceptions of Alex Woloch and Caroline Levine), I pursue a coherent formalist account of the mode often thought formless.

Chapters 2–5 craft formalist readings of realist novels that activate mathematical formalism in their exploration of political formalism. Since it is a maxim of this book's argument that realism merits and even demands formalist analysis, and that formalist analysis of novels requires sustained attention to the dynamic interrelation of their numerous literary elements and to the speculative whole symphonized by their parts, I make space for this sustained attention by devoting single chapters to single texts. Taking cue from the architectural fascinations of Brontë, Austen, and James, from the "old" institutionalism of Dickens and Trollope, from the architect Thomas Hardy's own pencil of nature, and from the radicalization of space and planarity in Lewis Carroll, these readings continue the method of thinking spatially about form. Each literary chapter elaborates a distinct facet of the dialectic of social form that the book addresses, the ungroundability yet essentiality of every order: *Wuthering Heights* illustrates how every sociality reckons with economic antagonism; *Bleak House* how every sociality faces questions of scale; *Alice's Adventures in Wonderland* how every sociality negotiates sovereignty; and *Jude the Obscure* how every sociality abuts sex. Remarkably, all of these texts have in common that their probing study of these absent foundations for social relations emboldens their constructivism; houses and institutions and letters and lines materialize as opportunities for agency, practicability, beauty, and making.

Chapter 2, "The Set Theory of *Wuthering Heights*: Realism, Antagonism, and the Infinities of Social Space," considers this extraordinary novel's preoccupation with boundaries, identities, and sets—one person and two, past and present, *oikos* (hearth) and *oikonomie* (law of the hearth, economy)—as decisive for its unique insights into the ineradicability of social antagonism and the multiplicity of social dispensations. Chapter 3, "The Limits of *Bleak*

House," reads in that paragon of expansive realism an unexpected absorption in questions of delimitation, diminution, and circumscription, probing why a commitment to limits—architectural, mathematical, institutional, political—constitutes realism's political imaginary. Chapter 4, "Symbolic Logic on the Social Plane of *Alice's Adventures in Wonderland*," explores this novel's overarching concerns with sovereignty, execution, and social ordering, suggesting that such political topoi glide encoded in the epistemology of symbolic logic, and that this text can itself be read as the symbolic logic—the reduction to the letter—of literary realism. Chapter 5, "Obscure Forms: The Social Geometry of *Jude the Obscure*," contemplates the excess of geometric imagery in this final Hardy (and, arguably, final realist) novel, asking how the ungroundedness of law signified by the break with Euclid figures the ungroundedness of formalized socialities as such, and why a surprising veneration of built and written forms nevertheless abides. These novel chapters linger over texts from pivotal points in literary realism's trajectory—*Wuthering Heights* at its inception, *Jude the Obscure* at its end, *Bleak House* at its acme, *Alice's Adventures in Wonderland* from its counterhistory. The progression across them suggests a movement toward abstraction, from the framed multiple narration of *Wuthering Heights* to the redactive precision of omniscience in *Jude the Obscure*. This abstracting momentum of the forms across the chapters repeats the cumulative tendency of these novels to zoom in on elementary social infrastructures: the built boundary in *Wuthering Heights*, the space of the law in *Bleak House*, the plane of constitution in *Alice's Adventures in Wonderland*, the letter of the law in *Jude the Obscure*. Together they chart a vast expanse of realist projects with a shared core of mathematical formalism and political formalism: realist novels abstract sociality, productively featuring the insuperable modelism of every social form.

Enlarging upon the elaborations of political formalism in the nineteenth-century novel and the momentum of abstraction across those novels, chapter 6, "States of Psychoanalysis: Formalization and the Space of the Political," and the conclusion turn to the twentieth and twenty-first centuries, advocating for the strategic value of political formalism in the present. In Lacan's notorious embrace of formalist mathematics I read an explication of the political valences of math, finding an extension of the arc of my novel readings, the abstractive winnowing of constituted social space down to its minimal-est unit of the letter or symbol. In the very recent political and cultural theories of Jodi Dean and Fredric Jameson, speculative heresies share a common unnamed project of esteeming the agency of form. Carrying the literary energies of the nineteenth century forward in time to the theoretical experiments of the twentieth and twenty-first, these concluding chapters articulate theses for political formalism today and in the future. Across all the chapters, my goal is to demonstrate the generativity of thinking the political formalistically, thinking form politically, thinking criticism constructively, thinking abstractions generously. I do mean this generativity to be at once theoretical and practical: we can arrive at new horizons of the goals of theorizing aesthetics and politics if we embrace that theory can be productive, interventionist, and constructive in its own right—not just secondary or descriptive. Theory at its best delivers the benefits of abstraction that mathematical formalism so limpidly sustains: inscription is not the obstacle to possibility but its enabling condition; projective representation uncorded from particulars need not inherently oppress particularities. For criticism informed by such theory, putting things together can become a necessary, newly attended complement to taking them apart.

Legible in the manifold chapters of *The Order of Forms* is something like a builder's guide: chapter 1 advocates for realism's function as an imaginative projection of social space that can inspire new constructions; chapter 2 surveys the shaky foundations of all constructions; chapter 3 highlights the delimited, reformable quality of elementary institutions; chapter 4 trumpets the outsize possibilities contained in the smallest inscriptions; chapter 5 resounds the exuberant beauty of building even when institutions fail; chapter 6 appraises the programmatic prospects of minimally constituted institutions; and the conclusion consummates in theory the speculative and affirmative projects of form that the early chapters see practiced in novels. With these elaborations of form's necessity and form's malleability, I hope readers will move toward building.

I began this introduction by suggesting that Marxian thought offers as yet unexploited resources for thinking the politics of aesthetics and the aesthetics of politics. At a moment when the trends in humanistic inquiry are resolutely anti-Marxist, antiformalist, and anticritical, the Marxian matrix still generates new ways of thinking about formalism and about critique, about how to make forms of sociality that are more just, and about what kinds of knowledge aid that making. In this essential striving toward futures, Marxism is forever kin to literature. The biggest debates in literary criticism have almost always concerned literature's relationship to history. While my position in that contest guides the following pages, this preoccupation with history in literary study has hindered our ability to account for and advocate for literature's ontological propensity for futurity and to therefore practice criticism as future-thinking. Literature makes in language something more than what already exists; it models futures possible. We can build with it.

1

The Realist Blueprint: For a Formalist Theory of Literary Realism

What does realism build? For its earliest, most preeminent theorist, realism builds houses. Across his theory and his art, Henry James figures realism's craft and construction of vibrant spaces with *architecture.*[1] As he put it in one of many such pronouncements, "A great building is the greatest conceivable work of art," and thus the writer as artist "has verily to *build*, is committed to architecture, to construction at any cost; to driving in deep his vertical supports and laying across and firmly fixing his horizontal, his resting pieces—at the risk of no matter what vibration from the tap of his master-hammer."[2] James's famous image of "the house of fiction" conjures a three-dimensional structure from which multiple and divergent points of view cast their gaze, but beyond this familiar spatialization of perspective, his repeated architectural language of engineered building gives shape to an account of how realist form works to produce an integrated world. For James, realism works architecturally because it projects coherent spaces independent of preexisting spaces but dependent upon laws of composition—because, in short, it evinces a formalistic regard for world-making. *The Order of Forms* advocates for such a regard, developing a notion of political formalism from out of the methods and innovations of mathematical formalism and aesthetic formalism. In the introduction, I have defined political formalism as esteem for the arts of social building, and the bulk of this book engages in formalist readings of major realist novels, for which this prefatory chapter necessarily establishes the conditions of possibility. Framing its affinities with architecture (the modeling of social space) and with mathematics (the modeling of possible space), I argue that realism is a speculative, abstract, nonmimetic form amenable to formalist address.

Jamesian Elevations

James provides great impetus for this speculative foray, since he articulated an imperative for theory, lamenting that even those few novelists he admired "had no air of having a theory, a conviction, a consciousness of itself behind it,"[3] and since his theory emerged in the dynamic interplay of his literary criticism and his literary form. Many of James's theoretical designations of the novel—"point of view," "the scenic method," "interior," and so on—function, as Dorothy Hale notes, to "spatialize writing."[4] Many of his signature stylistic gestures function similarly: his incorporation of the collective space of the theater into his fiction as what David Kurnick calls a "externalizing, centrifugal social will";[5] his frequent domestic settings; his use of metonymy to precipitate transitions in the flowing stream of consciousness; his representation of consciousness "spatially as being situated not inside the single self but outside, between persons";[6] and his incredible drive toward solidifying prose syntax, making paragraphs and pages into blocks and bricks, a masonry of densification that Seymour Chatman calls "nominalization."[7] So many elements of his form engage tropics of space and structuration, and Jamesian climaxes are perhaps the most pointed such element, pitching literary spaces in intensely architectural code. In what is only the most succinct climax, from the acutely constructive *The Portrait of a Lady*, Isabelle Archer's grim recognition of her plot is rendered thusly: "The truth of things, their mutual relations, their meaning, and for the most part their horror, rose before her with a kind of architectural vastness."[8] More roomily, *The Wings of the Dove* depicts Milly Theale's scheme to match being schemed as the militant occupation of a Venetian palace:

> She looked over the place, the storey above the apartments in which she had received him, the sala corresponding to the sala below and fronting the great canal with its gothic arches. The casements between the arches were open, the ledge of the balcony broad, the sweep of the canal, so overhung, admirable, and the flutter toward them of the loose white curtain an invitation to she scarce could have said what. But there was no mystery after a moment; she had never felt so invited to anything as to make that, and that only, just where she was, her adventure. It would be—to this it kept coming back—the adventure of not stirring. "I go about just here."[9]

Most voluminously *The Golden Bowl* magisterially confabulates Maggie's dilated anagnorisis, spatializing the time of realization into an exotic locale:

> This situation had been occupying, for months and months, the very centre of the garden of her life, but it had reared itself there like some strange, tall

> tower of ivory, or perhaps rather some wonderful, beautiful, but outlandish pagoda, a structure plated with hard, bright porcelain, coloured and figured and adorned, at the overhanging eaves, with silver bells that tinkled, ever so charmingly, when stirred by chance airs.[10]

In each of these passages, and in so many others, James's heroines discover the structures in which they are determinatively enclosed, and this very structural literacy facilitates their ultimate acts of freedom. His novels deploy architecture as an exotic figure for a fugitive uneclipsed sphere of social relations: architecture expresses comprehending sociality in all its banality and dimensionality.

Where the novels install this commanding trope of social volume, the Prefaces even more emphatically appraise it. Thus the image of the "house of fiction" circulates widely, yet inspires too ready domestication of its floor plan, too quick flattening of its elevation, too many culturalist studies of interior design. In fact, when the Preface to *The Portrait of a Lady* drafts that house, it arrays curiously conflicting figures: although James frequently invokes solidities like "bricks," "buildings," "cornerstones," and "foundations," he also accentuates the incommensurability between ordinary employments of matter and mortar and his extraordinary assemblages:

> The house of fiction has in short not one window, but a million—a number of possible windows not to be reckoned, rather; every one of which has been pierced, or is still pierceable, in its vast front, by the need of the individual vision and by the pressure of the individual will. These apertures, of dissimilar shape and size, hang so, all together, over the human scene that we might have expected of them a greater sameness of report than we find. They are but windows at the best, mere holes in a dead wall, disconnected, perched aloft; they are not hinged doors opening straight upon life.[11]

Not even the Pritzker Prize–winning conceptual architect Zaha Hadid could have built such a house, with its unreckonable number of pierceable, disparate windows. These infinite windows "are not hinged doors opening straight," permitting passage from exterior to interior or from fiction to fact; they are not even portals of illumination, but chimeric reverberations, penetrable fenestrations, holes within holes, queer openings casting an ontological paradox: since "dead wall" is the architectural term for a wall without windows, the fabrication here cleaves windows in a place without windows, lacunae unto their own nonexistence. The planar distortions and dimensional disjunctions of the house of fiction exceed what already exists, spatializing openings to the inexistent. James repeatedly associates architecture with such excesses—the innumerable, the infinite—outlining a paradoxical science of audaciously building impossible buildings.

Yet, for all the inventive intensity of Jamesian architecture, his edifices nonetheless hew to firm standards of integrity, to what he called "the principle of cohesion."[12] Employing architectural metaphors to convey the "proper fusions" that scaffold his visions, James labors under the imperative of precise engineering:

> For erecting on such a plot of ground the neat and careful and proportioned pile of bricks that arches over it and was thus to form, constructionally speaking, a literary monument . . . : a structure reared with an "architectural" competence . . . I should clearly have to pile brick upon brick . . . , I would leave no pretext for saying that anything is out of line, scale or perspective. I would build large—in fine embossed vaults and painted arches, as who should say, and yet never let it appear that the chequered pavement, the ground under the reader's feet, fails to stretch at every point to the base of the walls.[13]

When novelists fail, in James's estimation, as in the cases of Eliot's discursivity without dramatic intensity, Dickens's action without character density, Trollope's distension without limit, or Turgenev's simple "want of architecture," the failure rests in this dimension of architectural integrity—of proportioning and intercalation. Thus his renderings for the house of fiction famously tighten such "large loose baggy monsters" into crystalline design. His theory of the novel repeatedly advocates for "fusion"—the interrelation of parts (character, incident, description) but also the ultimate inseparability of "substance and form." The precisely built work is one in which it is "impossible to say . . . where one of these elements ends and the other begins" and one is "unable . . . to mark any such joint or seam."[14] James prizes structural integrity above all else; as he puts it, "The continuity of things is the whole matter."[15]

The preeminence of architectural tropes for James is vividly legible in that ambivalent edification of his corpus, the New York Edition. For this undertaking, James created illustrations that reinforce the powerful associations of his form and architecture. Originally envisioning a "scene, object, or locality" to be printed with each volume of fictional houses, James commissioned photographs that, in a fashion deeply reminiscent of the constructivism in Talbot's invention, prioritize the spatial dimensions of scenes and locality. The photographs display an almost singular focus on architecture: twenty-three of the twenty-four plates show structures, and even the sole exception—a portrait of the artist in ninety-degree profile—is arguably some kind of external section drawing. Colonnades, arches, bridges, gates, courtyards, grand halls, cathedrals, palaces, plazas, shops, neighboring clusters, houses, and doors, doors, doors—the photographs offer so many forms of open enclosures, of publics spectacular and mundane, of facades and their permeations,

FIGURE 3. Alvin Langdon Coburn, *The Doctor's Door* (early twentieth century). Frontispiece to *The Novels and Tales of Henry James* (New York Edition), vol. 19. Photograph: Harry Ransom Center, The University of Texas at Austin.

situations, relations. In the Prefaces to the New York Edition, James underscored the imaginary character of these spaces, prescribing that each photograph should "speak for its odd or interesting self"[16] rather than speak for a definite context or for the story; he similarly insisted that the settings of his works were themselves imaginary, a dislocation from recognizable geography, in the grand tradition of the decided fictionality of Trollope's Barsetshire, Hardy's Wessex, Eliot's provinces.[17] Richard Blackmur notes of the commissioning process that James was "insistent that no illustration to a book of his should have any direct bearing upon it,"[18] and the photographer Alvin Coburn's expansive use of filters and soft grain techniques enhance this effect of floating—dislocating the scenes from even themselves. Taken together with the pervasive architectural language of the Prefaces, the photographs offer a sister foyer for the fictions, firmly articulating the work of novelistic realism as that mathematically formal myriad production of unindexable space.

Spacing Realism

Jamesian architecture invites us to think form spatially, and to behold architecture as the art of forming spaces. In this it echoes the spatial imaginary of projective mathematics, while it also anticipates both the intermittent spatialisms ensuing in the history of literary criticism and the speculative theorizations in the history of architecture. Eons before the word "plot" takes on literary connotation, the *OED* indicates, it denotes first and foremost "a piece of ground" and secondly "a map, a plan, a scheme." These spatial grounds of the "plan or scheme of a literary work" suggest how much the plottedness ontologically comprises spatial projections, symbolizations of possible configurations of space.[19] Thus Michel de Certeau finds all narratives are intrinsically spatial: "They traverse and organize places; they select and link them together; they make sentences and itineraries out of them. They are spatial trajectories."[20]

I take inspiration for attending to literary architecturalist modeling from the mathematical radicalizations of the concept of model, the inscription of that which is not strictly available to experience. Wonderfully, the first use of "space" as a term in literary analysis in fact derives from mathematics. Mikhail Bakhtin professed to "borrow" from "mathematics" the concept of the "chronotope"—the unity of space and time—"almost as a metaphor (almost but not entirely)."[21] Just as non-Euclidean geometry raised the prospect that different orders of the universe can be defined by different space-time relations, Bakhtin extends his borrowing to argue that different literary genres can be defined by different chronotopes.[22] Nevertheless, Bakhtin was only so mathematical; he staked out the unity of time-space in line with formalist mathematics' radicalization of space, but he ultimately prioritized the temporal axis, emphasizing that plot-qua-action-transpiring-in-time is what founds the design of the narrative space.[23] Joseph Frank introduced alternative qualifications to such temporal paradigms with his now famous argument that modernist literature distinctly "intend[s] the reader to apprehend their work spatially, in a moment of time, rather than as a sequence."[24] In making this intervention, Frank emphatically situated spatial form in a modernism he found absolutely disjoint from realism—a disjuncture that remains sacrosanct. Yet James's theories, and indeed nineteenth-century fictions themselves, underline that realism too may be considered spatially.

Such consideration has been actualized only recently, in Alex Woloch's *The One vs. the Many: Minor Characters and the Space of the Protagonist.*[25] Woloch defines the novel as the asymmetric distribution of character space that models the asymmetric distribution of resources under capitalism, and goes on to define character space as "the intersection of an implied human personality . . . with the definitively circumscribed form of a narrative,"[26] the set of which spaces and their arrangement comprising in turn "the character-system."[27] Seeing the complex characterization of realism in spatial terms can in turn prompt investigations of the spatiality of other modal features of realism, such as its high degree of plottedness or its frequent omniscience.

The much lauded spatial turn of modernism appears, by the lights of these intermittent spatialisms, not as the repudiation of a realism more temporally obsessed (as evidenced in linear narrative, unfolding history), but as the prismatic extraction of realism's already extrusive projections of space in the abstract. After all, as Roman Jakobson inferred,[28] realism is decidedly spatial in its prioritization of the metonymic axis of contiguity above the metaphoric axis of continuity in the poetic temporalities of rhythm and meter in the epic. We could also note that realism's signature omniscience and free indirect discourse amount to nothing less than speculative projections of perspectival mergers and radicalizations of the space of presence, to wild projects in infrastructuralized extrusive extension. Realism experiments with knowledges, models the limits of knowledge, exercises what can be known and done when those limits are formalized. It is in this respect the close kin to mathematical formalism, the valorization of inscription as the condition of possibility for knowing that which cannot be experienced. Omniscience is, of course, impersonal narration, no matter how insistently critics try to personalize it; it is an abstraction that, as Jonathan Culler points out, reflects the abstraction of language itself.[29] A perspectival experiment that cannot be personalized, omniscience renders unanswerable Roland Barthes's question "Who is speaking?" Omniscience might furthermore be associated with the radicalization of space at stake in mathematical formalism, insofar as the omniscient point of view is an unlocalizable space, a metametaspace of transcendence of space, much like the agency of the letter or bracket in the mathematical formalization of infinite infinities. Like the bracket, too, omniscience is, Audrey Jaffe argues, a display of boundaries, since in order to

> demonstrate the ability to transcend the boundaries that confine characters, it must construct the very boundaries it displays itself transcending. Rather than being a static condition, then, the evidence of an unquestioned authority, omniscience is the inscription of a series of oppositions which mark a differ-

> ence between describer and objects of description . . . [,] an effect of narrative strategies, continually—in spite of and in distinct contrast to its invisibility—making itself felt.[30]

The impersonal abstraction of omniscience that is constitutive of realism necessitates, it seems to me, an impersonal account of its form, one that spatialism can provide.

Making this wager for the importance of spatial analysis is not meant to naively disregard time, nor to discount formalisms of time, such as music. But it is meant to evade the tendency of temporally oriented accounts of literature to invoke an embodied reader, shifting their object of inquiry from literary form to literary experience. This is the upshot of Catherine Gallagher's notable essay "Formalism and Time," which helpfully identifies inattention to time in the theory of the novel in particular, but ultimately offers less a formal account of time (duration, pace, length, measure) than observations on how readers experience the time of reading.[31] The phenomenological question (do human beings experience space only when thickened over time, do human beings experience time only when condensed in space?) must be distinguished from the formal question. More precisely, a rigorous formalism without recourse to phenomenology endeavors to grasp the being of form; formalization itself entails a certain priority of the spatial over the temporal. This is because even a poem as opposed to a painting (to take the exemplary opposition posed by Lessing, Keats, and other romantics) has a structurality that is agential and essential to its form independent of its apprehension. Outside the time of reading, it remains possible to access that structurality, to apprehend and appreciate it, in a register that consolidates the paraconceptuality at stake in the work. It may take a hundred hours to read *Bleak House*, but it does not take a hundred hours to cinch the synthetic thought that *Bleak House* thinks. Time is the experiential correlate of narrative and narrative length, but the form of the novel works to actuate a projection of the social space in its world, a projection perceptible, after the time of reading, as a blueprint or model.

To recall Lefebvre's emphasis on social space as *produced*, we can further refine this spatial conception of novelist modeling. Not for reasons of aggrandizement alone, he underscores that his assertion is so distinctive as to be virtually unthinkable: "To speak of 'producing space' sounds bizarre, so great is the sway still held by the idea that empty space is prior to whatever ends up filling it."[32] Bizarre and defamiliarizing, the literary production of space discloses the social relations in which space is always produced, in which politics is always formalization, in which there are no neutral empty immanent dimensions atop which art then unfolds. And then, a question: If space itself is produced, what can be the *art* of producing space?

What if we thought of realism as this art, a mode of production instead of a mode of reflection? Our relentlessly referentialist methods in literary study demolish the heights of James's constructivist conceit: build fiercely, soundly, cohesively, firmly—but without correlate. Build buildings whose infinite windows and crooked hinges, queer portals and speculative crevices, confound all who enter, defamiliarizing space itself. This essentially fantastical and estranging dimension of Jamesian architecture is no mere literary flamboyance—it is instead, I want to suggest, a magnification of the fantastic dimension implicit in the very architectural medium. For architecture at root is less the imposition of a pattern or order upon extant materials and space, less the erection of windows, walls, and doors around a given reality—less, in short, the kind of building with which canonical notions of realist mimesis would find their close analogue—and more a radical production of fluctuant realities.

Across a wide array of theoretical traditions, architecture lays claim to this radicalism, to production rather than representation, to creation of social spaces, to first-order formation. Architecture, Hegel philosophizes, is the first art, not only etymologically (*arche-tekne*), but because it limns the distinction between function and symbolism, between necessity and freedom.[33] Though Hegel discerns this liminality as a limit, a measure of architecture's inferiority to poetry, the firstness of architecture may be most thinkable precisely in its proximity to, rather than distance from, *writing*. Thus Derrida:

> At the outset architecture is not an art of representation, whereas painting, drawing, and sculpture can always imitate something which is supposed to already exist. . . . It is a *Riß* (rift, rupture) which should be thought of in its original sense independently of modifications such as *Grundriß* (groundplan), *Aufriß* (vertical section), *Skizze* (draft). In architecture there is an imitation of the *Riß*, of the engraving, of the ripping. This has to be associated with writing.[34]

A rend in the fabric, a rupture in reality, architectural outlining breaks (*Riß*) what is, performing the priority that Derrida eminently accords to writing. Such writing, it bears repeating, cannot be assimilated to representation. As Gérard Genette observes, "Architecture does not speak of space: it would be truer to say that it makes space speak itself."[35] For the architect Bernard Tschumi, this inscription without representation guarantees "disjunctions," the gaps between the forms of spaces and the uses to which they might be put, as well as more broadly the critical chasms between the social structures within which architecture is built (particular governments, particular economies, particular cultures) and its faculty for interrogating those structures.[36] Architecture ruptures; it realizes the priority and force of form.

Radically primary and radically critical, architecture wields power on the ground, and masters the practice of "space as the fundamental category of politics."[37] The politics of architecture, in the eyes of Le Corbusier, consists in its radical creativity, its core capacity to protract revolution from the mere seizure of power into the construction and constitution of new spaces.[38] Such politics surface when the medium is regarded formalistically; antiformalist thinkers such as Foucault have of course ascribed other politics to architecture.[39] In emphasizing the formalist approach to architectural politics, I embrace a tradition that outlines architecture's spatializing of the possible and reconfiguring of the political as the foundations of its intrinsic utopianism:

> There is no (architectural) project without exploration—through the imagination—of a possible, a future. Therefore, there is no plan without utopia . . . concrete utopia. . . . It seeks to conceive of a new space, which can only be based on an architectural project.[40]

That great surveyor of utopian functions, Ernst Bloch, stresses that the relationship is bidirectional: not only is architecture utopian, but utopia is essentially architectural, for it is nothing other than the "anticipation of a space adequate for human beings."[41]

In the abstract, architecture does not represent, depict, denote, or refer —it rather takes place, makes space, composes shape, inaugurates contour; it negates and exceeds what exists. Antimimetic, political, radical, architecture produces social space, and in this, I propose, rests at once the spirit of mathematical formalism and an isomorphism with realism. Realism fabricates volumes of sociality and voids of totality that inspire the mapping of extant spaces and incite the design of other spaces, but that must not be construed as the referential representation of a definite society. In concrete practice, architecture often attenuates its imaginary, relenting to the exigencies of engineering, subjectivizing material, financial, political, cultural limits; this encounter with limits is built into realism's architecture—that endorsement of temporal, physical, social limits that distinguishes realism from romance and science fiction. Though critics habitually conflate realism's adherence to these limits with a "reification of the social status quo,"[42] we might rethink this very recognition of constrainedness as realism's utopianism. The structuration of social space offers manifold relations, yet relationality itself is delimited above all by the impossibility of achieving a whole representation of its sphere. As James inimitably put it,"Really, universally, relations stop nowhere, and the exquisite problem of the artist is eternally but to draw, by a geometry of his own, the circle within which they shall happily appear to do so."[43] Architecture names the plastic mediation that is the imaginative construction of social space; realism is its literary instantiation.

Estranging Realism

My investigations of realism as the projection of social space originate in the interplay of Jamesian architecture and Marxist theories of space. Yet what is so remarkable to me about Jamesian architecture is how very remote and strange it appears today, when subsequent generations of professional theorists have elaborated the flatness and formlessness of realism. The analysis below walks through these accounts before attempting a re-approach to realism's architecture via another opening, the abundant architectural criticism of the greatest living theorist of realism, Fredric Jameson. Architecture serves here as a trope for the internally consistent composition of forms (aligned as well with the axioms of mathematical formalism), and for the integrally produced spatial volume that exceeds flat mimesis.

As a medium analogue for realism, architecture seems by most scholarly standards unusual, since the dominant approaches to realism have tended to emphasize the newspaper, the photograph, the telegraph, and the map, all while effectuating a sense of realism's formlessness. Such unusualness marks the important difference between technologies of relay, with their overarching implications of mimesis, and the art of building, which operates less as representation than as production. What if, then, architecture might provide some touchstones for theorizing what it is that realism produces?

Realism's products have been hard to fully perceive, since across a variety of methods and schools, from Marxism to deconstruction, new historicism to computational humanities, realism signifies most often the least formed, least artistic aesthetic, requiring interpretative frameworks other than formalism, and unavailable to theorizing on a grand scale. Assigned the job of representing the extant world, relaying the real, realism appears *formless* and hence unapproachable through formalist reading and unabstractable in theory. Within literary study it is common from a variety of methodological and political standpoints to refuse a theory of literature more broadly—championing instead literature as the singular, the resistance to theory, the anti-abstraction. But realism would seem to be the most acute case of this resistance, a formlessness that distinctly disables any possible theory, any general designation. Instead of formulating the tendencies of the mode in order to think with them, of fathoming literary history itself in terms of capacities and aesthetic attributes, critics default to claims that realism lurks everywhere and nowhere, "a syndrome" or set of "antinomies."[44]

We can track this untheorizability and this formlessness in numerous places. Realism's apparent remoteness from aesthetic formalism is the logical culmination of the now preeminent methods in the study of nineteenth-century realism, computational humanities and new historicism. Where literary formalists study literariness as a discrete function of language, the quantifiers and contextualizers share a common core that wholly equates literary language with referential, expressive, ordinary language. In the case of computational humanities, the very premise that algorithms might count instances of specific language units and that such counting would be illuminating roots itself in the presumption that language is so unambiguous and iterative as to enable quantification.[45] Precisely this conviction that literature is information already orchestrates the new historicist embrace of literature as evidence of lost presence, as portal for answering "the desire to speak with the dead."[46] This common core of reducing literary language to the calculable/evidentiary datum begets a rueful irony: in the interest of scientized knowledge (speaking with the dead to know more accurately what were their ontologically positive realities; shedding cumbersome interpretations to produce verifiable quantitative results about literature), the specificity of the science's object—its literariness—has been utterly abrogated.

It is no accident that these preeminent methods of the past forty years have been led by Victorianists like Catherine Gallagher and Franco Moretti, since the critical heritage for the study of Victorian literature consistently enforced the view of realism as the most referential, least literary of possible objects. Beginning with one of the first comprehensive literary critical works on the novel, Ian Watt's *The Rise of the Novel*, realism has been understood at once as the key determinant of the novel genre *and* as curiously unformal—a referentialism that excises the bounds of art. In Watt's skillful schema, the novel's essential realism consists of an individualizing and particularizing framework, "detailed presentation of environment"[47]/"solidity of setting"[48] and, what he deems the "most important," a prose style that "restricts itself almost entirely to a descriptive and denotative use of language."[49] This decisive referentialism determines the novel's "formlessness." As he indelibly writes, "The poverty of formal conventions would seem to be the price it must pay for its realism."[50]

Watt's findings extend and reinforce the seminal work of Eric Auerbach, whose *Mimesis* appeared in English just four years before *The Rise of the Novel*, defining realism as a transhistorical, multigenre tendency toward "the representation of daily life"[51] in a "serious" rather than comic manner. René

Wellek's pivotal work of 1961 also upholds this view, naming realism "the objective representation of contemporary social reality"[52] and despairing of the possibility of producing a coherent account of its stylistic features, concluding ultimately that realism suffers always from the "pitfall" that it might "lose all distinction between art and the conveyance of information"[53] and that "in its lower reaches realism constantly declined into journalism, treatise writing, scientific description, in short, into non-art."[54] The subliterary surmisal on this thin line of referentialism also founds George Levine's landmark 1981 study, *The Realistic Imagination*, which explores a plurality of realist practices and praises realist self-consciousness, promoting the ultimate definition that realism "always implies an attempt to use language to get beyond language, to discover some nonverbal truth out there."[55] This abiding referentialist fallacy forceloses a formalist theory of realism.

Oddly enough, deconstruction, the very literary school most committed to exploring literature beyond referentialism, has often peripheralized realism. Major theorists such as Jacques Derrida and Paul de Man demonstrably prefer poetry to prose, and the resultant literary histories often stress a romanticism–modernism continuum on which realism is hardly a blip.[56] Critics in this vein deftly champion self-reflexivity, irony, and fragmentation—often positing realism as a contradictory ideology of linguistic naivete and political totalization. J. Hillis Miller is a notable exception, a lifelong reader of realism also sustainedly engaged with deconstruction; he often makes self-reflexivity and knowingness the ultimate attitude of realism. He proposes, contra George Levine, that realism's self-referentiality demands attention to a dual process of figuration and defiguration, and that it "is not a mimesis in language of something nonverbal, but language about language," and in turn that this ultimate concern with language ferries the truth of social construction: "A novel does not represent a nontextual reality in a textual condensation. . . . The social world is already a written record or memorial."[57] Although Miller's deconstructive emphasis on self-reference destabilizes the mimetic paradigm, to more adequately analyze realism's form might require sidestepping the referential/self-referential debate altogether and tracking other functions of language, such as the performative—the production of a new order of things.

Traditional criticism, new historicism, deconstruction, and digital humanities have each in their own way posited that realism is inaccessible to formalism. But nowhere has this lack of formalism proved more vexing than in Marxism, which, with peculiar simultaneity, and somewhat befitting its long history paralleling these other trends, has been the most influential school in propagating antiformalist theories even as it has also been the only tradition to indicate real directions for a formalist theory of the novel. Like many other things that may be his fault, Friedrich Engels had already sent literary Marxist criticism down an overly referential, antifigurative path in 1888, when he wrote that "realism, to my mind, implies, besides truth of detail, the truthful reproduction of typical characters under typical circumstances."[58] Fredric Jameson, not for nothing a student of Auerbach's, has most often defined realism as "propagation of a belief in the referent"[59] or as having "a vested interest, an ontological stake, in the solidity of bourgeois social reality."[60] For a tradition in which history is form (the socially formalized matter, the narratively formalized multiplicity, that which, Marxists from Hayden White to Tom Eyers illuminate, is only available as form), realism can be merely the formless mirror. In place of form, realism correlates to the extant world as cause and referent; it courts the categorical ignorance of its aesthetic formal features irreducible to narrative; it seems to authorize the categorical mistake that art *re*presents an object that presents itself independent of representation. Prominent recent efforts to advance Marxist aesthetic theory of the contemporary have once again taken up realism, and here too Alberto Toscano, Annie McClanahan, Leigh Claire La Berge, Alison Shonkwiler, and Joshua Clover generally prize reference above all else. For Marxists, realism thus paradoxically occupies two poles simultaneously: the paragon of ideology—the imaginary resolution of real contradictions, the false suture of a partiality as a totality—*and* the paragon of artistic truth-telling, the gold standard of representing actualities behind the veil. Impossible though it may be to identify individual works that constitute "actually existing realism," the impression that the mode on the whole can best be grasped through notions of referentiality and social documentary remains commanding as a critical paradigm.

The missing Marxist theory of realist form is particularly confounding when we consider that one of the inaugural texts of Marxist literary criticism, which happens to be almost exactly contemporary with James, employs "architecture" as a pivotal trope. Even across the self-described political awakening in the middle of his intellectual career, Georg Lukács consistently understood realism as this productive building of sociality, and he hinged this understanding to figures of architecture. In the early, romantic, and riveting *Theory of the Novel*, the gap in phenomenality is almost transcendental, but loosely historicized as "modernity." Since "a totality that can be simply accepted is no longer given to the forms of art" there is a burden that "weighs too heavily upon its [art's] forms: they have to produce out of themselves all that was once simply accepted as given; in other words, before their own a priori effectiveness can begin to manifest itself, they must create by their own power alone the preconditions for such effectiveness—an object and its environment."[61] Where ancient Greece enjoys a spirit of connectedness pursuant to social totality, modernity has only the novel, a *merely formal* totality, a project to aesthetically produce totality in form. Novels are most essentially grasped as the awareness of their own formalized quality, the unshakably aesthetic and compensatory valence of their confabulation. Such attitudinal pathetic irony gives shape to the novel's only formal difference from the epic, a difference Lukács conspicuously deems "architectural": contrasting "the epic mentality's total indifference to any form of architectural construction,"[62] is a realism "self-conscious that it must have a strict compositional and architectural significance."[63] In this way he evokes architecture—the deliberate building of social space—as the trope of realist form.

Lukács's formal insights remained intact across his Marxist conversion. In *Theory of the Novel*, Lukács had acknowledged the challenges for formalist theories of realism when realist form was so hard to define, "a problem of form whose formal nature is much less obvious than in other art,"[64] yet, as we have seen, he called upon architectural tropes to mark out this formal nature. Much later, these tropes continued to offer an alternative to the mimetic paradigm, since "the Marxist conception of realism is not to be confused with any photographic reproduction of real life," and is instead anchored in structural and construction metaphors of integrity and calibrated composition.[65] That is, even after Lukács learned to blame capitalism and reification for the dispossessions and disillusions of modernity, architecture perdured as the trope of realism's distinct form. In seminal essays like "Narrate or Describe?" and "Reportage or Portrayal?" Lukács sieves good from bad composition with the criterion of balanced integration. True realism, as against naturalism, melodrama, or modernism, inheres in the integrality of every aspect of the composition. No effects without causes, no details without events, no individuality without sociality, no agency without determination. Lukács takes the trope of architecture to its ultimate form-follows-function Corbusian height: every element a purpose, every form a communist synthesis of every part's contribution according to ability and receipt according to need; volume and dimensionality wrought of fused elements. Dimensionality is the ultimate criterion of a good mode for Lukács, since he indicts "single dimensionality in the technique of representation"[66] as a trait of idealism, and poses materialism in literary construction as an "indissoluble unity of the what and how,"[67] a "concrete integrity of subjective and objective world,"[68] a responsiveness to the dialectical interrelationality of a situation. This dimensionality of integrality is an aesthetic mandate for formalizing historicity in all its dialectical possibility, and it is also that upon which Lukács rests the very definition of form itself. I quote at length so we can track the flow from dialectical historicity to formal dimensionality and political possibility:

> Every historical event is both integrally and uniquely new and also a product of historical development. . . . A poet is concerned not with what has actually happened but with what is possible. The possible, considered both positively and negatively, the maximally possible . . . represents the issue of the moment confronting the human species. . . . Literary forms develop from the theoretical and practical exploration of these concrete maximal potentialities to the ultimate. Not in the sense of mere formal techniques, for the transformation of a history or chronical into a verse might actually result in unprecedented innovations in prosody without producing true literature, but in the sense of true form, in the sense of the genuine creation of form, in the sense of the integration of the *what* of the social historical question with the *how* of the formal artistic response. Of the unity of content and form Hegel said: Content is nothing but the transformation of form into content, and form is nothing but the transformation of content into form.[69]

Formalism emerges in this analysis as the being-toward-fusion of an aesthetic sensibility that dialectically beholds the work of art in its determination and in its autonomy, the terrain of the present in its past derivation and future deviation, and form in its metabolic metamorphosis of its other into itself. These dynamic dialectics foment a motion of knitting integrity, which is the production of that very architectural dimensionality—every weight a counterweight, every element in situ, every feature constituted by, of, and for every other—which Lukács ultimately takes as the constitutive criterion of the work of art. Again and again he insists upon "intensive" construction rather than "extensive" reflection, on the dialecticity that gives great art its internally consistent, refiguratively resonant, intercalated dimensional wholeness. "Every work of art must stand on its own";[70] lacking "interpenetration,"[71] improper construction falls down.

Floor Plans of Utopia

The foundational tropes of architecture and integral construction in the virtually coeval works of James and Lukács gesture toward an as yet unactualized formalist theory of literary realism: realism is architecture, a projective composition of integral space. It is therefore a matter of no little interest that one of the other very most prominent theorists of realism, Fredric Jameson, also elaborates a profound theory of architecture, even though he does not link the two. Indeed, while architecture appears to him as an art of projective modeling with utopian dimensions, realism largely appears anchored in description. From *The Political Unconscious* up through *The Antinomies of Realism*, Jameson has defined realism as "absolutely committed to the density and solidity of what is—whether in the realm of psychology and feelings, institutions, objects or space"[72] and has labeled this fidelity realism's "inherent conservatism," its "oppressive" "reification."[73] At the best, in what he calls the "ideal of realism," the literary mode promises a "narrative discourse which unites the experience of daily life with a properly cognitive mapping"[74]—but this best is rarely attained. Whether oppressive or liberating, realism appears as the referential capture of what already exists, even if what exists, as in bourgeois modernity, is fluxus and change. Thus Jameson's ultimate formulation of realism as

> the "objective" function . . . : the task of producing as though for the first time that very life world, that very "referent"—the newly quantifiable space of extension and market equivalence, the new rhythms of measurable time, the new secular and "disenchanted" object world of the commodity system, with its post-traditional daily life and its bewilderingly empirical, "meaningless," and contingent *Umwelt*—of which this new narrative discourse will then claim to be the "realistic" reflection.[75]

This antiformalism in his literary ontology sits tightly against the formalism of his literary methods of actual textual engagement, and perhaps stems from the paradox of the novel itself, that formless form. As he defines it, "The novel is the end of genre. . . . It is not an outer, conventional form"; and therefore he emphasizes "the novel as process rather than as form."[76] At issue for us, then, is the possibility of upholding the Jamesian/Lukácisan precise sense of integral form but to do so in concert with the Marxist explorations of the sociality of form that found political formalism.

Jameson announced his fascination with the aesthetics of space and with spatial logics as the defining feature of postmodernity in his original essay on postmodernism (later to become his most influential book).[77] In particular, he describes the "mutation in built space" that postmodern architecture effectuates, and he anatomizes the body's response, which is one of bewildered disorientation and perceptual incapacity, and then he proceeds to analogize this individual dislocation to "the incapacity of our minds, at least at present, to map the great multinational and decentered communicational network in which we find ourselves caught."[78] This cartographic dilemma raises for Jameson the issue of aesthetic theory's "repudiation . . . of the pedagogical and the didactic"[79] and occasions his call for "a new (and hypothetical) cultural form as an aesthetic of cognitive mapping."[80] He is very careful to repeatedly, assertively declare that "the cognitive map is not exactly mimetic,"[81] and I would underline that this nonmimeticism has not been fathomed by those who have taken up the concept, much to its detriment as an instrument for aesthetic analysis.[82] For Jameson the designation of cognitive mapping as an "aesthetic" cannot be mapped onto the Althusserian opposition between ideology and science, phenomenal experience and abstract knowledge. Rather, what is important is the "symbolic" character of this other kind of compassing, the "radically new forms" in which such a mediation of the tension between "situational representation on the part of the individual subject" and "that vaster and properly unrepresentable totality which is the ensemble of . . . structure as a whole"[83] becomes possible. The aesthetic is, in other words—in this schema that Jameson explicitly details as a Lacanian modification of traditional Marxism—in fact a deeply Kantian category, in its paraconceptual alternative to the opposition of intuitions (experience, ideology) and concepts (science). The aesthetic stands as a different, privileged kind of knowing.

If, though, the Kantianism of Jameson's aesthetic would position it transversely to the transcendental categories of perception (time and space), this is not quite the route he takes, since the nonmimetic map retains for him a crucial spatial aspect; Jameson is keen to define this aesthetic via its proximity to, rather than distance from, the axis of "pure reason" that is *space*. In this he accentuates tendencies in Marx's own thought, since the Marxian theory of history is complemented by a parallel, if tacit, theory of space. One thinks, for instance, of the seminal role of Engels's experiments with exploring urban space in *The Condition of the Working Class in England* or the utopian projection of better orders of forms in *The Manifesto of the Communist Party*. Jameson picks up this spatial emphasis and privileges spatially engaged aesthetics as sites of possible cognitive mapping—namely, architecture and cinema.[84]

It is in his architecture writings where the aesthetic of cognitive mapping is best revealed as necessarily spatial without being mimetic, where the prospect of spatial figurations rather than spatial imitations is best developed. I loiter in those writings for a bit because I think they might help renovate Jameson's own account of literary realism, bridging it to the theory of realism as the projection of social space that Henry James helped us to begin. Jameson's architecture criticism exalts endeavors that reimagine massings and gradings, installations and institutions, closures and openings. Much like James's impossible effusions of millions of windows and confounding forays through queer hinges, Jameson's buildings innovate fabulous openings; much like James's structural cohesiveness, Jameson's buildings contrive dynamic totalities. His architectural appraisals listen to spaces that James heard "speak for [their] odd or interesting self," making space thinkable as the groundwork of sociality and social possibility, carving gateways to utopia. For James and Lukács, architecture embodies the structural integrity of the novel. For Jameson, architecture most prominently bodies forth ponderings of utopia. Engaging the space between them, we can begin to track the utopian potential of the realist novel's architecture—to think realism aslant of reference, to think its creative constructions in their other-worldly richness, to think its formalist mathematical models of spaces beyond experience.

Over a number of historical movements, Jameson reads in architecture great utopian potential. His superb essay on Frank Gehry's Santa Monica house, for example, revels in the way Gehry's subsumption of a classic pink clapboard bungalow within corrugated steel and chain-link amounts to "an effacement of the categories of inside/outside,"[85] activating a dialectic of interstitiality that performs the sort of mediated openings that can ballast utopias. In Robert Gober's architectural sculptures like "Untitled Installation," Jameson similarly venerates formalizations of between-ness and dialectical suspension. A doorframe separated by depth from a door leaning against a wall, Gober's incorporates "what might once have been called painting, sculpture, writing, and even architecture," becoming a work of multimedia in which "there is, first of all, no 'representation' to look at."[86] Moving through the installations, Jameson locates utopia on the threshold of fantastical vestibules, windows in dead walls and doors to nowhere. Utopia here pivots on the aestheticized framing of space itself, delineating extant constellations, exposing the artifice and contingency of constellation as such, precipitating other spaces.

Where the postmodern aesthetic activates openings, the *post*-postmodern produces enclosures that, in their very boundedness and limitation, offer equally utopian generations. Most exemplary for Jameson is Rem Koolhaas's vigorous pursuit of the large form—often a macro-cladding enveloping solids and gaps. Jameson zeroes in on the contradiction dramatized between exterior and interior:

> Large scale now produces . . . *incommensurability*. . . . The contents of the various large-scale projects can also be seen as a selection of all the geometric forms and solids imaginable: an enormous random collection of solids, cones, cubes, pyramids, spheres, and so on, such that what they are housed or collected in (as it were the notorious "class of all classes") does not itself fall under any of those geometrical types or categories and must be dismissively referred to as a "block."[87]

The tension between the déclassé block and the particularized solids that it houses, as well as the secondary tension of junctures and misjunctures between the voids and divergent solids, activates a zone of contradictions precariously cantilevered into a delimitable whole. And it is finally this antagonistic whole that Jameson admires, for it eloquently bespeaks an "ambition to grapple with the totality of the social itself."[88] Totality for Jameson means the "properly unrepresentable ensemble of society's structures as a whole"[89]—the mode of production, the relations of production, ideology, *and* their negations, the coexistence of other structures, along with the epistemological impossibility of fixing these dynamic negations and relations. Projects like Koolhaas's are not therefore *representations of* totality but enunciations of the question of such representation: mediations of space, aestheticizations of logics that rivet and contradictions that unhinge.

Aesthetic totalization is positioned by Jameson as the distinguishing hallmark of utopian projects: "It is precisely th[e] category of totality that presides over the forms of Utopian realization: the Utopian city, the Utopian revolution, the Utopian commune or village, and of course the Utopian text itself."[90] "The text itself" is the thorny point for us here; Jameson has notably studied the utopianism of science fiction, conspiracy cinema, and allegory, but he hardly rates realism on his scales of utopia, going so far as to argue that "truly Utopian forms . . . drift out of the province of realism altogether" and that "realism has a vested interest, an ontological stake, in the solidity of bourgeois social reality."[91] But the question of totality obliges us to read Jameson against himself. After all, his scandalous willingness to proffer Walmart as a paradigmatic utopia should teach us that the place of no place might be right where we least expect it.[92] By extension, what has so often been decried as the most conservative of all the novel's revolutionary modes might offer something quite radical. Taking the point that utopian modes and genres are characteristically concerned with totality, should we not also reciprocally observe that modes animated by what Jameson deems "the desire called totality" have utopian inflection? "The desire called totality" works as a name for the libidinal register of the orientation Lukács locates in realism's retaining the sensation of totality after its social dissolution ("das dennoch die Gesinnung zur Totalität hat"). We have already mentioned that Lukács contrasts "the epic mentality's total indifference to any form of architectural construction,"[93] with a realism self-conscious that it "have a strict compositional and architectural significance"[94] and equally self-conscious about "show[ing] polemically the impossibility of achieving"[95] a representation of totality, and thus we might deduce that the encounter with totality *as a problem* originates realism's architecturality. If realism addresses itself to totality, might it not meet the criterion for utopian form?

Architecture's performance of the problem of totality is precisely what enchants James, and what intrigues Jameson. Jameson reads "the desire called totality" palpably exhibited by post-postmodern architecture, while James and Lukács elevate architecture as a figure of total integration in an architectural period we could scarcely deem modern; from their joint fascination, then, emerges the prospect that the question of totality and totalization actuates a faculty of architecture as such (and this is avowedly in diverse architectural movements).[96] In James, as we have seen, architecture densely casts impossible totality—the aesthetic wholeness of fantastical space. Architecture attracts James as prism for the art of fiction precisely because a building's parts are so necessarily parts of wholes: to manufacture parts without regard to whole is to engineer dilapidation; to take architecture apart is to demolish, to lose the thing itself.[97] Architecture provides a vernacular for James to house his craft of fictive construction, and it likewise provides Jameson with a craft to figure the utopian projective construction of other worlds:

> Counterhegemony means producing and keeping alive a certain alternate "idea" of space. . . . [Architects] are able to form conceptions and Utopian images of . . . collective ensembles that express and articulate original social relations (and needs and demands) of a collective type. . . . Such Utopian "ideas" are as "objective" as material buildings.[98]

The articulation of original social relations, the art of the aperture, the *Riß* of the plane, the experimental formalization of a spatial ideal—these are architecture's utopian practices, and they are the very purview of literary realism.

Jameson comes closest to fathoming realism as the construction of social space in his essay "The Realist Floor Plan," in which he credits realism with manufacturing the lifeworld of capitalist modernity. Glancingly remarking the importance of a "characterization of 'realism' less passive than the conventional notions of 'reflexion,' 'representation,' and the like,"[99] he proceeds to think "this productive function" as the illustrative instantiation of what has properly been produced elsewhere:

> The ideological mission of the nineteenth century realistic novelists . . . is not merely to produce new mental and existential habits, but in a virtual or symbolic way to produce this whole new spatial and temporal configuration itself: what will come to be called "daily life", the *Alltag*, or, in a different terminology, the "Referent"—so many diverse characterizations of the new configuration of public and private spheres or space in classical or market capitalism.[100]

When it is productive, literary realism partners with socioeconomic forces to inaugurate new conditions. Even as he thus grants productive agency to the literary, he merges that production with the broader mode of production, forcelosing the imaginative, utopian, counter-factuality of the literary.

But acknowledging this agency should prompt other insights: What if this productive function were thought in less determined, more "relatively autonomous" terms?[101] What if this floor plan were extruded into a blueprint?

Architecture improvises paradoxical openings, practices an art of integrity, disorients space. Realist architecture improvises social cohesion, images a mode of social production at once free and constrained, defamiliarizes realities. In its precise calibration of lintels and joists, its ingenious assemblage of interlinking strata, realism proffers not a unified meaning to which its various levels can be resolved, but an aestheticization of necessary and contingent webs of relations, a spatialization of implication and determination, a mediation of the particular by the universal and of totality by its impossibility. Put differently, realist structural integrity is the aestheticization of dialectics.

Speculative Theses on Axonometry

Realism's integral modeling of social space braces the forms that constitute sociality, enunciating the political formalist truth that there is no world without form. Realism's enchantment of quotidian worldly forms animates a constructivist marvel for what can be made. Realism encompasses not *the* world but *a* world, drafting a structuration of social space that does not reify the extant order of things even though it acknowledges the inevitability that constructed realities take on ontological solidity. Realism's exploration of the city, governmentality, labor, and law affirms *that there is* institution, but does not inherently affirm any particular institution or form thereof. Realism investigates the insuperable dilemmas that destabilize social grounds, the impossibility for any immanent social space, the provisional solutions that contingent constellations afford, the paramount political question of totalization. Realism's casting of variegated nets, networks, webs, and systems for interconnectedness affirms the insuperability of human interdependence. Realism's experimentation with omniscience and its limits, focalization and its curtailments, free indirect discourse and impersonal grammars, affirms that consciousness itself is spatial, and that no steady point of view for relations avails. Realism's evocation of secular causality, democratized providence, and impeachable knowledge affirms that collectivity is a project without logic, an antagonism without solution, a world without natural order. Realism's interrogative impetus (what is reality? what is real? what processes substantiate realness? what could be real?) queries the possible, and thus incites thinking and building more utopically than utopian fiction's normativity. Realism contemplates indispensable elements of human affiliation, models relational space, conducts charettes for sociality. Realism is not the index of fact but the house of fiction; not reference, not evidence, not representation; realism is architecture.

Realist architecture asks for spatially astute reading practices, attending to realism not as symptom but as mediation, not as determined reflection but as determinate negation, not as ideological content but as utopian form. It asks in short for reading practices that actually sustain its own formal dialecticity. Novels know that the worlds they build are artificial, artifacted, designed, and this is how they know that the same is true of any world; in their self-concept they effectuate political formalism. We owe it to them to persuasively advocate for the making of new worlds as the very work of literature. If we could more robustly fathom the literary as figurative, as spatially inventive world-mapping but also world-making, as mathematically formal projective modeling, as critical in its very negation of the already made, its very exceeding of what exists, as utopian in its very exertion to build something else, we might activate literature's contributions to the most important Marxist formalist project, building new formations against rapaciously imperialist capitalism.

The readings that follow are speculative exercises in attending to realism formalistically, reading for its architecture, its mathematical radicalization of space alongside its affirmation of structuration. The chapter orders are chronological—but only because they make vivid cumulatively thereby the problematic of abstraction in and as sociality that most interests us. From the framed multiple narration of *Wuthering Heights* to the astonishing oscillation of first- and third-person narration in *Bleak House* to the destabilization of perspective and distillation of omniscience in *Alice's Adventures in Wonderland* to the harrowing incisiveness into the schema of things in *Jude the Obscure*, abstraction enfolds a blending of perspectives, an abrupt delimitation of perspectival bounds, a precipitous careening amid and betwixt worlds, an engrossed remoteness of beholding totalizations. Each of the novel chapters has some occasion to grapple with quotidian architecture (the houses and frames of *Wuthering Heights*, the delimited, repeated domicile "Bleak House," the distinctive buildings of Wonderland, the many construction projects in the architect Hardy's final novelistic composition). But these first-order analyses quickly open more broadly onto the realist blueprint, realism's endeavor to model social space—onto an order of form itself: to each text's intercalation of literary elements, and that composition's animating drive toward the projective dispensation of sociality. Formalist reading for realist architecture thereby refines our grasp of political formalism, that affirmation of the merely formal, perennially reformable sociable infrastructure.

2

The Set Theory of *Wuthering Heights*: Realism, Antagonism, and the Infinities of Social Space

It is the largest concern of this book to pursue political formalism as an alternative to anarcho-vitalism, an alternative that affirms form itself as the provisionally shaped synthesis of collective interdependence. Inspiration for this alternative rests in the surprising affinities between the contemporaneous projects of Marxian materialism, mathematical formalism, and literary realism, which each accord a decisive priority to form as the precondition of possible space. My approach to these affinities, as to the questions of political imagining they advance, originates in literary critical methods. Thus the main chapters of this book are dedicated to formalist literary readings that endeavor to exemplify how attending to the composition of relations within a novel is an intellectual practice that bears upon the political question of how or even whether to compose relations in the outside world. Chapter 1 argues for literary realism as an axis of political formalism by proposing to redefine realism in formalist terms as the modeling of possible social space, an aesthetic endeavor to sensuously contemplate form as infrastructure for life. In this chapter I begin to practice the reading strategies attendant upon that theory. Taking up the conjuncture, in 1847–48, of *The Manifesto of the Communist Party*, set theory, and *Wuthering Heights*, I explore how this extraordinary novel vividly enunciates a political theory of economic antagonism that refines Marxist insights into the strife that unsettles every social space by enfolding those insights into mathematical problems of representing infinite possible dispensations of space. Even as it searchingly surveys the insuperable negativity of class antagonisms, this novel inscribes a deep, mathematical esteem for positive structuration in every register of its form—through its frame narration, its architectural poetics, its pronounced patterning, its mathematical cosmology, and its overarching denaturing of economies. The aesthetic qualities of social formalization forever open the lot of new building.

Universality and Antagonism

Political formalism affirms the merely formal quality of political dispensation. It is the obverse and corollary of a politico-ontological affirmation of antagonism, that gap in relationality that precludes immanence. The conceit that equates formlessness with liberation underestimates antagonism, locating social contradiction purely in the inadequacy of forms, rather than in their ungroundability. Any theory of the social that portends a solution to this ungroundability falls short of contending with the extent of social negativity—the awesome lack of natural, immanent, sufficient relations. Even though Marxism is a dialectical procedure of negativity that addresses the unshakable contingency of politico-economic relations, this very error of underreckoning with the ungivenness of sociality has sometimes dogged it, insofar as Marxism has been seen to overstate the role of capitalism in human immiseration, mistaking the end of capitalism for the end of struggle. Yet, as we have read in the founding documents of *The German Ideology*, Marx's materialism forthrightly and capaciously articulates the priority of sociality to the individual, the necessity of formed collectivity for species survival, and the historical variability of any form of this social space.

In *The Manifesto of the Communist Party*, however—Marxism's other founding document—we can find some origin of this failing. In the spring of 1847, as he sought Belgian refuge from Prussian oppression, Karl Marx answered the call of comrades to compose a manifesto articulating propositions for the people. "The people" had ephemerally emerged as a subject in England and Europe in the Glorious Revolution and the French Revolution, and, as the communists saw it, the engines of contradiction were roiling toward another apparition. "A specter is haunting Europe,"[1] Marx opened, hailing the spirited prospect of collective seizure of the means of production and collective determination of the sociality to come. Printed in February 1848, *The Manifesto of the Communist Party* ultimately predated by mere days the advent of its constituency's new semblance, in the Springtime of the Peoples, when uprisings and mass demonstrations in dozens of countries pushed back against systematic dispossession and asserted rights to democratic governments. *The Manifesto* proleptically advocates for upholding what will have been those revolts, for developing not-yet-organized parties of workers to supersede the revolutionary conditions sown by bourgeois society—and it emplots such efforts as universal history: "The history of all hitherto existing society is the history of class struggle" ("Die Geschichte aller bisherigen Gesellschaft ist die Geschichte von Klassenkampfen").[2]

How are we to understand this weird little word "all"? There is something surprising about an ontological claim coming from the founders of historical materialism, which so usually seems license for skepticism. Ontologically, the "all" proclaims, history is the history of class struggle; "class" and "struggle" both pertain to the essence of the human. Across recorded civilization—freeman and slave, lord and serf, bourgeoisie and proletariat, oppressor battling oppressed—history is what hurts, and modern capitalism merely "simplifies" the hostilities.[3] *All* of human existence is collective interdependence, *all* of human existence is the lack of an immanent form for this interrelationality; and thus *all* of human existence is the struggle over the shape of the quintessentially necessary but radically arbitrary socius. Historical materialism, often presumed a particularizing enterprise, is here paradoxically universalizing, addressing the irreparably antagonistic character of human social relations, where antagonism signals not psychological strife but the material void whence social form hails.

Marxism's commanding account of human sociability's essential nonessence has too often been overshadowed by its more pressing indictment of capitalism. We think of Marxism as the critique of the capitalist mode of production, but we think less often of it as a formalism of the political that reveals the ungroundedness of all modes of production. This very trajectory in its future reception is already precipitated by the rhetoric and genre of *The Manifesto* itself, whose hyperbole and topicality, sloganeering and presentism, stand in tension with Marxism's erstwhile universal ontology. In *The Manifesto*, a *universal* unsolvable problem (*all* hitherto existing history is the history of social antagonism) is provided a *particular* solution (the overthrow of the specific regime of private property, the specific kind of antagonism), and in the process the particularity occludes the universality. The political urgency to unseat the capitalist mode, in 1848 as in our own spectacularly immiserated grotesquely privatized present, risks conceptual trouble: the communist horizon gets falsely conflated with ending antagonism as such. Both the theory and practice of Marxism have been hindered by this risk; our ability to fathom a sociality more adequate to human flourishing that also does not present itself as natural or groundable suffers when the capitalist simplification of antagonism simplifies antagonism as such.

The genre of manifesto may not be quite suited to this politically and philosophically important task of complicating simple antagonism, but perhaps another genre is. In this chapter, I call upon *the novel* as a mode of thinking uniquely helpful for elaborating the multiple prongs of political formalism: acknowledging the universal antagonism, admitting social form's ungroundedness, condemning particularly capitalist domination, and yet prizing the energy of social formalization anyway. *The Manifesto* has a theory of universal antagonism that particularizes itself so much we can't see it that way. A novel, however, might be just the kind of paraconceptual constellation that is able to think universal and particular simultaneously—that is able to think dialectically, that is able to think the contradiction between all possible antagonism and a subset. Emily Brontë's astonishing *Wuthering Heights,* in the very same 1847–48 England of *The Manifesto,* is such a novel, merging Marxist ontology of antagonism with mathematical rigor of universalization with aestheticized form. Through its unique interest in the objectivity of economic antagonism, in the ubiquity and ductility of social forms, and in the paradoxes of inscribing infinity, *Wuthering Heights* theorizes the unending negativity of the social in a way that preempts the risks of romanticizing a communist end. Instead, this novel suggests that economic antagonism ought be the premise, rather than the refutation, of social forms; learning that every economy lacks grounds authorizes more constructive attempts to build them anyway.

As I read the novel formalistically, I also continue the project in *The Order of Forms* to triangulate political formalism, aesthetic formalism, and mathematical formalism, resounding Marx and Brontë with a third framework from that same nodal point in history, the revolutionary discovery of mathematical set theory. Set theory comprehends infinite multiplicity with the aid of symbolic abstraction. If one of Marx's core insights is that we cannot understand social relations merely by experiencing them directly and must therefore make recourse to abstractions, formalist mathematics offers itself as a parallel affirmation of what abstractions can do. The formalist revolution in mathematics offers models of relations that are less content-filled than social theory, and it does so at the exact moment in intellectual history when political thought most needs to break away from the empirical. In autonomizing models from what exists, formalist math allows the thinking of the inexistent, the charting of new extents. The formalist endeavors this book studies unite in a radicalization of space: an effort to conceptualize, aestheticize, and formalize the riven planes on which take place both historical pasts and possible futures. The intersection of the critique of political economy, the insurgent realist novel, and formalist math refracts infinite spatial possibilities, expansively open fields of relationality, and the prospect that formalizations of sociality otherwise than private property will never dispatch with ungroundedness but may powerfully enable new freedoms.

The Manifesto seems to collapse capitalist social antagonism and all possible social antagonism—it seems, in another idiom, to mistake capitalist antagonism for the set of all possible antagonisms, of which capitalist antagonism is merely a member. One possible explanation for this mistake is the unprecedented totalization of capitalism in Marx's time. The social process of enclosure greatly exemplifies this totalization, and, as we will see, it is a particularly salient example for *Wuthering Heights.* From the middle of the eighteenth through the middle of the nineteenth century in Britain, millions of acres of communally utilized land were privatized through thousands of legal acts; Parliament systematized these small laws into a cohesive policy with the General Enclosure Act of 1801. Such seizures, sometimes violent, impose new conditions: closing effective commons; generating private property that could in turn be monetized; casting subsisters onto the wage market. As an example of particular impositions, however, enclosure also exemplifies the tipping point at which such impositions posit a new generality. In Carolyn Lesjak's succinct phrase, enclosure was "at once a series of discrete events and . . . a catastrophe," the violent annihilation of an entire way of life rooted in the commons and the common right.[4] If the discrete legal acts of forcible seizure embody particular totalizations, the General Act of 1801's generalization of catastrophe exemplifies a general totalization: a new "way of life" becomes reality, eviscerating preexisting alternatives. The decimation of communal living constitutes at once an economic crisis for those who must now sell their labor rather than their products, and a political crisis that Marx calls "expropriation of the people,"[5] the abnegation of any notion of common, communally bound existence. Once the laborer is freed to sell himself as commodity, he seems to himself and to others as an individual. Capital produces this semblance; it produces the lack of a commons as a prelude to the individualism that founds its ideology and its mode.

The problem of how such totalizations are to be thought has often been debated by Marxists, since social processes with discrete, contingent histories transpire simultaneously but heterogeneously with the overarching tendency of the system to amass ever greater extent, scope, and necessity. Universalizing in its very essence, unaccountable in the mere terms of what precedes it, unfixable at a definitive period, totalizing capitalism raises the specter of the diminishing returns of historicism, of how historical materialism might demand a different method, one that apprehends the kind of synchronic totalization that enclosure effectuates, the kind of structure that capital effectuates. It is this necessity of synchronic thinking, often also known as structuralism, that *The Manifesto* seems to me to obliquely perform. At a certain point in time (1848 it would seem), the history of capitalism ceases to appear as a discrete history of a particular mode of production and its attendant relations of production, and begins to appear as the history of "all hitherto existing" relations, or, at least, as the history whose end would also end all hitherto existing relations; diachrony becomes synchrony.

The Manifesto's ultimate minimization of the universal history of antagonism obscures the material fact of the abyssal negativity of human sociality, equating that fact with capitalist exploitation. Human life is constrained and bonded, finite and interdependent, a material ontology Marx also inscribed in his frequent praise for Aristotle's *zoon politikon*: political being is the being whose very existence depends on the collective (as Hegel might put it, in the universal there is life, in the particular only death), yet the collective enjoys no possible givenness and can only be wrought of politicized formalization. The open question of the form responsive to these constraints mandates that, even after the abolition of private property, the future history of human society will continue to be that of political antagonism over social space, class struggle by other means. The problem is how to sustain "antagonism" itself, how to ensure both in theory and in practice that antagonism is at once the preeminent force *against* capital's immanentization (history is the history not of the value form but of the class struggle) and simultaneously that antagonism is the force *after* capitalism. What social forms are less simple than capital versus labor, accommodating more complex antagonisms? What forms could mediate their own internal dialectic of contingency and necessity, contrivedness and indispensability?

This problem of sustaining antagonism, thinking universal history abstractly from within the regime of universal abstraction, and formalizing sociality anyway, this is *the* problem that to me defines the shared space of Marxism and the novel. Whatever the historiographic debates internal to Marxism about synchrony and diachrony and their possible dialectical rapprochement, what the theorizing proper to the novel form offers Marxism is a speculative experiment in dynamizing the synchronic: mobilizing the synchronic as the kind of thinking sufficient to totalization, the kind of thought that can brace simultaneously the totalization of capitalism and the coexistence of pre-, post-, or noncapitalist class struggles, the thought that preserves less the diachrony of contingency than the structure of the transcendental antagonism, the thought of social structuration as such. A robust synchronic logic born not of error (failing to always historicize) but of formalism (attending to the composition of structure).

Marxism can in turn offer the novel not so much a diagnosis of its determination, a sociology of its production, an audit of its failures to accurately, referentially represent the extant world, but much more: intense focus on form (form was after all what distinguished Marx's critique of political economy from what came before[6]), and the practice of dialectical critique,[7] sufficient critique, critique in full dimension, critique as *both* the laying bare of a form or space *and* the utopian pursuit of other forms, other spaces, critique responsive to the dialecticity of the form itself. Marxism shares the novel's own utopian impulses, its project to reimagine the social spaces of lived reality, and it is this commonality that forever justifies Jameson's claim for it as "the untranscendable horizon" of novel reading.[8] Marxism brings the project of dialectical critique to the novel, and in return, the novel offers Marxism the special dialectic internal to synchronic logic, the thought of totalization *and* the thought of the structures in a parallel universe with that which is total now. There were other pasts, there are other futures, contingent apertures revealed by the novel's mediation of social structuration.

Such emphasis on the Marxian topoi of utopian energies and dialectical dynamism in the novel form circa 1848 will strike many Marxist literary theorists as strange, since 1848 hinges of course the irredeemable turning point in Lukács's historicization of the novel genre.[9] Close on *The Manifesto*'s publication, the people surged as the subject of anticapitalist struggle. But after the burn (and after London, that imperial and financial if not cultural capital of the nineteenth century, never lit), the spent revolutionary credit of the bourgeoisie irrevocably impoverished the novel. Lukács saw a brief zenith of actually existing realism, alive with dialectical dynamism and political optimism, descend into the moribund determinism and rank conservatism of the naturalist nadir. Perhaps, though, we can take 1848 as a rather different fulcrum in the institution of the novel—take Lukács's own literary determinism and recast a rather different dynamism. For it is none other than 1848, after all, that gives us an alternative threshold, not the end of realism but the beginning of realism's real phase, the moment when the historical novel's master trope of diachrony became the subsumed novel's actualized synchrony. This would be then the moment at which the proper terrain of the realist novel, and its finest property, become the antagonism cleaving all social space, the moment when the rift in space and the nonimmanence of what is called reality become not so much *representable* as *mediatable*, subject to both synthesis and negation. This would be the moment of *Wuthering Heights*.

Housing Problems

Wuthering Heights demands the kind of synchronizing and reading I above referred to as "dialectical," so my attention will be to the form of this novel, to the formalist question of the way figurative structures in the novel (types of narration, repeated images, the arrangement of events into plot, the values pronounced by character, the stylization of setting, the letters of names, the structuration of chapters and volumes, ellipses and hyperboles) all synthesize one another. This synchronicity in the aesthetic of the novel, as I have suggested up to this point, encircles a particularly adroit capacity for critical synchronic logic, a capacity for animating synchronic logic as multidimensional, with a dynamism all its own. Radical synchronic thinking, instantaneous representation of the extent of what exists and the extent of what could be, is also the promise of mathematical set theory, which endeavors to rigorously formalize infinity infinities. Where there is a certain risk of a flatter synchrony in *The Manifesto*—a risk that the antagonism materialism distinctly perceives as defining all of human history would be domesticated by the nullification of private property—in the very same year *Wuthering Heights*'s peculiarly heightened synchrony and its mathematically inflected figurative system sustain simultaneously the total hell of private property *and* its underlap with the all of class struggle, underscoring a different truth than *The Manifesto*. For *Wuthering Heights*, property is merely one guise of the irreducible, withering antagonism of the economic, the irrepressibly negative void of any *nomos* for every *oikos*. Holding open this antagonism may be the indispensable prolegomena to any future critique of political economy. Political formalism absolutizes antagonism so that every institution of social space may be countenanced in its formedness and reformability. Only in perceiving sociality as transcendentally negative can we sustainably build new forms against the capitalist simplification of hostilities. And only in sieving the particular guises of social antagonism from the universality of antagonism can we approach the political formalism that I have been arguing is crucial for more just relations. *Wuthering Heights* posits the indelible thesis that social antagonism is unending, larger than capitalism and the regime of private property, but also that social formations, in all their stylized structure, remain necessary, malleable, constructible.

While private property comprises the definitive logic of modernity, it does not definitively exhaust the problem of human sociality; while property is *Wuthering Heights*'s central concern (the fight for control of a house, the question of who is proper to the family unit, the enigma of the property of the self), it is not the novel's only concern. The plot certainly offers a thoroughgoing critique of property—aristocratic families are in shards, common lands are enclosed, property battles and propriety disputes abound—but that plot is formally contextualized in a way that also offers far more. From the novel's pervasively spatialized images, motifs, setting, and narrative mode all pressing on frames, boundaries, hearths, thresholds, all querying architecture's foundationlessness, and from the animalities and alliances of the human, civilization's discontents, all unsettling social space, we get an enfleshed materialist theorization of the universality of class antagonism. This theory endogenous to *Wuthering Heights* is an essential premise of political formalism. Property prevails as the modern logic for the ordering of space, but even in its abolition the intractable enigma of how to formalize sociality will remain. In privileging the complexities of space—no possible configuration of space is peaceable, yet configuration as such is inescapable—*Wuthering Heights* holds open the gap between the particularly capitalist antagonism and economic antagonism in general. Furthermore, in aestheticizing spatial relations so vividly, the novel insists on the formal quality of social shaping.

In chapter 1, I proposed architecture as a foundation for an antimimetic theory of literary realism as the practice of producing social space, a practice that accords with certain material limits but that is also constitutively utopian. Literary architecture means much more than literature *about* architecture, but it is notable that *Wuthering Heights* is fascinated with architecture as a trope for the framing of space; this fascination immediately puts social space in question, asking not only what happens to relations when they are anchored by private real estate, nor only what happens when that anchor is upended by mercantilism and finance, but also whether any possible arrangements of house and home would ever evade violent conflict and contingent law. Architecture is this novel's master trope of social structuration, built from the ground up starting with the *frame*, which happens to also be set theory's enabling constraint. Aestheticizing the brackets of social forms, *Wuthering Heights* limns what they offer, simulating set theory's bracketing of infinity to fathom its multiplicity.

Wuthering Heights is a house of a novel, and we must loiter in this house, for the way the novel builds itself around structural and architectural tropes unlocks its constructivist imaginary. Architecture is never self-identical in this novel, but always contradictory—the site of conflict and contestation and construction. The title, portal to the story, activates a built form inflected by the regime of property, a house with a proper name. Yet this proper name "Wuthering Heights" denominates questions of structural integrity and elemental assault. "A significant provincial adjective,"[10] Lockwood tells us, "wuthering" conjures "pure, bracing" "atmospheric tumult."[11] To make a house wuthering, a high house wuthering, is to activate numerous tumults: blustering wind, decaying heights, withering critique. In a stroke, this nonsense portmanteau conjures architecture as trope of shifting social stratifications. Inalienable "real estate" palpated in its alienation: the house can be acquired, the domestic eviscerated, the property improperly repossessed, an erstwhile immutable now on the move. Both heights as a location and house as a construct are variable, unstable, shifting, under attack, and "house" stands first for the setting of social transformation—all that was solid liquidating into the moorland mists.

Crucially, the architectural imaginary equally opens a mathematically formalist one, since the novel apprehends these transformations in an instant rather than over time: in place of any history of the house (think of Jane Austen's opening gambits on estates and entails) we get a formal vision. Lockwood immediately remarks: "Happily, the architect had foresight to build it strong: the narrow windows are deeply set in the wall, and the corners defended with large jutting stones."[12] Before he even enters the house, that is, our narrator celebrates its canny design, the prevision of the maker, who knows his shelter is at odds with nature and thus takes care to reinforce its boundaries and protect its permeable points. A house, in attempting to install a space of culture in the fields of nature, to rebut climate with buttress, appears above all a project of differentiating: nature from art, outside from in, "exposed" from "defended." The boundary patrol of *Wuthering Heights* commences in earnest from the first scene—not simply from Heathcliff repelling the interloper he has himself contracted, but from the interloper making such a fine study of the materials of boundaries, and their vulnerabilities, and then "inspecting the penetralium." The ensuing orientation sketches nothing less than a floor plan, replete with realist detail:

> One step brought us into the family sitting-room, without any introductory lobby or passage: they call it here "the house" pre-eminently. It includes kitchen and parlour, generally, but I believe at Wuthering Heights the kitchen is forced to retreat altogether into another quarter, at least I distinguished a chatter of tongues, and a clatter of culinary utensils, deep within; and I observed no signs of roasting, boiling, or baking, about the huge fire-place; nor any glitter of copper saucepans and tin cullenders on the walls. One end, indeed, reflected splendidly both light and heat from ranks of immense pewter dishes, interspersed with silver jugs and tankards, towering row after row, on a vast oak dresser, to the very roof. The latter had never been under-drawn: its entire anatomy lay bare to an inquiring eye, except where a frame of wood laden with oatcakes and clusters of legs of beef, mutton, and ham, concealed it. Above the chimney were sundry villainous old guns, and a couple of horse-pistols: and, by way of ornament, three gaudily painted canisters disposed along its ledge. The floor was of smooth, white stone; the chairs, high-backed, primitive structures, painted green: one or two heavy black ones lurking in the shade.[13]

In these architectural panoramas, narrative itself works as the extrusion of spatial details into the social relations they inform. Lockwood studies the flow from room to room, the functions of the rooms, the material of the floor, and the exposed beam-work of the roof that "never had been underdrawn" (filled in with plaster). Floorboard to rafter, end to end, "row after row," the narrator surveys with "inquiring eye," perspicuously takes in the space, its infrastructure, and the relations it fosters. The kitchen is heard rather than seen, except for the glimmer of the abundance, the pots and meats hanging from the rafters; the center for producing the provisions of life obscured except in its din. It is unclear, even to the penetrating eye in the penetralium, how food and family get made, and this conundrum of making life ascends as a prime mystery for this novel to investigate. When Master Heathcliff instructs Joseph the servant to "take Mr Lockwood's horse; and bring up some wine," Lockwood instantly surmises, "Here we have the whole establishment of domestics," and wastes no time judging the failing housekeeping ("No wonder the grass grows up between the flags").[14] From such an opening we can glean that narration takes as its conditioning pretext the inventorying of social space, the interpretation and regulation of domesticity, and the querying of who belongs inside the bounds. *Wuthering Heights* offers "house" as a manifold figure: a microcosm of larger-scale social arrangements, a den of class differences, human-animal conflicts, and infinite labors amount to a "hearth [that] was an absolute tempest,"[15] both object of and setting for social antagonism. These figures assert not only that class struggle happens in and through the domestic and the sheltering, but that class struggle is in some fundamental sense equivalent to the ungivenness of the social spaces for making human existence. All of hitherto existing history is the history of class struggle, because class struggle is the name of the objective negativity of the indispensable social relation.

With its extensive tropology of architecture, the novel orients us toward a spatial episteme. Its references to time paradoxically reinforce the axis of space: "1801" is the novel's first word, impressing the year of the General Enclosure Act—and the Act of Union with Ireland—as the origin of 1848; yet on that same first page the novel signals the irrelevance of diachronic origins in hastening to the gate of the house, an arc labeled "1500." Time is not specific but repetitive, not linear but cyclical, history subordinate to structure, the structure of enclosure itself, of the gate and the doors, windows, thresholds, and frames (including the frame narrative) that this novel obsessively worries.[16] In this way the novel commends synchronic thinking. Dates are not origins, but inscriptive markers of repetitive expanse, symbols of sets. Enclosure actualizes a new planarity for history, a massive new extent that arrests the history before catastrophic totalization. "Time stagnates here,"[17] Lockwood observes, and the vacillating intercourse between his present-tense narration and Nelly's past-tense narration effects this indifference of single temporal registers. To tell this story, narrative time itself must be not one but two: juxtaposed, and spatially defined (Nelly narrates at Thrushcross Grange, Lockwood at Wuthering Heights). Taking a house for its title and for its setting, the novel launches the action at the gate of the house with a homeless man newly renting, and quickly climbs into the floor plan, the bedrooms, and inside a sleeping chamber within the bedroom, only to have, in its first climax, the boundaries of the house permeated by the open window and the insinuating ghost of young Catherine. It then expels the interloper into the harsh clime, and takes his reincorporative convalescence at Thrushcross Grange as the occasion for the framed narrative: Nelly relays the main story to him as he recovers in bed from his snowy disorienting journey outside. The story ends exactly where it begins, the novel's final scene repeating its opening architectural survey in its concluding appraisal, tuckpointing the structures that outlast lives, the forms that rebut withering, the foundational relationality that indifferently weathers all comings and goings. This spatialization of diachrony, this nondevelopmental narrative, suggests that the type of historical logic assembled in this novel works not diachronically, in arraying the past as narration, but synchronically, in addressing the structures that organize space and perdurate the present: all of history has always been antagonism. Yet, of course, *Wuthering Heights* is not a blueprint or a photograph—it opts for narrative as the form in which to performatively produce this structural idea. Brushing the friction between the synchrony of structural rendering and the diachrony of narrative, the novel thus enthuses about the capacity of varying modes of representation to accommodate the structural truths of antagonism. Building up forms that register their own groundlessness is a greater ambition than hypostasizing formlessness.

Such registering reposes in this book's spatialization of narrativity, which it intensifies by doubling frames, folding Nelly's narrative within Lockwood's, and Isabella's within Nelly's. The frame within the frame underscores the contingent quality of any frame. Writing is the instituting of a frame, which could well have been another. There is no dispensing with frames, however, since only through a frame can the medium of space actualize a sociable formation. *Wuthering Heights* literalizes this point in associating all of its frame narratives with specific spaces.[18]

The spatial imaginary that organizes narratives and motivates the frame imagery is consolidated in the novel's conclusion, which echoes its opening, again repeating the logic of synchronic indifference to diachronic development. In a dramatic doubling of the opening, the closing finds Lockwood returning to the house for another appraisal, a doubling of setting and situation that again prioritizes the spatial above the temporal, signaling the stasis of any linear development and the centripetal pull of the circle. He remarks on its largeness:

> Both doors and lattices were open; and yet, as is usually the case in a coal-district, a fine red fire illumined the chimney: the comfort which the eye derives from it renders the extra heat endurable. But the house of Wuthering Heights is so large that the inmates have plenty of space for withdrawing out of its influence.[19]

In the hearth, a fire—yet the house itself affords withdrawing from its force. Not all of structure is exhausted by antagonism; the framing of social space hosts breathing room beyond the heat. Even buildings that avow the conflicts and ungrounds at their heart can still offer shelter and support and beauty.

Hell on Hearth; or, Every *Oikos* Is a Polis

Wuthering Heights activates a distinctive synchronic thinking to achieve its theory of antagonism. It spatializes narrativity, and it condenses its setting to ramify the ubiquity of social strife, fathoming the universal history of class struggle by figuring the *hearth*, the spatial heart of the house and the elementary space of sociality, as an inferno of insuperable conflict. The novel gives us the house as setting and crucible of abiding antagonism—in the power play over the deed to the property, evocative as it is of transfers between propertied aristocrats and moneyed bourgeois, but even more comprehensively in the power struggle at the literal spatial heart of the house, the staggering violence and hostility on the hearth, that spatial component of every economy, every *oikos*. The hearth is the particular space privileged above all else in this text (the words "hearth" and "fire" are used an average of once every three pages), and from the first usage "the hearth was an absolute tempest of worrying and yelping."[20] Site of fiery agon and fierce connection, the hearth is where Nelly narrates to Lockwood, where the main alliances in the story are initiated and sealed, where many of the violent blows are thrown, where animal carcasses accumulate and animal brutality proliferates, where Catherine pronounces at the novel's climax, "Nelly, I am Heathcliff"[21] (about which more momentarily).[22] An Old Frisian, Old Saxon, Old German word for "fire, floor, ground, dwelling, family residence," "hearth" is a baseboard signifier for the spatialization of relations—the establishment of a ground plan for human interdependence, the earth plus an *h*, and the heart plus an *h*, the fused materiality of body and environs; "heath" interrupted by a primal "r," irruptive lettering of the socius amid vast wild evergreen. When *Wuthering Heights* situates its love and war on, at, and before the hearth, it enunciates its truth: fires and the place they require are elemental to human relations; human relations require this minimal order of space. With the omnipresence of the hearth, *Wuthering Heights* relays that this elementality is not romantic, not pastoral, not our past, but material, antagonistic, our present. Through hearthiness *Wuthering Heights* substantiates its essential realism, its essential query of reality; making the space of social relations strange, foreign, Gothic, unpredictable, unsafe, inverting genre expectations, and granting nothing bucolic or stable. Everything is conflict, every domestic zone is endless war, every dispensation of dwelling is baseless.

The antagonism the house spatializes is therefore not just any antagonism, but what we read in *The Manifesto* (and *The German Ideology* before it) as the transcendental antagonism, the nongivenness of social space, the nonimmanence of the base social field, the vacancy of the *oikos* at the beginning of the world/*oikoumene.* Aristotle inaugurated the thought of this space as a polymorphous unit of the social, the form of appearance of the ontological priority of the polis before individual life:

> The *oikos* is the association established by nature for the supply of man's everyday wants. . . . This state is a creation of nature, and man is by nature a political animal (*zoon politikon*). . . . The whole is of necessity prior to the part.[23]

Abstract political formations precede and are foundational to life itself; the *oikos* is their concrete countenance, their primitive structure. It is so even though, and because, it has no particular shape. Formations of the *oikos* are variable and ungeneralizable, even as they serve an indispensable material function (this is true theoretically and practically, as anthropologies of Aristotle point out[24]). Human existence materially depends upon relationality even though the form of that relationality is not materially given, even though that relationality is eternal class struggle, and even though that relationality is itself instrumentalized, valorized, and thus relativized, by capitalism. Marx recapitulates Aristotle:

> It is only in the eighteenth century, in bourgeois society, that the different forms of the social union confront the individual as a mere means to his private ends, as an outward necessity. But the period in which this view of the isolated individual becomes prevalent is the very one in which the interrelations of society (general from this point of view) have reached the highest state of development. Man is in the most literal sense of the word a *zoon politikon* [political animal]: he is not only a social animal, but an animal which can develop into an individual only in society.[25]

Wuthering Heights pursues this "most literal sense" of politics by centralizing the antagonisms of human political affiliation, routinely rendering the hearth, that spatial core of any *oikos*, as the scene and stuff of strife. Through what I take to be an acute intensification of how the novel genre's imaginative world-making generally performs the mediation of sociality, this novel makes its own version of *The Manifesto*'s striking ontological claim, tarrying over the spatial quality of the transcendental class struggle: the struggle pertains to the configuration of the necessary socius, the formalizability of the primal social space. With its recurrent representation of the hearth, its contestation of the house, its doubling of the house with Thrushcross Grange, its endless fascination with the wall and the window and the barrier, the novel multiplies the spaces of the social, infinitely diverse in their dispositions even though unified as setting for antagonism. It uses abundant spatial imagery to evoke the copresent history that universalization obscures, the history of precapitalist antagonism and the future history of ineluctable struggle after capitalism; it foregrounds the property relation, conducting a withering critique of the private, but it maintains a solid background of the antagonism of all possible economic relations, all possible laws of the hearth, every possible *nomos* of the *oikos*, every possible *oikonomike*.

Bracketing Antagonism

Wuthering Heights ramifies *The Manifesto*'s problematic of synchronic and universal history, and it does so, I have begun to suggest, in part by resounding the revolutionary spatial imaginary of another matrix from 1848: mathematical set theory. Sets and classes and orders and frames saturate this novel's figurative system, strikingly echoing the discovery of the mathematical possibility for formally registering infinite space. Set theory refracts the novel's practice of the airy, arbitrary, but enabling dimension of schemes for formalizing relations, be they logical or social. Through the enabling inscription of the bracket {}, set theory makes demarcations that facilitate the aesthetic thinking of an infinity inaccessible to experience, a spatial diversity and distributional possibility only operable via formal denotation, and aesthetic relay of the truth that no configurations of space are totalizable or immanent. In educing these affinities between the novel and math, this argument takes Augustus De Morgan's lead in considering mathematics an imaginative enterprise (he maintained that "the moving power of mathematical invention is not reasoning but imagination"), one with direct affinities to the project of world-making that joins literature and politics; and it approaches the novel through a formalist lens.[26] Rather than discussing Brönte's education or the novel's iterative references to mathematics, I read the narrative frames, redoubled plot structure, infinity of Heathcliff, and imagery of limits as aestheticizations of emergent set theory. I look, in other words, for the novel's aesthetic modalities of thought as the scenes of engagement with the nonfiction project of formalizing mathematical expression of the sublimely inconceivable: infinite infinities.

Formalist mathematics poses the question of the construction of internally coherent systems, the question of how to construct representations in such a way that fundamental truths emerge in all their situatedness; these questions quickly open onto the aesthetic realm, the revelation, paramount in literary realism, of the real as constructed, of the constructedness of all possible representations, of the value that lies in what becomes possible with ultimate constructions. What Marx, math, and realism have in common, *The Order of Forms* argues, is twofold: (1) the materialist insight that political antagonism over social space defines human existence universally and (2) the corollary dialectical affirmation that any particular *formalization* of space will be radically aesthetic, equal parts arbitrary and necessary, instituting limits and effecting partiality, but nonetheless liberatory for all that. The intensity of spatio-structural thinking in 1848 is a lost urgency our 2019 present would do well to recover. These nineteenth-century theories of the ordering of social space could strategically renovate the twenty-first-century vogue for antisocial anarchy, the refusal of order, organization, and the letter. They could open, in short, onto a formalism of the political that affirms order's essence while foregrounding its madeness.

The role of an enclosure in defining and totalizing vast extents, and differentiating such vastness from other parallel universes, poses a central question for the early mathematical set theory of 1847–48.[27] Circa 1848, Karl Marx and Emily Brontë both alight upon this unshakable strife that sculpts history into so many successions of possible social spaces variantly responsive to antagonism; set theory is a third vector, another modality for thinking spatially and thinking synchronically. With a strange consistency across England, the Continent, and Russia in 1847–48, mathematicians established the first formulations of the theory of sets. A set is a class of objects of intuition that can be bound up into a whole through a law; set theory has three root ideas: that it is possible to rigorously codify the relationships between incommensurate classes, that forms of rigorous representation are possible even where empirical experience is not, and that space is simultaneously infinite and divisible. When *Wuthering Heights* aestheticizes the rifts between romantic cosmos and realist order, it prompts us to read set theory as political theory, mathematics as social science. As Peter Hallward explains of set theory, in the turn to formalist mathematics, intellectual abstractions "could no longer be understood as the transcription of certain elementary, self-evident aspects of homogenous physical space, but were recognized to be irreducibly relative to a particular *model* of space."[28] *Wuthering Heights*'s spatial imaginary homologously courts this recognition (that schemes for civilization are not transcribable from a natural order). Circa 1848 may thus be the point at which we can mark the simultaneous discovery by literature and math of the purely formal, inorganic quality of any matrix for human constellating of the antagonistic universe.

Although there are no such easily derivable social rules for class relations, early set theory codifies three fundamental set relations: the union (all of set A and all of set B are united in a new set), the intersection (all the elements that are common to both A and B constitute a new set) *and* its corollary the complement (the uncommon elements, the underlap between sets, constitute a new set), and finally the subset (every element of set A is also an element of set B). In 1847, Augustus De Morgan discovered laws for connecting these basic relations together, providing a basis for fathoming relationships among sets that exceed easy verifiability. For example, if I wanted to understand the union of the set of whole numbers less than 4, and the set of whole numbers less than 8, I could simply count up the elements, but if I wanted to understand the union of an infinitely large set, like the set of all whole numbers greater than 4, with another infinitely large set, like the set of all prime numbers, no such empirical check would be possible. De Morgan's laws provide a way out of this predicament—in which either I can count on my fingers, or I can throw up my hands and shout, "It's infinite!" shedding no light on that set—by allowing something else to be said, especially something about the under- and overlaps between two different infinite sets. Even though it is not possible to calculate or enumerate infinity, the possibility of symbolically representing infinity becomes actual. In other words, his laws enable thinking infinity differently, thinking infinity as difference: instead of "It's infinite!" as the only possible predication of what then appears as a mystical, unified transcendence, De Morgan's laws allow the schematization of differences that sunder the field of the infinite.

Set theory as a whole thus radically disturbs the romantic conception of infinity as a boundless beyond, openness without any closure—by inserting limits within this uncountable horizon, exposing heterogeneity at its heart. In the view of Georg Cantor, the architect of additional advances in the theory a couple of decades after De Morgan, set theory replaces the notion of infinity as the ever-receding horizon of a temporal sequence of "the addition of ones" with the atemporal, crystalline structure fathomable in "a single act of abstraction."[29] By way of abstraction, set theory radically unseats a diachronic paradigm of perceptual truth (infinity is temporal, accessible to experience if only we were immortal) with a synchronic paradigm of formal logic (infinity is spatial, available to conceptualization because we are finite). This synchronic paradigm orients itself precisely toward the thinkability and heterogeneity of space and refigures what we have already seen as the difference between diachronic accounting of capitalist continuity and synchronic inscribing of capitalist totality.

In the introduction to this book I had occasion to discuss the ways that the epistemic consequences of these shifts are nothing less than revolutionary, ushering in a specifically mathematical instance of the modern shift that Foucault identifies in the human sciences, from *resemblance* to *representation*.[30] In place of the Aristotelian paradigm in which mathematical truths are grounded in our perception of the world, set theory installs a new norm, in which mathematics emerges as a mode of modeling, of arbitrary aestheticization—the standard of value for which is no longer the truth of correspondence, but a usefulness despite its inapplicability to nature. The fact that I cannot perceive in reality a negative or transfinite number, that I cannot intuit non-Euclidean space (non-Euclideanism is another significant break in the period, to be studied in chapter 5), does not in the least compromise the perfectibility of the abstraction on its own terms, the thinking a form enables us to do. When the knowledge attainable by both the arts and the sciences is understood as representational rather than reflective, productive rather than mimetic, the constructedness of reality becomes thinkable, with matrices of relation, formal logics, and law as such liberated from their putatively organic origins.

In joint enterprise with the mathematical discoveries of the same year, *Wuthering Heights* reckons with this gap between nature and law, material and model, primal disorder and posited order, limning the chasm of form and antagonism. In multiple aesthetic dimensions (narratological, thematic, figurative, syntactic), it problematizes order and dismisses diachrony, while prizing form and elevating synchrony. A novel of chaos, its world is "a world of things to order,"[31] and "order" and "disorder," as both nouns and verbs, appear at staggeringly frequent intervals across the text. These "things" quite explicitly concern the insuperable tautologies of inexplicably interposed foreign elements ("A stranger is a stranger";[32] neither Lockwood nor Heathcliff nor Hindley's nameless wife can be integrated), the mixing of "the gentry" and "the lower orders"[33] (Linton and Isabella with Heathcliff and Cathy), and the merging of different sets (Thrushcross Grange with Wuthering Heights; the dramatically withering *ancien régime* with the voraciously acquisitive middle class of originless merchants and financiers). The manifold obstacles to order are at once social and psychological, generic and aesthetic, and the novel's ultimate refutation of order—the "dangerous excesses" noted by one of the first reviews—aestheticizes in literary form the set theoretical priority of cardinality over ordinality, structure over sequence, synchrony over diachrony.[34] It brackets the question of the order of things and their denumeration, and pursues instead the thinkability of sublime magnitudes and recursive differentiation.

Although political implications seem far from set theory, in its exercise of total abstraction it performs the kind of formalist thinking that *The Order of Forms* advocates, the kind of ability to grasp the formalism in and of political relations. Set theory's investigation of space, and of space's thinkability via formalized boundaries, of the thinkability of coexisting, conflicting, total extents, amounts to an abstract sustaining of antagonism: there are infinite possible configurations of space, no possible configuration is immanent, any given configuration is a product of inscription (the bracket, the writing of the formula), the fact that any given configuration operates as a totality does not gainsay the existence of other parallel totalities. Just because capitalism totalizes itself does not mean that other possible social constellations cannot be built; just because capitalism "simplifies" the social antagonism as such does not mean that its overcoming would dissolve all antagonisms. This sustaining of antagonism in the abstractions of set theory might remedy the pitfalls of *The Manifesto*'s bombast; *Wuthering Heights*'s own version of sustaining antagonism is less abstract, but no less theoretical.

Form Affirmed

It is pivotal for my argument that this novel's thoroughgoing inquiry into the universal antagonism and the corollary ungroundedness of social forms is not tainted by the ecstasy of formlessness with which *The Order of Forms* quarrels. Rather, *Wuthering Heights* enacts an emphatic principle of formalization in its own highly crafted, highly stylized, highly patterned, exuberant form. The novel's affirmation of aestheticized constellations of the socius amid their ungivenness is writ large in its own incredible structuration—its frame narration and frame imagery, its constitutive symmetry, its fascination with doubles and synchronicity, its compositional rigor. Abstract form, this structuration seems to say, exceeds and outreaches the aberrant passions, wild heathens, and anarchic immoderacy the story displays.

We have already focused on the frame narration; another overarching facet of this structuration is the symmetry between the two houses—Earnshaw and Linton, each two syllables, each one son and one daughter—and the drive toward merging the two halves: Mr. Linton's son marries Mr. Earnshaw's daughter, and the only child of their union marries successively both of her cousins, Mr. Linton's grandson and Mr. Earnshaw's grandson. Another is the convergence of the boundary-gate-window-frame imagery and the frequent use of "frame" as a verb with the repeated references to the exilic quality of the world of the novel, its profound isolation and totalized extent.[35] But perhaps the most striking facet of the novel's own structuration is its hyperbolization of "the two," the double doubled, the squared cubed, repetition cardinalized. The form of *Wuthering Heights* mobilizes twoness and repetition as figures of synchronicity: two volumes, two houses, two families, two temporalities (the present of Lockwood and the past of Nelly), two inexplicable Heathcliffian arrivals, two Catherines, two Lockwoodian approaches from outside on the first and last pages. The birth of the second Catherine in the second volume's second chapter doubles Catherine's nonidentity with herself, confirming her astonishing insistence "Nelly, I am Heathcliff."

"Nelly, I am Heathcliff" is the most memorable and disturbing—and short—sentence in all this great book, and it is a sentence emblematizing the novel's resistance to enclosure and to property, punctuating the novel's formations of colliding opposites in provisional syntheses, inscribing its striving after robust copresence, critical synchronicities. Her statement is a prohibition, in the vein of more advanced set theory, against self-belonging, an insistence that a proper "one" cannot exist, for a set cannot own, contain, or belong to itself. Catherine and Heathcliff's joint maxim that, in Badiou's words, "the one is not" forswears the concept of integer, forecloses any possibility of counting all the numbers between any two whole numbers such that the one could be distinguished from the two.[36] Crucially, the novel equitably distributes this synchronicity of the nonidentical: Catherine is not even singular or self-identical in her doubling of Heathcliff, for Heathcliff is in everyone, and thus, so is she: "We've all as summut uh orther side in us."[37]

Like the signs of formal mathematics, these unities are inscribed by the intertwined and repeated letters in the intertwined and repeated, doubled names. "This writing was nothing but a name repeated in all kinds of characters, large and small,"[38] Lockwood tells us—the internal rhymes of shared final syllables in Linton and Hareton, shared first syllables in Hindley and Linton; the limitation of surnames to three (Heathcliff, Earnshaw, Hareton, repeated) and the repetition among these three of the three letters *E-A-H* that also spell Catherine. Heathcliff trespasses everywhere: he is the double of the dead Earnshaw son for whom he is named, the double of Nelly who is both inside and outside the family, the double of Edgar in his love for Catherine, the double of Hindley as a tyrannical master, the double of Hareton as an excluded savage, the double of Isabella in her volatile rebelliousness, the double of his son, his second, and the double of the father who brings home an unaccountable booty from elsewhere.

And, he is also the double of his most obvious opposite, Lockwood, in a way that finally punctuates the indifference of antagonists, the irrelevance of counting, the generality of antagonism. For just as the condition of possibility of the narrative is the intrusion of the foreigner Lockwood, the condition of possibility of the story is the incorporation of the exotic Heathcliff. While Lockwood spends the narrative giving an account of his time at Thrushcross Grange, he offers little in the way of explanation for the familial and economic circumstances that drove him there, and drove him to return again a year later. Heathcliff's arrival and return are even more dramatically unaccounted, the great enigma of the novel is excessively doubled—his is "a Cuckoo's" "history" . . . "where he was born, who were his parents, and how he got his money,"[39] "he has nobody knows what money";[40] there is no accounting for where Lockwood came from, nor where Heathcliff came from, and even less accounting for the primitive accumulations that enable his return to and conquest of the Heights. In his unaccountableness and his twofold subversion of the "compound order" of "the whole establishment" at Wuthering Heights, Heathcliff is the ultimate avatar of the irrelevance of precise reckoning, exact counting. What is important in his plot is not diachronic specification but structural possession, cardinal representation, the sheer imposition of an abstract principle.

Catherine's impossible but vital identity with Heathcliff repeats Heathcliff's nonidentity with himself: radically adopted, radically homeless, radically insurgent, radically usurping, he functions as an acquisitive avatar of the middle class, as Terry Eagleton has formidably argued, but equally an avenging visage of slavery, as Susan Gillman has advanced, of that property extremizing the violence of all property, and equally an exemplar of the proletarian prospect of the bourgeois, as elaborated in *The Manifesto*, to attain universal subjecthood, to revolutionize class itself.[41] Ultimately, as Jameson has implied, Heathcliff cannot function as a character in any coherent literary sense, so much as illustrate the very determination of the notion of character by capital itself.[42] Heathcliff's very mobility among social strata, the overfiguration innervating this most engrossing of all novelistic protagonists ever, performs his violation of classes, the arbitrary character of their inscription.

In training its gaze on and activating its dramas in an elementary social space, this novel makes the house, like the hearth and the heath, a site of mediated aestheticization.[43] From this specific spatial trope, it moves outward toward a generally spatialized form, one that sets to work upon questions of synchronic historicity and social formalization. In its dynamic spatiality,

Wuthering Heights models political formalism, that multipronged hold in which avowing that "the history of all hitherto existing society is the history of class struggle" makes possible not the reduction of antagonism to private property, but the contestation among formal configurations of "class."

Like the revolutionary fervor in Springtime of the Peoples in 1848, set theory confronts "class" as a construct upon which the organization of space depends, but a construct that cannot be made grounded or self-identical. A set cannot contain its own principle of setting. Individuals share crucial features with the other members of their sets, cementing the cohesion of the class, yet any individual could also exceed its class in forming class connections extrinsic to its primary set. Classification as such is essential, universal, inevitable, and useful, but class composition is in flux.

For class struggle to be universal encompasses a certain universality of class as such as well; any formulations of the communist revolution as the abolition of class run aground in reaching for an immanentization of the social field, as if exclusion and stratification could be canceled. It is the exclusiveness of forms that engender the fantasy of formlessness, but that fantasy has proved debilitating for theory and for struggle. Far better to engage in the production of forms whose exclusions are more provisional, more rotational, more mediated. The nonimmanence of economic relations guarantees class difference, subjective instantiations of the objective antagonism, yet not all political economies naturalize such difference. A formalistic ontology of political structures, for instance, can support a formal equality among those whose lives they enable and support the approximating pursuit of all that that equality is owed, by constantly recombining classes and constantly rebracketing members in formulae and edifices like direct political representation, equal access to actualization in education and health, equal protection in the wuthering climate.

That revolutionary agency interpellated by *The Manifesto* in 1848 rests with the class that can think itself as the elevation of antagonism to a universal maxim, as the sustaining of this antagonism. As Marx put it elsewhere, the proletariat is "a class which is the dissolution of all classes, a sphere of society which has a universal character because its sufferings are universal, and which claims no particular right because the wrong committed against it is not a particular wrong, but wrong as such."[44] Complementarily, Peter Hallward clarifies that "the proletariat is not that class which seeks an improvement of its place, and still less, that aims to usurp the place of the bourgeoisie; it is that force beyond class whose coming into existence destroys the very concept of place in general."[45] But of course the challenge of this agency not identical to itself is how to give it a form of existence, how to make space for living together within the very ruins of the concept of place. Set theory thinks this challenge in a different register: the set of all sets is not a set; it cannot be coherently collected into a whole, yet this impossibility can be written in formal language. Just as "communism is for us not a *state of affairs* which is to be established," a content to be substantialized, but rather a ceaseless practice, "the *real* movement which abolishes the present state of things,"[46] the proletariat is not a subject to be positivized, but rather a relation to be taken up toward universality in its negative formulations, toward the universality of the negative, the universal history of antagonism, the universality of social form. The proletariat is the agent of a political struggle not merely for more equitable distribution but for the enabling structuration of social forms to positively promote human flourishing. Any form for the relations in infinite space, whether the layout of a house, the frame of a narrative, the symbolic logic of a set, or the dispossessions of the private, will not dispel antagonism; the set of private property differs from the set of all antagonisms; the best forms build their own positive operability from out of their avowal that they are limited by these absolute negativities.

Taking up this impossible relation requires all available imaginative reinforcements. It requires the dialectical and utopian relentless critique of everything existing as the law of the hearth, the unwavering discernment of antagonism and the unsentimental affirmation of formalization, cartographies of the space of social antagonism not coextensive with the space of capital, multidimensional trajectories where Marx and Brontë and math are in sync. The prism of their intersection refracts the materialist truth that the quicksand of any social order sinks not every benefit of the order of forms. Premier among such benefits, as set theory's radical inscriptions perform, may be the faculty of forms to concretize abstractions, to mediate antagonism. If, as *The Order of Forms* has been arguing, it is the politics of the novel form to intervene in the dispensation of worlds, it is the politics of *Wuthering Heights* to broker no resolution to worlded antagonism, no end to politics other than the righteously raging "unquiet slumbers"[47] of its own ending sentence, no consolation but in formalism itself. In place of resolution, even the sorely needed resolution of destroying private property, it tenders only the frame of a different synchronicity, one that negates capitalist universality not by a mythical diachronic before or beyond, but with the dialectical present of the universal antagonism and universal structuration here, now.

3

The Limits of *Bleak House*

Every limit is an ending, but also a beginning.[1] Political enthusiasm for formlessness puts limits in question: Why constraints? Why law? Why order? Why forms? Limits stipple the shapes of social space into perceptibly high relief, and so often their exclusions overshadow their installations. In something like a face–vase problem, mutually exclusive regard for limits stands at the heart of the difference between anarcho-vitalism and political formalism: one position sees only what the contours prohibit, while the other dialectically descries what the contours enable. To better grasp this difference, as well as to curtail it, this chapter mobilizes the formalist mathematical conceptions of the "limit" as a metaphor for what limits generate, why they are necessary and unavoidable, and how they can be embraced. I read this metaphor as animating Charles Dickens's *Bleak House.* An eminently maximalist text, endlessly esteemed as "massive," pedestaled as the very archetype of realism, *Bleak House* famously encompasses the biggest city in the nineteenth century and the foundational institution underwriting it, the law. Yet the form of this novel turns out to be conspicuously delimited in ways that pinpoint a surprising *minimalism*: bounded settings, a tight repertoire of architectural tropes, a small cast of pivotal actors, incomplete plotting, and the iconic split narration whittle and winnow this novel's amplitude. These basics performatively graph the generativity of limits for producing social space, scaffolding what *Bleak House* calls "the whole framework of society."[2] Readings regardful of these capacious minima need not stretch to embrace the variability and expanse of composed, formed relationality. Prizing limits finds footing for the constructive impulse: if you want to build, you have to start somewhere.

The magnitude of *Bleak House* rolls off the critical tongue, and a long legacy of readings by both Victorianists and non-Victorianists intones its ultimate realism, "an anatomy of society" gyring centrifugally from novelistic instance to sociological insight.[3] Paradigmatically, a recent and quite commanding reading by Caroline Levine celebrates *Bleak House*'s enormity, citing in particular its generous length as key to "capturing the complexity and power of networked social experience," and its dazzling breadth as key to theorizing networked sociality.[4] For Levine these dimensions amount to *Bleak House*'s "radical expansion of the usual affordances of narrative form."[5] In a different tenor, in her brilliant analysis of the biopolitics of *Bleak House*, Emily Steinlight attends to "the virtually unthinkable problem suggested by the term *supernumeraries*, or the paradox of a total in excess of the total,"[6] underscoring the aesthetics of the innumerable as they evince the emergence of the mass as the subject of fiction. Aesthetic largeness as a condition of possibility for social largeness: *Bleak House*, by virtue of its well-nigh innumerable characters, its multiple strata, its roving length, achieves an effective representation of that outsize referent, social totality.

But what if *Bleak House* achieves social realism through means other than mass? At the very beginning, already in the second chapter, the narrator intones of Chesney Wold: "It is not a large world. Relatively even to this world of ours, which has its limits too (as your Highness shall find when you have made the tour of it and are come to the brink of the void beyond), it is a very little speck."[7] Even in the eventual diegetic movement beyond those aristocratic quarters, this remains an emblematic principle for this novel's form: it addresses itself to these limits, perches itself at the brink of the void, and thus apprehends the affinity between the bounds of the fictional world and the bounds of this world of ours. Its project is not the manufacture of the expansive, but the investigation of what hinders expanse, what hems the speck. For reasons other than mine, James Buzard has observed that readers of *Bleak House* often "lack a forceful enough appreciation of the energies of *limitation* that structure" it.[8] Energies of limitation one might easily meter in realism's modal production of social space—limits of mortal temporality and material phenomenality, of physics and fusion that hold the structure up. *Bleak House* is familiarly the paradigmatic instance, the most extreme and most wholly adequate exemplar, of Victorian literary realism; this chapter therefore tests my formalist theory of realism against the limit case. Space is the medium of social relations, and one of the most dogged questions of formalizing the social is that of the *scale* of relations, the extent of space, the feasible arena.[9] From telescopic philanthropy to a self-consuming lawsuit, from grandiose delusions to architectural replications, from deportment to combustion, from in medias res beginnings to ungrammatical endings, from mixed narration to inordinate length, *Bleak House* arrays at every level of its form (plot, characterization, theme, imagery, narration) questions of apt scale, appropriate size, effective organization of relational space.

I argue that it is this formal writing of limits—the formalization of limits—and not the exceeding of them—that comprises *Bleak House*'s realism and indeed its political formalism. The smallness of *Bleak House* frames its insights into the fundamentals of composed relations; Dickens mobilizes a dialectic of form in his production of institutions, laws, and other social architectures, charting minimal structuration in its maximal prospects. To undo the habitual political equation of freedom with formlessness, literary critics can ably explore how literary works might theorize the benefits of form's limits. Shaping social space in any particular way means excluding other ways, but it also means instating arrangements for elementary social goods, like fair housing policy. Institutions, organizations, and social formations operate limits, through which in turn their functions and distinctions gain efficacy. As theorists ranging from the anthropologist Victor Turner to the pedagogue Paolo Freire to the francophonist Tracy McNulty all illuminate, limits elastically enable the construction of social space, its thinkability as constructed, and the imagining of possible reconstructions.[10] Limits are not just destructive but constructive.

Constructions and their spatial rhetorics orient the etymology of "limit" as well as its mathematical specification. From the Latin *limes*, *limitus*, a limit is first a boundary or frontier of a plot of land, and then becomes generalized. Spatiality orients the extensive figurative meanings; a limit is a "bound beyond which something ceases to be possible," a spatialization without which there is nothing. "Limit" here in many ways figures what the preceding chapters have termed "form," insofar as the limit is a shaping of space that constitutes sociality, an inscription inherent in social formalization. The political power of formlessness often derives from its attack on limits, refusal of exclusion, and valorization of flow. In outlining political formalism as an alternative affirmation of form, I advocate for the strategic value of provisional limits, for the constant deliberation of form with special help from the mediating faculty of aesthetics, and for a certain ontological facticity of social form: our collective interdependence requires a shape. At the base of this position rests a conviction that even though political imagining has so often held form and formalism to readily signify stasis and proscription, there are other valences of form. The revolutionary mathematical formalism of the nineteenth century opens pointedly toward these other valences, exalting what forms can do, and especially how form works as a vehicle for superseding the perceived, intuited, experienceable, referable bounds of the possible. The construct of "limit," first developed in the nineteenth century by Augustus De Morgan,

James Wood, and the Royal Society, illustrates the fortuitous plasticity of form, limning a point of successive approximation never absolutely reachable. Fathoming the exclusions of form via limits in the mathematical sense, as strategic designations and heuristic inscriptions that enable more than they foreclose, casts rather differently the contest between form and formlessness.

The provisional approximacy that mathematical limits denote figures in *Bleak House* the approximate character of political institutionality, the abstract, departicularizing character of the law, and the smallness of worlds: confined spaces, constrained perspectives, small repertoires of replicated forms. Through such figures *Bleak House* approaches a minimalist attitude toward social infrastructure, one that instantiates the mereness of the affirmative regard for forms in political formalism. Recognizing social infrastructures as small, limited, provisional, approximate—as, in short, *formal*—correlates with the recognition of their necessity and their ungivenness. Because forms are formal, they can be reformed; because social life is built, it can be rebuilt. Projections of politics that only espouse dismantling and not construction impede the practical composition of relations. Just as reflexive anti-institutionalism thwarts institution-building, so too it blocks the tactical appraisal of institutional dispensations in their particular offerings. In its magnificent composition of an enchanting expanse from out of a small frame, *Bleak House* performs the maxim that the provisional institutes of made worlds are beginnings, not just endings.

Limited, Inc.

The problem of the limit holds the conceptual center of *Bleak House*, through its premise of the suit in Chancery. Though, as Dickens insisted, his text is lacking a definitive single historical referent—and thereby sets its sights on a general dynamic—*Bleak House* does evoke a precedent of wide reach for English legal history: a suit begun in 1797 and not resolved until the mid-nineteenth century, whose contentious core was the subject of "accumulating at compound interest" (the concluding phrase of the opening paragraph of *Bleak House*). Upon his death in London in 1797, a Swiss-born director of the Bank of England established a trust of £600,000, not to be touched until a hundred years later. In response to this projected outlandish accumulation (approximately £1,000,000,000), Parliament passed a bill in 1800 imposing a twenty-one-year limit on the life of a trust. Since the Thellusson will organized itself as an attempt to circumvent the widely observed (then and now) Anglo-American common-law Rule Against Perpetuities, which limits the reach of a will to twenty-one years after the death of the last-mentioned person alive at the time of the will's enactment, the 1800 Accumulations Act strengthened the Rule Against Perpetuities by clarifying that the estate could not accumulate new earnings after twenty-one years from the death of the grantor; after twenty-one years, an estate must distribute its income rather than compound its income. Against compound interest, but more explicitly against the sheer accumulation of growing a trust just for the sake of growing a trust, the Accumulations Act fundamentally imposes a limit. In taking as its pretext the notion of a legal case whose impetus is the legal instituting of limits to private accumulation, and in complementing this pretext with the conceit that all of an estate could be expended in legal costs contesting the distribution of an estate, *Bleak House* organizes itself around the essential mechanism of legal limits—the law as vehicle of limit, the law as force against its own limits, the law as limited by this self-reflexive, self-consumptive relation. Since such a function of law accords with the ubiquitous laments of limit setting that political formalism opposes, it seems crucial to point to this specific value of constraining the accumulation of wealth—a constraint that is an enabling sine qua non for any communalizing, redistributive justice.

If the story centers limits in this precedential function, the novel's plot (its manner of arranging the story) assigns yet more weight to what limits offer. *Bleak House* begins in medias res. The case has been on for decades and "has in the course of time become so complicated that no man alive knows what it means,"[11] as Jarndyce explains to Esther:

> The lawyers have twisted it into such a state of bedevilment that the original merits of the case have long disappeared from the face of the earth. It's about a will and the trusts under a will—or it was once. It's about nothing but costs now. We are always appearing, and disappearing, and swearing, and interrogating, and filing, and cross-filing, and arguing, and sealing, and motioning, and referring, and reporting, and revolving about the Lord Chancellor and all his satellites, and equitably waltzing ourselves off to dusty death, about costs. That's the great question. All the rest, by some extraordinary means, has melted away.[12]

The novel refuses any standard plotting around the central legal conceits—there is no origin of the legal story, no flashback to the legator's intent nor rival versions of the will—*and* there is no resolution of the legal story: the estate consumes itself in court costs, rendering irrelevant the determinations of who the true beneficiaries are. Stark repetitions in the text further this sense of absolute installation. Despite its destruction, despite its being "a monstrous system," the law repeats. Numerous deaths by implosion—Nemo, Gridley, Krook, Richard—echo the collapse of the houses in Tom All

Alone's, and foretell the self-consumption of the suit in Chancery.[13] Gridley's own case serves as a Jarndyce & Jarndyce precedent at a slightly diminished scale:

> The suit, still undecided, has fallen into rack, and ruin, and despair, with everything else—and here I stand, this day! Now, Mr. Jarndyce, in your suit there are thousands and thousands involved, where in mine there are hundreds. Is mine less hard to bear or is it harder to bear, when my whole living was in it and has been thus shamefully sucked away?[14]

A thoroughgoing logic of repetitive destruction for parties and places connected to the case relays not only the reach of its influence, but also its imperviousness and self-perpetuating dynamism. The many cases in Chancery are alike, the major vector of Chancery is to reproduce such likeness. Things continue, even when they explode. Law manifests as that which cannot be begun or ended, as the limit beyond which there are no social relations of which to speak, no social spaces to map.

We can therefore read in the central tropes of Chancery a thought about the structuring force of the law accompanied by the irrelevant content of the law, a thought constitutive of political formalism: law is premise, law is impetus, law is tautology, law is originless, law is repetitive; law is not plot.[15] Indifference to the law's particulars issues less an indictment of legal institutions than a license of law's universal character, its organizing form. *Bleak House* prioritizes this abstract register of the law in its plot's refusal of resolution and refusal of origin, in its narration's ongoing present tense, in its conclusion's notorious gerunds: law as present, law as persistent. Even though this novel has consistently been read as patterning a plot that excoriates the legal system, we could say more precisely that *Bleak House* builds its very form—plot as well as setting, and characterization and narration—by *ratifying* law through a formalist lens. We might thus conclude, quite counter to D. A. Miller's influential reading of this novel's panoptic disciplinary agenda, that in *Bleak House* the law, even if reviled in its Chancery incarnation, nonetheless fundamentally appears *as limit*, as a merely formal writing in place of an impossible function, as a writing that formally institutes the "whole framework of society."[16] Far from a headquarters of carceral power, this constituting inscription directly admits its own formality. Limits successively approximate that to which functions tend, indicating the unclosed quality of form's aspirations.

As the historical precedent of the Rule Against Perpetuities partially underlines, something calculative entwines with the philosophical or political conception of the limit. And indeed, the broad intellectual milieu of *Bleak House* activates with important advances in formalist mathematics the idea of a limit as that which enables structuration. Mathematical limits, first formalized in the nineteenth century, express the tendencies of sequences and functions, and therefore denote the boundaries of topological space. A limit wrests something finite from something infinite, delimiting infinity into finitude, cordoning finite space from infinite space.

Mathematical limits come into play when the relationships in question are essentially *indeterminate*—when we know that there are relations, but not how to write them (a lesson we have seen that *The German Ideology* teaches us in a different language). The value of $1 \div \infty$, for instance, is strictly indefinable and inexpressible. The movement toward formalization often culminated in abstractions capable of *representing* that to which it is impossible to *refer*; one such formalization answers precisely the predicament of an indeterminate function by substituting a claim about the tendency of the function. Thus, while the value of $1 \div \infty$ cannot be calculated or expressed, we can formulate a tendency: that as 1 is divided by larger and larger numbers approximating infinity, the function tends toward zero. In this act of formalization, the approximate and the tendential are demarcated the "limit"—as in "the limit of the function 1 divided by x, as x nears infinity, is zero." In the formula, we write $f(n) \to L$. The function approaches a limit; limit becomes the name for that which is being approached. The rigorous codification of this naming is one of the achievements of George Boole's *An Investigation of the Laws of Thought*, published a year after *Bleak House*. For Boole, a limit distills the formalist trajectory of mathematics we have noted in England after the 1840s, a trajectory toward types of representation whose formal, abstract, or symbolic quality opened new bounds of what was possible to think and to know. Just as, in his prior work, he had established that the mathematicization of logic could render new logical conundrums thinkable and old logical conundrums solvable, in this project Boole underscores how limits support a working definition of undefinable dynamics.

Boolean expositions of limits had wide uptake and continue to direct computation and computers in our present. Even Karl Marx grew busy with differential calculus, leaving behind little-studied, wonderfully weird mathematical manuscripts from 1881–82. His goal in the manuscripts seems to be to apply differential calculus to more effectively represent economic processes mathematically, and to intervene in the increasing habit of economists to do so at the expense of acknowledging the politics of economics. Interspersed among his many equations and explanations rest brief meditations on the possible dialecticity of math, the inherent qualitative moments in its quantitative arcs. Differential calculus especially promised this dialectic, since its variables could be approached not as mere magnitudes, but as genuinely dynamic factors on the move (as *essentially* varying). The problem of provisionally distilling the movement among and relationship between variables in such a way that honors their dynamism yields, as Marx put it, "the negation of the negation generally,"[17] whereas solving for magnitude "leads literally to nothing." Arithmetic adds up to "a damned useless mass of details,"[18] but calculus rhymes with the dialectic. The mathematician doing calculus attains dialectics through awareness that the math of differentials "operates independently on its own ground,"[19] a self-reflexive conceptuality in and for itself.

For Marx as for mathematicians, the motif of the limit in differential calculus represents a minimalist writing of maximal possibility, a writing that underscores its own groundlessness the better to host new relations. The undefined horizons of the infinite cannot be positively instantiated in operative representation—there will always be exceptions, alternatives, exclusions to any formation. But a too-simple opposition between the limit and the limitless, between structure and flow, does not aid better building. The mathematical trope of the limit allows the elementary inscribing that makes thinkable the tendency of the letter, the formula, and/or the law to approximate the unrepresentable. Working definitions, make-dos, improvised provisions—these strengths of mathematical form surrogate the merits of social forms overlooked in the destituent paradigm.

If the limit in mathematics names the drawing of a line beyond which lies the infinite, and in so doing sequestering a subinfinite about which it becomes possible to make claims and establish relations, this very operation of enabling inscription seems also to be at stake in *Bleak House*'s smallness, and in what I have theorized as realism's modeling of possible social space. The novel works on the problem of social relations, but it executes this work figuratively rather than referentially, through practices of limits rather than through practices of documentation. It does not represent a whole world, a span of London, a reified totality—quite to the contrary, it represents small pieces of worlds and the limits these bring about, the building materials of social infrastructures upon which undefined relations can be elaborated. Arch among these pieces stands the cipher "house": contained, manageable, locatable sociality, but constitutively differential for all that. In chapter 1, we explored ways that constructive architecturalism can motivate a formalist understanding of the projective abstraction at the heart of literary realism, and in chapter 2 we tracked such projecting in the importance of tropes of the house and the hearth in *Wuthering Heights*, where they figured above all the fascinating constructedness of social space ungrounded by abiding negativity. In *Bleak House*, "house" evokes limit, a minimal structuration that enables the undefined to unfurl, repeating across time and space, scaffolding relations of multiple shapes. Through a pervasive rhetoric of the house, this novel installs the walls beyond which lies the unbuilt, surveying the spatial terrain that constitutes the social field.

The House of *Bleak House*: Domestic Architecture Scaling Social Space

Bleak House orders itself around two cornerstones: the law in its elemental formalism, and the house in its elemental structuration. Why is a book about the law also a book about a house? I argue that together these two motifs compound a political formalism: the infrastructural forms of collective life are essential but simply formal (viz. the diffuse undefined premise of "law") and thus subject to perpetual rebuilding (the proliferating, decentering house trope). At the center of *Bleak House* dwells, to state the obvious, a house. "House" furnishes the banner under which the famously sprawling, expansive, encyclopedic novel of institutions and urban life takes place. The banner wasn't chosen lightly; of Dickens's dozen potential titles for the novel, "Bleak House" differed drastically from the others, all of which featured "Tom All Alone's." Deliberately elevated, "house" works as the crux of a novel whose first word is "London," a novel whose tremendous study of networks and affiliations and forms of social, political, biological connection propels it outward from its context. And not quite any house, but *bleak* house, a paradoxical amalgam of light and dark, the *bleach* of too much illumination and the *bleary* of too much wind, the place where exposure to the elements of sun and air dramatizes the need for shelter, the place where the darkness meets the light. A strong tradition of scholarship on Victorian domesticity by Nancy Armstrong, D. A. Miller, Mary Poovey, and others reads in "house" the strict opposition of the domestic to the institutional, the private to the public, the intimate to the bureaucratic. But I want to suggest that this particular novel pronouncedly figures domestic space as metonymn of social structuration tout court.[20] *Bleak House* launches its investigation of social systems from a house; it assembles the house as the organizing principle from which other organizing principles radiate. In short, *Bleak House* positions "house" as the limit of social space par excellence. The law is an absolute, and the house metaphorizes the absolute's constructedness. Or, the law is the impossible function; the house formalizes that function, localizing it in an inscription. $F(n) \rightarrow L$.

The novel takes "house" as its central figure, proffering houseness as the prism for scalar questions. From broad Indo-European roots commonly indicating "hide" as in "skin" and as in "conceal, protect," "house" evokes a shell that is shelter, a metaskin that secretes lives, a building for habitation. House augurs the elementary social space, the fundamental physical form installed at the nature/culture divide, the human-animal's initial materialization of its nonnatural life. The sociologist Pierre Bourdieu describes houses therefore as templates for the legibility of culture as such: the house "is the principal locus for the objectification of the generative schemes; and through the intermediary of the divisions and hierarchies it sets up between things, persons, and practices, this tangible classifying system continuously inculcates and reinforces the taxonomic principles underlying all the arbitrary provisions of this culture."[21] Literary houses would seem to redouble this rendering legible, a redoubling that accounts for literature's irreducibility to projects of particular social "reinforcement." Indeed, for the philosopher Michel de Certeau, reading as such is akin to inhabiting, in ways that estrange space.[22] The process of reading the house that *Bleak House* engenders activates then a double operation of rendering social space legible, and rendering social space strange; houseness in its manifold incarnations, its fundamental forms of association and social installation, its paradigms of institution that build upon these foundations—these are the questions of political formalism upon which the text works.

In a manner at once plain and profound, "house" orders the form of *Bleak House* by arraying its setting. The spaces the novel enters are houses, many of which share a common blueprint in Bleak House, which, we learn, has had as many names over time—"The Peaks," then "Bleak" (dark), then "Bleak" (light)—as it has had locations in space—replicated in London in Esther's residence and in Tom All Alone's, and replicated in New Bleak House. Houses of law, of aristocracy, of debt, of orphans (Chancery, Chesney Wold, Coavinses, Krook's, boarding); houses as buildings, dwellings, shelters, clusters of buildings (Tom All Alone's). In these settings unfurl contradictions at the heart of houses, the insufficiency and ill-fabrication of every house, domestic deportment and good housekeeping. Crucially, although often embraced as the acme of Dickensian urbanism and institutionalism, and thus as the epitome of Victorian realism, *Bleak House* depicts urban space and public orders not directly but as extrapolations of the domestic spaces in which its action markedly cloisters.[23] The events of this expansive novel take place in a limited number of places: house-places, either residences or dual-zoned residence-businesses. Roughly in order as they appear, we have the house of Chancery, Chesney Wold, Windsor, the Jellyby residence, Krook's residence; Bleak House; the Brickmaker's cottage; Snagsby's residence; Tulkinghorn's residence; the Bleak House in London; Turveydrop's; Charley's residence; Kenge's quarters; the Smallweed residence; George's gallery; the Bagnet residence; Boythorn's estate; Symond's Inn; Skimpole's residence; Richard's residence at Deal; the Rouncewell residence in Iron Country; the new Bleak

House at Yorkshire. One stratum predominates among these spaces: neither the grounding degradation of poverty nor the swaying heights of aristocratic Great Houses, but the hybrid professional/domestic habitats of the middle class. Manifold and malleable spaces of working for living, houses project assemblages of social space that accommodate many functions.

The prevalent house-settings and especially their domesticity map the smallness of institutions, their minimal scape. Projective schemes for relations shape the ensuing social spaces, with functional, load-bearing walls; in this sense even the most expansive form, like a law applicable to all, generates limitedness as one of its phenomenal effects. This large novel consistently effectuates limitedness, including through its logic of setting: institutions other than houses are surprisingly rare. One visit to the courtroom (four in the antechambers), one visit to a theater, one visit to a prison, three visits to taverns. Even more exceptional are the scenes that could be said to be "urban" insofar as they take place on the street, in public: one scene in the debt collector's alley, and three scenes in the district of Tom All Alone's. Most exceptional are events of interstitial location, events of transit: the road to Bleak House when it is first introduced, and the two climactic chapters in which Bucket and Esther journey in search of Lady Dedlock. All this manual counting reveals that *Bleak House* manifestly conceives its breadth of social relations as transpiring within very delimited spaces; it contextualizes "the social" as the set of relations that obtain within narrow confines, with some notable bridges among compounds. In this smallness, in this houseyness, in this meditation on limits, it enunciates a truth of political formalism: structures organize every space, and much can be flexibly hosted in so little room; to conceive of politics as only the thrust of formlessness and not the glue of reforming makes for poor political imagining, out of doors and unconstructive.

Setting attains that great Jamesian/Lukácsian integration with the other aspects of novelistic infrastructure in this novel through explicit extension of "house" to the offices of characterization and plotting. In *Bleak House*, houses are personified, and in turn serve as the novel's main means to represent persons, its foremost technology of characterization, with lengthy description of houses actively substituting for interior focalization. The Dedlocks' London house, or "house in town," is persistently personified ("the Dedlock townhouse stares at the other houses in the street of dismal grandeur, and gives no outward sign of anything going wrong within"[24]). Characters as disparate as Mrs. Jellyby and Mr. Tulkinghorn are first enfleshed through description of their houses. Housekeepers and housekeeping are recurrent characters and motifs; the most masterful housekeeper is of course the novel's first-person narrator, whose narrative owes its limits to her movement within and between different houses. When Esther learns of her mother's identity from Lady Dedlock, her narrative dispatches with that climactic revelation in two paragraphs of retrospective summary, but then immediately lingers for pages of description of Chesney Wold, a better evocation of her "place" than any personal melodrama.

Similarly, the plot itself derives from the setting. The delimited spaces of *Bleak House* link to one another by physical resemblance and physical proximity, ramifying the spatial limits of houses with spatial limits of contiguity; spatial contiguity itself could be said to drive the plot, insofar as numerous crucial events take place by the grace of place, by confluences of presences in improbably contiguous, implausibly small spaces. Take the very first scene of London in Esther's narrative, far more urban than the opening paragraph in the third-person narrative, in its almost classic rhetoric:

> "I admired the long successions and varieties of streets, the quantity of people already going to and fro, the number of vehicles passing and repassing, the busy preparations in the setting forth of shop windows and the sweeping out of shops, and the extraordinary creatures in rags, secretly groping among the swept-out rubbish for pins and other refuse."[25]

But as soon as this bustle and range blow in, the field dramatically narrows; no sooner has the expanse of the great city outstretched than it contracts:

> "So, cousin," said the cheerful voice of Richard to Ada, behind me. "We are never to get out of Chancery! We have come by another way to our place of meeting yesterday, and—by the Great Seal, here's the old lady again!"
>
> Truly, there she was, immediately in front of us, curtsying, and smiling, and saying, with her yesterday's air of patronage:
>
> "The wards in Jarndyce! Ve-ry happy, I am sure!"[26]

All of the largeness of London leads to the absent centrality of Chancery, and to the coincidences and connections to its populace. Relational coincidences gain their due (as when Rachel, an old attendant of Esther's in her orphan home, resurfaces as Mrs. Chadband), though more prominent are the spatial coincidences. One miraculous instance involves Richard's happening upon Deal as a place to reside, Esther's happening to visit him there, and their happening to see Alan Woodcourt on the pier there precisely as he disembarks from passage to India; then happening to be in the same hotel as the one he chooses for his stay (chapter 45). Woodcourt is again the subject of another chance encounter at a late hour, in terrible weather, in Chancery Lane, and the oddness of the encounter is repeatedly exclaimed by all sides, as if "in a strange country."[27] A chance meeting with Caddy in the city delays Esther's arrival at the climactic final hearing on the cause of the suit in Chancery, facilitating the belatedness of the action, the resolution without resolution, the offstage denouement (chapter 65).

But most staggering of all these tiny metonymies is the way London turns out to be so small as to consist of only one poor crossing sweep in the whole of the place, so findable that Lady Dedlock alights upon him the instant she tries. In the chapter titled "Tom All Alone's," the discarded original title for the entire novel, the aristocrat travels incognito to "the ruinous place,"[28] and directly to the crossing, where she beckons to Jo, "Come here," and immediately inquires, "Are you the boy I have read of in the papers?" The incongruity of the question has been foreframed by the meditation on Jo's illiteracy ("It must be a strange state to be like Jo! To shuffle with the streets, unfamiliar with the shapes, and in utter darkness, as to the meaning, of those mysterious symbols . . . ! To see people read, and to see people write, and to see the postmen deliver letters, and not, to have the least idea of all that language"[29]). And so, Jo only fittingly replies, "I don't know nothink about no papers. I don't know nothink at all." While Lady Dedlock succeeds in extricating from Jo much that he does know about the death of Nemo, and while this knowledge interestingly consists of "place" ("Can you shew me all those places that were spoken of in the account I read? The place he wrote for, the place he died at, the place where you were taken to, and the place where he was buried?"[30]), the narrator knows, or tells, nothing of how Lady Dedlock came to be in precisely the place Jo occupies. She reads in the newspaper that a boy has testified, and instantaneously locates a single boy in the midst of the world's largest metropolis.

Jo the paradigmatic "type" of the destitute urban poor, a homeless orphan whom police and church alike order to "move on," turns out to be uniquely, paradoxically singular. When Lady Dedlock asks him whether Nemo's state resembled Jo's own, he replies, "O not so bad as me, I'm a reg'lar one, *I* am!"; and he repeats this epithet in chapter 19. Regular, typical, representative—but a regular *one*, exceptional, singular. This oneness of Jo, I mean to suggest, establishes another level at which the text thinks about limits. Only one Jo, a someone who links No One to Lady Dedlock, underworld to upper echelon, "the place in Lincolnshire, the house in town, the Mercury in town, and the whereabout of Jo the outlaw with the broom";[31] Jo is the node the novel poses in answer to its own ur-question of connection. This single hinge, this peculiar pivot, the random act of kindness that distinguished Nemo to Jo and the hyperlegibility that improbably allows Lady Dedlock to locate him, the vehicle of contagion that brings Esther to her illness, the helplessness that belies

Skimpole's harmlessness—this quilting point that holds together the whole book—this is another register by which *Bleak House* crafts its own smallness, fashions its delimited direct connection rather than diffuse network.[32] Not many threads, but one. Worlds turn upon irreducible limits, singular specters of their constitutions.

Bleak House studies limits by operating a spatial imaginary of hyperbolic domestic confinement, implausible contiguity, and the singular node. Subplots reiterate this thoroughgoing formal engagement with limits. Richard Carstone's tragically limited *Bildung*, for instance, presents a young man unable to pursue professional development, and unable to grow emotionally, whose trouble ultimately stems from being unable to perceive the limits of the case in Chancery. It is his everything, but it is not everything; it is millions of pounds, but his portion could never substitute for a living. Richard suffers from an inability to perceive or instantiate limits, and the novel punishes him for this failure. The novel's excoriation of Mrs Jellyby surely also enacts its insistence on limits, as her "telescopic philanthropy," presented as an alternative to "the limited vision that could see anything but Boorioboola Gha"[33] and bearing always "serene contempt for our limited sphere of action,"[34] is castigated for searching too far afield while overlooking the nearest to hand; women's projects ought have a more domestic scope.[35] Critics of course argue whether this plot arc, a conflict framed but never resolved, wields a critique of the British Empire alternately anti-imperial or insidiously nationalist in its domesticity, but at a minimum we can say that the Jellyby plot provides another instantiation of limit. In multiplying these instantiations, the novel underscores the infinite project of installing limits, the unfinished business and ungroundable schemes of delimiting social space. Social scale is rendered here a subject of intense scrutiny and irresolvable strife, enunciating the political formalist insight that every social formation contends with the problem of its own extent.

A certain hysteria about limits characterizes, improbably, both Mr. Turveydrop the master of deportment and Sir Leicester Dedlock the master of Chesney Wold; through the comedy around both of these figures we can discern the novel doesn't offer a facile endorsement of just any limit—it is, rather, keen to differentiate good limits from bad, general limits from particular. Outmoded versions of structuration and limitation are cause for concern: Mr. Turveydrop deplorably "fully believes he is a member of the aristocracy"[36] and deplores that "we are not what we used to be in point of Deportment. . . . We have degenerated. . . . A levelling age is not favourable to Deportment."[37] The same sentiment of course also airs repeatedly in the recurrent image of "the floodgates and the framework of society" within Sir Leicester's discourse. Deployed by Sir Leicester but also by the narrator, the image connotes a constitutive delineation of social relations for "the cohesion by which things are held together."[38]

Sir Leicester laments "the confusion into which the present age has fallen; of the obliteration of landmarks, the opening of floodgates, and the uprooting of distinctions."[39] It is his own, albeit mockably partisan, variation on the 1848 *Manifesto of the Communist Party*:

> All fixed, fast-frozen relations, with their train of ancient and venerable prejudices and opinions, are swept away, all new-formed ones become antiquated before they can ossify. All that is solid melts into air, all that is holy is profaned, and man is at last compelled to face with sober senses his real conditions of life, and his relations with his kind.[40]

The narrator presents the image in all its metonymic glory:

> From the village school of Chesney Wold, intact as it is this minute, to the whole framework of society; from the whole framework of society, to the aforesaid framework receiving tremendous cracks in consequence of people (iron-masters, lead-mistresses, and what not) not minding their catechism, and getting out of the station unto which they are called—necessarily and for ever, according to Sir Leicester's rapid logic, the first station in which they happen to find themselves; and from that, to their educating other people out of THEIR stations, and so obliterating the landmarks, and opening the floodgates, and all the rest of it; this is the swift progress of the Dedlock mind.[41]

For Sir Leicester, floodgates are essential to frameworks; there is no sociality without the imposition of certain limits to flow. For the narrator who remarks upon the overhasty metonymizing in Dedlock's logic, the deadliness of the locks in the floodgates, Sir Leicester's fault seems to be that his mind already commits the inattention to limits that he ostensibly portends; too quick catastrophizing and too clumsy causality are a graver threat to the framework of society than "progress" of "education" and "station." Thus whether in the aging aristocrat's worldview, or in the omniscient narrator's showing-up of that worldview, the motif of frameworks and floodgates evokes disagreement and mistake, essentiality and contestability. "House" presages a former framework of society, houseness sways; the house may remain the name of the new framework but that will entail radical revision to the root of what house signifies. This novel undertakes that resignification; it proliferates locales and meanings of houses as the scale at which it conducts social thinking, the unit at which social totality is practicable and fathomable.

The Absent Center of Political Ontology

Supreme as a technology for this proliferation—and performatively evocative of that formalism that simultaneously takes structuration as given and takes any given social shape as contestable—is the crucial decentering of the center. Even as Bleak House manifestly centers *Bleak House*, that center displaces itself: its appearance within the narrative is dramatically delayed and forestalled, and the energy of the text as a whole can be thought to articulate this nonidentity of the novel and this one house, and nonidentity of this house with itself. House is limit, the mathematical inscription of a dynamic tendency, a shorthand for the impossible-to-ground yet indispensable functions of law. Bleak House isn't mentioned until the third chapter and not visited until the sixth; it is less the setting for the novel than the destination, but when that destination at long last arrives, in chapter 64, it is not Bleak House itself but the replica, also called Bleak House. In all its centering pull, Bleak House recalcitrantly differs from itself, a space reiterated and renovated across the text. Having first gained its name from its state of disrepair and traumatic history, the house metamorphoses into a polar variant already held in title—from dark dereliction to bleachy domesticity, and transforms yet again in franchised replication elsewhere:

> There is, in that city of London there, some property of ours which is much at this day what Bleak House was then; I say property of ours, meaning of the suit's, but I ought to call it the property of costs, for costs is the only power on earth that will ever get anything out of it now or will ever know it for anything but an eyesore and a heartsore. It is a street of perishing blind houses, with their eyes stoned out, without a pane of glass, without so much as a window-frame, with the bare blank shutters tumbling from their hinges and falling asunder, the iron rails peeling away in flakes of rust, the chimneys sinking in, the stone steps to every door (and every door might be death's door) turning stagnant green, the very crutches on which the ruins are propped decaying.[42]

Rebuilt in London, Bleak House makes a common estate of Tom All Alone's, in common condition of disrepair. In inverse, as official Bleak House enjoys restoration, the degraded physical structures of its London twin typify dereliction. The structures of these tumbling, decaying ruins—more than any archetypal suffering individuals—vividly hand down dispossession. When the elemental structuration troped by the house breaks down, the law is exposed in its disorder, the social in its injustice. But the promise of better building lights up the plotted pursuit of Bleak House, the continuous construction of instantiations that mathematically approximate hospitable social space.

This tension between the centrality of the house and its decentering in replication and renovation writes itself into the very first references to the house in the book, which we have already noted come at some delay. Before the house physically appears, the text underscores that a copying, technologically reduplicative dissemination destabilizes the inscription of its name. The name is given, in its ungivenness, written on the wall of one of the more richly detailed spaces in the novel, Krook's shop:

> She had stopped at a shop, over which was written, KROOK, RAG AND BOTTLE WAREHOUSE. Also, in long thin letters, KROOK, DEALER IN MARINE STORES. In one part of the window was a picture of a red paper mill, at which a cart was unloading a quantity of sacks of old rags. In another, was the inscription, BONES BOUGHT. In another, KITCHEN-STUFF BOUGHT. In another, OLD IRON BOUGHT. In another, WASTE-PAPER BOUGHT. In another, LADIES' AND GENTLEMEN'S WARDROBES BOUGHT. Everything seemed to be bought, and nothing to be sold there. In all parts of the window, were quantities of dirty bottles: blacking bottles, medicine bottles, ginger-beer and soda-water bottles, pickle bottles, wine bottles, ink bottles: I am reminded by mentioning the latter, that the shop had, in several little particulars, the air of being in a legal neighbourhood, and of being, as it were, a dirty hanger-on and disowned relation of the law. There were a great many ink bottles. There was a little tottering bench of shabby old volumes, outside the door, labelled "Law Books, all at 9d." Some of the inscriptions I have enumerated were written in law-hand, like the papers I had seen in Kenge and Carboy's office and the letters I had so long received from the firm. . . .
>
> He touched me on the arm to stay me, and chalked the letter J upon the wall—in a very curious manner, beginning with the end of the letter and shaping it backward. It was a capital letter, not a printed one, but just such a letter as any clerk in Messrs. Kenge and Carboy's office would have made.
>
> "Can you read it?" he asked me with a keen glance.
>
> "Surely," said I. "It's very plain."
>
> "What is it?"
>
> "J."
>
> With another glance at me, and a glance at the door, he rubbed it out, and turned an "a" in its place (not a capital letter this time), and said, "What's that?"
>
> I told him. He then rubbed that out, and turned the letter r, and asked me the same question. He went on quickly, until he had formed, in the same curious manner, beginning at the ends and bottoms of the letters, the word JARNDYCE, without once leaving two letters on the wall together.
>
> "What does that spell?" he asked me.
>
> When I told him, he laughed. In the same odd way, yet with the same rapidity, he then produced singly, and rubbed out singly, the letters forming the words BLEAK HOUSE. These, in some astonishment, I also read; and he laughed again.

> "Hi!" said the old man, laying aside the chalk. "I have a turn for copying from memory, you see, miss, though I can neither read nor write."[43]

The space of the house's copying, its writing on other walls, vestibulates the house itself; before the narrative arrives at Bleak House the center has already been replicated and disseminated. In thus arraying so many relations via the writing of the name, the novel positions domestic construction, the architecture of social space, as the essential metainstitution propelling the legal system, the real estate system, the family system, the class system, the public health system, the manifold domains of the administration of life. Institutions diverge and fail, but the construction project remains.

Like the originless, plotless formalism of the law, the haziness and obscurity surrounding the house even in its foundational meta-ness survey the ungiven ground for the orders of sociality that human animals erect. No wonder then that when the text finally visits Bleak House, profound disorientation ensues; the perceptive senses can scarcely integrate the paradoxical light dark ("There was a light sparkling on the top of a hill before us, . . . "That's Bleak House!" . . . Presently we lost the light, presently saw it, presently lost it, presently saw it. . . . We alighted in no inconsiderable confusion"[44]), and the interior proves no enlightenment:

> It was one of those delightfully irregular houses where you go up and down steps out of one room into another, and where you come upon more rooms when you think you have seen all there are, and where there is a bountiful provision of little halls and passages, and where you find still older cottage-rooms in unexpected places with lattice windows and green growth pressing through them. . . . But if . . . you . . . turned up a few crooked steps that branched off in an unexpected manner from the stairs, you lost yourself in passages, with mangles in them, and three-cornered tables, and a native Hindu chair, which was also a sofa, a box, and a bedstead, and looked in every form something between a bamboo skeleton and a great bird-cage, and had been brought from India nobody knew by whom or when. . . . You might, if you came out at another door (every room had at least two doors), go straight down to the hall again by half-a-dozen steps and a low archway, wondering how you got back there or had ever got out of it.[45]

Within this Escher art, essential space does not reveal itself; doors and steps and passages stupefy in their abundant accommodation, and domesticated imperial spoils quarter a staggering too-muchness of possible shapes. As Benjamin Bishop observes, this passage employs "excessive metonymy," through which "shapes overlap, converge, and transmute into each other. These discontinuous transformations . . . uncover a raw materiality caught up mid form, suspended within and held by the morphing that carries matter into intelligible form."[46] Esther's very procedure of spatial detail might therefore be seen as one that tends toward a distillation of the purely formal lines of design and description/inscription, one that tends toward a formalist sense of the limit writing that constitutes manifold social spaces.

A crucial dislocation thus disperses the center of this multicentered novel: it is not quite possible to know where one is at Bleak House nor to inhabit a precise space from which broad relational nexuses can be consolidated. Such absences demark the novel's political formalism, its contemplation of social relations in terms of galvanizing abstractions whose insubstantiability does not gainsay their utility. Bleak House is difficult to perceive, difficult to fathom, decentered from the novel it entitles, reiterated in its London establishments (the household Esther and John take up there, as well as the properties in Jarndyce to which it is kin), is replicated in the New Bleak House John Jarndyce commissions, is always already as a copy of itself, is accessed only tendentially, is approachable as a limit rather than as an idyllic beyond. An overarching project to visit and revisit Bleak House, to make and remake other houses in its likeness, to compare other households to its highness, to disseminate its model plan, propels the book forward. Like Esther's famous embodiment of "a pattern," the iterability and portability of the house imply its own availability as pattern, model to follow. Matthew Beaumont helpfully argues, "*Bleak House* contains a multitude of bleak houses . . . none of which are called Bleak House. The title of the novel refers . . . to this multitude of bleak houses, this collective Bleak House."[47] Domestic space, the novel tells us, proliferates, replicates, recalibrates, differentiates; individual installations of the house are so many limits making habitable and legible the otherwise infinite. Instead of a natural order of things, instead of a paragon of domesticity that a society ought to copy, the novel presents us with original copies, and original obscurities, whose most originary qualities are not particular relational contents, but formal inscriptions of lines. *Bleak House* therefore extends the formalist ontology of politics that I have identified throughout this book as the essence of literary realism: it marks out forms as abstract, projective models for the relations they enable.

Our Mutual Narration, Delimited

If the novel's systematic rhetoric of the house promotes the approximacy of limits, the enabling openness of written form, it seems only time to suggest how such exploration motivates this novel's most radical formal feature: the split narration. First and third, past and present, embodied and abstract, the novel sunders its perspective, tracking the constraints of what is written. Alex

Woloch notes that the split evokes "the basic condition of the novel, as genre, torn between first- and third-personness," but he notes as well how hard it is to observe this condition, how unremarked Dickens's formal experimentation passed until after significant uptake of the Jamesian spatial theory of the novel.[48] I want to extend this essential spatialism proper to the split. As readers of the late twentieth century and onward did notice, the two narratives formally delimit one another—at least in principle, as one uses the first-person pronoun and the past tense, while the other uses third-person pronouns and the present tense; one represents subjects the other cannot. However, it must be pointed out that they importantly approach one another throughout, showing how much limits can generate access to what they seem to seclude: Esther's very first sentence is in the present tense and her very last sentence too; her narration becomes progressively less embodied and more eventful, climaxing in the sequence on the trail of Lady Dedlock; her narration becomes more temporally convoluted, resulting in several passages of doubling-back in time toward the end of the book; the third-person narrator sometimes employs the first-person pronoun, and has no more interior insight than Esther does.[49] Most profoundly, we can see the narrative convergence across the split in a mutual circumscription of the pivotal events in the plot, and a mutual orientation to space. In this dynamic of divergence and convergence, we can almost read a mathematical graph of functions and their asymptotes, of tendencies and their limits. The very modality of the split but not absolutely split/variable not random narration formalizes the de-essentialized representability of social space: there is no comprehensive view, there are no comprehensibly grounded relations—there are only variable, but designable, arbitrary installations. Such is the map of infinite space in mathematical formalism, and of social space in political formalism.

By circumscription, I mean the tendency of this "massive" book to exclude from the récit some of the most evental moments in the story. Within the third-person narrative, the deaths of Nemo and of Krook, which respectively sets in motion Lady Dedlock's demise and comprises the most memorable and controversial artistic point in the text, are each relayed perfunctorily after the fact offscreen. In similar fashion, albeit inflected by gendered modesty, the introduction of Alan Woodcourt into Esther's narrative happens completely belatedly to his presence in the story; he is added via subtraction: "I have forgotten to mention—at least I have not mentioned—that Mr. Woodcourt was the same dark young surgeon whom we had met at Mr. Badger's. Or that Mr. Jarndyce invited him to dinner that day. Or that he came."[50] More surprisingly, the climax of Esther's plot, the revelation of her parentage, transpires in a face-to-face conversation summarized post facto. In all of these and many other instances, the discourse of the novel calls conspicuous attention to its own boundaries, to the many events and affects it cannot relay—not merely periphera, but essential pivots. The narrative can only approximately graze the very most important of plot developments and character experiences, by tracing out their noniteration, writing the limit to their representation. Most intense of all such moments of limit narrativity is, of course, the asymptotic concluding nonconclusion, the novel's final sentence, a fragment that is also an ellipsis: "I did not know that; I am not certain that I know it now. But I know that my dearest little pets are very pretty, and that my darling is very beautiful, and that my husband is very handsome, and that my guardian has the brightest and most benevolent face that ever was seen, and that they can very well do without much beauty in me—even supposing—".[51] There, the very punctuation of the entire novel, the very end of termination of the narration function, is impossible to fully attain, and inscribed as a graphic line. With its ellipsis, *Bleak House* formally distills its fascination with the limit.[52]

The circumscriptive curtailing of narrative content reiterates the circumscriptive bounding of narrative space. Both narratives share this feature of general spatial confinement. Although Esther is titularly a housekeeper, and the third-person narrator is conventionally a worldkeeper, and although readers who celebrate the paradigmatic realism of *Bleak House* regularly remark the omniscient narrator's omnipresence, both narrators in this text actually remain equally domestic, equally confined.[53] The third-person visits more total spaces than Esther, but still dwells in the domestic, and the only truly interstitial chapters in the novel (the pursuit of Lady Dedlock) belong to Esther. The main image of narration that the text offers, an image now infamous as the paradigmatic emblem of omniscience, highlights mobility among spaces: "We may pass from the one scene to the other, as the crow flies."[54] But we must remark that this image appears *only once* as applied to the narrator, and that as a rule the third-person narrator moves contiguously—even in this signature image, the flight of omniscience is girdled by the flight plan of contiguity and resemblance: "It is but a glimpse of the world of fashion that we want on this same miry afternoon. It is not so unlike the Court of Chancery but that we may pass from the one scene to the other, as the crow flies."[55] Mostly, the contiguity to which the third-person narrator is subject follows the travel of the law, the physical path of Tulkinghorn the lawyer. Indeed, the only recurrence of the crow accentuates the limits of omniscience by a strange abridgment; the crow returns only to find *narrative* mobility wholly dependent upon its compression into *character*:

> Mr. Snagsby standing at his shop-door looking up at the clouds sees a crow who is out late skim westward over the slice of sky belonging to Cook's Court. The crow flies straight across Chancery Lane and Lincoln's Inn Garden into Lincoln's Inn Fields.
>
> Here, in a large house, formerly a house of state, lives Mr. Tulkinghorn. . . .[56]
>
> Mr. Tulkinghorn goes, as the crow came—not quite so straight, but nearly—to Cook's Court, Cursitor Street. To Snagsby's, Law-Stationer's, Deeds engrossed and copied, Law-Writing executed in all its branches, &c., &c., &c.
>
> It is somewhere about five or six o'clock in the afternoon, and a balmy fragrance of warm tea hovers in Cook's Court. It hovers about Snagsby's door. The hours are early there: dinner at half-past one and supper at half-past nine. Mr. Snagsby was about to descend into the subterranean regions to take tea when he looked out of his door just now and saw the crow who was out late.
>
> "Master at home?"
>
> Guster is minding the shop, for the 'prentices take tea in the kitchen with Mr. and Mrs. Snagsby; consequently, the robe-maker's two daughters, combing their curls at the two glasses in the two second-floor windows of the opposite house, are not driving the two 'prentices to distraction as they fondly suppose, but are merely awakening the unprofitable admiration of Guster, whose hair won't grow, and never would, and it is confidently thought, never will.
>
> "Master at home?" says Mr. Tulkinghorn.[57]

The sequence effectuates a delay and then a repetition, highlighting the strange descent of the crow into the body of Mr. Tulkinghorn. Though one might read this association of omniscience and the law as tantamount to registering the omnipresent, regulative powers of omniscient narration, one can hardly fail to read how it equally dramatizes the limits to omniscience, the unsustainability of flight, the flightiness of disembodied abstraction.

The tight interlocking of the third-person's domain becomes a metanovelistic principle in one of the book's most stirring sequences, imparting a reading method receptive to intercalated registers:

> What connexion can there be between the place in Lincolnshire, the house in town, the Mercury in powder, and the whereabout of Jo the outlaw with the broom, who had that distant ray of light upon him when he swept the churchyard-step? What connexion can there have been between many people in the innumerable histories of this world who from opposite sides of great gulfs have, nevertheless, been very curiously brought together![58]

Bleak House, Levine and others note, studies a remarkably strange, asymmetrical, incoherent set of linkages—"the law, disease, philanthropy, the space of the city, class, gossip, and the family tree"[59]—but we can also add that "house" constitutes the metalink that accommodates this baggy lot; house is the connection there can be. For all this connective tissue, the stuff of the house perches in question—who should live in it, under what auspices (housekeeper, wife, sibling, ward), by what lights (bleak dark, bleak white), in what frame of mind (Jarndyce or the crazy old man), in the country or the city (the property replicated in London), original or copy (the property replicated in Yorkshire). The house of fiction holds together the intricacy of space and sociality, of architecture and association; the infrastructural forms of collective life fold ductilely around multitudinous endeavors.

We might be inclined to fathom the split narration as something like an effort to diversify, a project to cover more bases: *Bleak House* is massive, and thus one mode of narration requires the supplement of another mode. But since I have been arguing that *Bleak House* is not massive, and that it is this minimalism, rather than its referentiality, that cues its thinking about social space and social totality, I locate the split narration as a site of delimitation: far from shoring each other up and achieving some total narration via perspectival supplementation, the first- and third-person and the oscillations between them serve to underscore the limits of each mode. This literary formal structure makes a profound point about political forms: there is no total scheme for the relation of the world; no narration without limits; no art of the social unmarked by its own artifice. Esther is limited by her inability to inhabit the role of narrator ("I have a great deal of difficulty"[60]), by her feminine self-diminishment and withholding, by her confinement within spaces rather than movement "as the crow flies." Indeed, on this point, it is crucial that the times when Esther's narration most closely resembles the omniscient narration are when she is on the move, in the chase after Lady Dedlock. But if the omniscient narrator enjoys unique mobility, there too are profound limits to where it will go: to Tom All Alone's, but not to any poor character other than Jo unless they are meeting with a more affluent character; to Lincolnshire and London but not to India with Alan Woodcourt, nor to Booriboola Gha with Mrs. Jellyby's minions.[61] What is more, beyond this geographic and economic delimitation, the omniscient narrator does not attend or present the most important events in its plot: Nemo's death, Krook's death, Richard's death, Lady Dedlock's death, the lawsuit's final hearing, and Esther's discovery of her parentage *all* take place offscreen or in Esther's narrative or both (since in Esther's narrative events frequently show up only belatedly and perfunctorily).

The variability of the narrative switching also suggests a constant, random abutting of limits; there is nothing regular about it as regards numbers of chapters or pages (sometimes the switch is after one chapter, sometimes two, three, four, five); there is nothing even about the alternation; the narrator has more continuous sets of chapters (a span of five chapters, which Esther never gets, from 25 to 29, and four spans of four chapters, versus Esther's three, from 3 to 6, 35 to 38, and 59 to 62). There is, in short, no pattern, even among the distribution: while the narrator has only one more chapter than Esther (thirty-four to her thirty-three), Esther commences three more serial parts than the narrator (eleven to its eight), but then again the narrator has five installments purely from its perspective, while only one is wholly Esther's. Esther's narrative appears to be more personal, in that it relays both her perception of events and her plight to take up the right home, and in that its knowledge is attained through social interaction, visits, dialogue, and often consists of the personal feelings and personal struggles of the other parties in those relationships. The omniscient narrator, though generically better disposed to present such intimacies, remains tonally aloof, and makes scant use of free indirect discourse. The omniscient narrator moves among houses more quickly than Esther can, but often only by following characters' motions: Tulkinghorn, Bucket, the men of the law who travel freely and insert themselves inquisitively, uninhibitedly. The perspectival limits effectuated by the variable narration bring into consideration the impossibility of a consistent point of view from which to register "the whole framework of society." Like the very partisan partiality that impugns Sir Leicester when he speaks this phrase, any possible representation of "society" will be limited by its own situatedness. With its remarkable narrative construction, then, *Bleak House* delivers a political formalist theory of the dispensation of social space and the artful ungivenness of any such dispensation.

The novel's overwhelming attention to *houses* as frameworks within which abstract forms take less abstract shape directs our attention to form as spatialization, to the installation of social matrices via local infrastructures of buildings, mixed-use establishments, and residences. *Bleak House* takes the dynamic overlaying of the law and the house, inscription and architecture, as a crucial impetus for the novel form. In thus laminating the architectural constitution of lived social space, *Bleak House* novelly articulates political formalism. Superimposing tropes of displacement, replication, inauthenticity onto tropes of architecture and housing onto tropes of legal suits and legal regulations, *Bleak House* highlights the aesthetic facets of social structuration: the art, the artful, the artless, the arbitrary formalizations of social relations. Moreover, because these tropes initiate reaching reflections on limits, we can read realism otherwise than the mimetic mandate writ large. If *Bleak House* can legitimately be understood as the apogee of Victorian realism, then realism must mean much less representativeness, much less bigness, and much more this limitedness. Realism emerges by the dark light of *Bleak House* as the fictive production of social space in accordance with limits—limits of finitude and mortality, of available materials, of temporal linearity and corporeal indivisibility, of structural integrity—most of all, the limit functions of inscription and installation, institution and law. It emerges as that affirmation of form and elaboration of structuration at the heart of political formalism, a galvanizing prompt to remake sociality with inspiration other than limitlessness, so that what is written and composed can more adequately host.

4

Symbolic Logic on the Social Plane of *Alice's Adventures in Wonderland*

At once, three propositions. Mind this form, because the arc of this chapter bends ultimately toward its own three propositions.

A	Nothing is better than eternal happiness.
B	A ham sandwich is better than nothing.
C	A ham sandwich is better than eternal happiness.

If, dear reader, the middle of this book finds you needing a break, you might be favorably disposed to the sustenance of sandwiches. But you might also detect something fishy about this ham syllogism. The deduction of a conclusion from two related premises that share a common term absent from the conclusion (here, "nothing"), syllogisms are not inherently fishy—only, their being right hinges on the uniformity of the common term. Here, the signifier "nothing" in A (negative universality; there is no exception) is unequal to itself in B (negative presence; there is no thing); not all nothings are equal, but a true syllogism requires that nothing means nothing more than what it means.

Nothing contrived or unusual about this particular fish ham; this pickle already dogs the very first page of the Victorian textbook *Symbolic Logic*, by Charles Dodgson, which commences with a graphic illustration of underlapping universals:

A	That story of yours, about your once meeting a sea-serpent, always sets me off yawning.
B	I never yawn unless something is totally devoid of interest.
C	That story of yours, about your once meeting a sea-serpent, is totally devoid of interest.

Always and never—what Dodgson calls the "universal affirmative" and "universal negative" and Kant called dynamic and mathematic and Lacan called masculine and feminine: contradictory universalities, that taken together yield falsehoods, antinomies, nonrelation. To guarantee the syllogism's truth, it is imperative to disambiguate signifiers (ensure the singularity of nothing): hence Dodgson's text first tries to lay out unambiguous definitions, and then substitutes for the linguistic presentation of the syllogism the algebraic notation: symbols, letters, operators, and diagrams subtracting semantic excess. All cats understand French; some chickens are cats; some chickens understand French. Nothing intrinsically incorrect in this formulation: it strictly follows rules of interrelation. Only extrinsic sense complicates things. Rewritten with letters and symbols, the extrinsic is prohibited, the intrinsic perfected. In this, Dodgson followed the headmost Victorian logician George Boole—Boolean algebra and the computer, you know—whose own practice of symbolic logic not only subtracted semantic excess, but also expressly grasped that meaning lies not in words themselves, but in their arranged relation. The meaning of the word "cat" does not emanate from c-a-t but from "pat that cat" or "cat ate rat." Symbolic logic, Andrea Henderson observes, makes the formal, ungrounded character of language a matter of explicit principle.[1] Well before structuralist linguistics and surrealist aesthetics the Victorian revolution in logic comprised the direct avowal of this ungroundedness, the direct inscription of the arbitrary and conventional essence of formal systems as such.

I say "revolution" because that is indeed how intellectual historians often characterize the profundity of the epistemological shifts ushered in by Victorian mathematics, a set of reconfigurations of the basis of human knowledge even more upending than Darwin. These shifts—effected by symbolic logic as well as non-Euclidean geometry, set theory, differential calculus—all reorient mathematical knowledge from a description of the world to a projection of possible worlds, and thus establish mathematics as *formalism*. Deductive not inductive, abstraction above empiricism, consistency before concretude, symbolization beyond meaning, formalist mathematics elevates representation in distinction from description in a move Foucault hails as pivotal for epistemic modernity.[2] In contrast to the view that behind signs are things, formalization sunders signs from things, to the benefit of both signs and things: what is signifiable exceeds the order of things, and this very excess may eventually precipitate new things.

This "benefit"—this probing of the possible—stems from the core irony of formalization. By reducing theorems to formulae and words to letters in the interest of exactitude—so that nothing means nothing more than what it means—the formalists also multiplied hypotheses. As the mathematician Augustus De Morgan explained this philosophical corollary to symbolic reduction in 1859, "Pure logic and pure mathematics are the only fields of the possible and impossible. All that is thinkable is possible; all that is impossible is unthinkable: that is so far as our knowledge can go. We cannot *know* the impossibility of anything we can conceive without contradiction."[3] Sit with this tension: formalist mathematics is simultaneously the minimal-est, supremely precise denotation, *and* the maximal-est, supremely speculative connotation—the thought of the possible, the drive to infinitize the possible.

Proposition A

As the consummation of mathematical formalism, symbolic logic foregrounds the constructedness of universals and their negations (to return to our old ham sandwich); opens the heterogeneity of infinity and the aleatory horizons of different dispensations of possible space; and radicalizes the constituting power of the signifier (anything that can be written is possible). This chapter is structured by three propositions, and we come now to the first: symbolic logic effectuates mathematical formalism as idiomatically or theoretically *political*, as assembling concepts and questions also proper to the political. It's rather a big proposition, so we can put it in the form of the syllogisms to which you are now accustomed: politics is the art of the possible; math is also an art of the possible; math is politics.

What should strike us, literary critics in the twenty-first century, about this math of the nineteenth century, in the faculty of formalism to comprise not just an aesthetic method but an epistemology and indeed a political theory, is the different, *affirmative* valence mathematical formalism accords to form, structure, law. Form is not delimited containment but prismatic projection of other spaces. Structure is not transcendental determinativness, but immanent agency. Law is not an emanation from nature or what exists, but an axiomatic writing that creates new possibles. Humanists of many stripes understand their scholarship as contesting the law, negating institutions, dismantling universals, undoing generalizations, fleeing from form—promoting particularity, hybridity, concretude, formlessness. We authorize these political conceits with reference to traditions ranging from Foucauldian historicism to new materialism, queer antinomianism to deconstructive poetics, standpoint epistemology to anti-instrumental reason, and imagine that dissolution is emancipation, while composition is domination. To give form is to oppressively contain—and thus the study of art favors fragmentation, unmaking, decomposition. Privileging modernism over realism, openness over closure, transgression over synthesis, irony over telos, methodological protocols and theoretical truisms in the study of art have celebrated forms that undo their own formedness. But quite opposed to all this, a mathematically inflected political formalism affirms the constituting power of abstraction to make possible alternate, heterogeneous, disparate social spaces. Mathematical formalism opens a different purview onto form: integral forms make new relations possible. Abstractions also liberate. There's your lesson, then, from math to politics: formalism emerges in the nineteenth century as an approach to composed generalization, consistent form, and speculative projection; this framework opens up completely remarkable insights about the politics of form that we professional critics of aesthetic form have not yet absorbed in the twenty-first century.

Symbolic logic's linguistic formalism extracts a parallel formalism of the political: if all systems function by virtue of their internal consistency rather than their external import, can we not also say that all socio-symbolic orders of human sociality function rather than signify, obtain as structure rather than as meaning? Now, much as such formalism gets accused, in vast archives of critical theory from Adorno to Agamben, of subtracting the subject and minimizing the particular in the service of the instrumental rationality of "the administered world" in all its bellicose totalitarian fascist glory, there remains the counter prospect of a different politics of math. The politics of logic, as Claude Lévi-Strauss or Paul Livingston might define it, would quit lamenting the ordering of life and quit longing for anarchy, turning instead to the question of better and worse orders, a question only possible if the primacy of order is admitted.[4] The only true universal is not the affirmative substantive good lunch or good life, but the negative planarity of social structuration as such. Even as all socialities erect themselves always already dislodged, there can be no unstructured collective existence.

One might arrive at this preliminary proposition about symbolic logic's entailed political theory with the help of the philosopher Alain Badiou, the anthropologist Claude Lévi-Strauss, or the psychoanalyst Sigmund Freud, or any theory committed to the symbolic structuration of social life. But since literary critics do so like induction, we can arrive the other way, taking up the politics of mathematical formalism via its preeminent literary instantiation, *Alice's Adventures in Wonderland*—a text written, you will have noticed, by none other than the author of the symbolic logic textbook with which we began, Charles Dodgson. Dodgson's novel distinctly integrates the quandaries symbolic logic names—axiomatic rules, universal signifiers, hyperspace consistency—with the overt political dynamics of sovereignty, law, and the business of life and death. In laminating these domains of logic and politics together, the novel suggests that they are tropes of one another, interanimating. To read this work as a whole—to read it, that is, formalistically—is to reckon with this intersection of symbolic logic and the political, to receive *Wonderland*'s political formalism.

In its overt form, this fiction couldn't be further from the precision of symbolic logic: an unruly maximalism, it is at once a children's picture book, a travelogue through insane terrain, a nonsense glossary, a fantasy digest, and a novel in twelve parts, yet any fool can see that the book is chockablock with logic games, a veritable parody of rigorous proofs, each scene leaping from one proposition to the next. An immediate mystery: Why does a logic novel take such illogical license with literary form? A *murder* mystery: Why does this ironic and logic poetic play transmute so often to the deadly serious business of beheading? Through and through, on virtually every page, *Alice* confronts the specter of violent death at the will of the sovereign, the text working itself into nothing less than a treatise on sovereignty, including individual agency, collective power, judicial law, monarchic authority, and what Michel Foucault and Jacques Derrida both define as the ultimate sovereign expression, the death sentence:[5]

> There was a dispute going on between the executioner, the King, and the Queen. . . .
>
> The executioner's argument was, that you couldn't cut off a head unless there was a body to cut it off from;
>
> The King's argument was, that anything that had a head could be beheaded, and that you weren't to talk nonsense.
>
> The Queen's argument was, that if something wasn't done about it in less than no time she'd have everybody executed, all round. . . .[6]
>
> "They're dreadfully fond of beheading people here; the great wonder is, that there's any one left alive!" Alice says.[7]

Threats of violent death punctuate most of the episodes in *Wonderland*, and the Queen's threats are the most constitutive: she is always "in a furious passion, stamping about, and shouting 'off with his head' or 'off with her head' about once a minute,"[8] and at the last minute "off with her head" punctures wonderworld, ending the framed narrative. This is a book that insistently juxtaposes wordplay and the ambiguity of the signifier to death sentences and the whim of the sovereign—that makes, indeed, of this juxtaposition a comprehensive equation between the sovereign decision on death and the sovereign decision on the signifier; it is called a "sentence of execution" because the order to execute analogizes the order constituted in the sentence. The power to decide death is the power to fix the word, to posit the axiom, to sheerly assert that there is a regime. Mystery solved: this axiomatic character of sovereignty is an insight of symbolic logic. Where a classical logic of sovereignty pretends to grounds and transcends to essences, holding that the king is the king because he is himself, symbolic logic sustains the realization of nongroundedness: the king is the king because his subjects are his subjects, because he occupies a position within a differential system that is purely formal and wholly immanent. The imposition of form, the authorization of a regime, the positing of an axiom: these are radically constituting acts whose purely synthetic power wears the trope of violence. Alice objects to the King at the book's climactic conclusion, "That's not a regular rule: you invented it just now," and he instantly replies, "It's the oldest rule in the book."[9]

Wonderland draws a straight line between the sheerly formal, sheerly instituted quality of mathematical laws and the radically imposed, radically contingent quality of social law as such. As Alice bangs her head against the bounds of the world, deduces norms from the idiosyncracies of gesture, and fights to delimit contradictory universalities, the book repeatedly asks where rules come from, and in its insistent repetition the question flatly refuses answer. There is no farther beyond than the necessity and facticity of structuration; the theory of the political is not an origin story, not a diachronic narrative, but a synchronic formula. This is symbolic logic's positive political theory, its mathematical formalism extrapolated into a "political formalism."

Yet relativizing rules in this way is not a game; the "great wonder is that there is anyone" even alive—rules are matters of life and death; relationality precedes identity; minimal institutionalization is required for anyone to be left alive. The inventive, playful children's tale is also alarmingly adult; *Wonderland*'s genre ambidexterity articulates these two unlike things into a single thought: the life of a child is a grown-up business, mature cohesion required for infant survival. Political order may hold the constant prospect that life ends in execution, but order also sustains the very beginning of life. There are no worlds, in three dimensions or four, untainted by the absurdity of their confabulation. Invented, unfounded sovereignty is the only foundation, improvised rule the only rule. Any given formalization of systematicity is ungrounded, but that does not gainsay the system's effectivity or necessity—nor, and this is the crucial point, its availability as a space of play. The fanciful pen of *Wonderland* writes a different accent to the blankness of every order: no longer an indictment of illegitimacy or an altar for lament, the formalism of the political opens onto the exuberance of reform, new constitutions, new buildings, new spaces. The marvelous, funny, beautiful adventure of this book takes shape atop this formalist regard for formalized sociation; it turns the null of law into ground zero for creative fun. Such is the political ontology cast by the book of wonder.

In this brief chapter, I consider the tight isomorphism of the form of *Alice's Adventures in Wonderland* and the form of symbolic logic. Of the novels I engage in *The Order of Forms*, *Wonderland* is the most explicitly enmeshed in the worldview of mathematics—written by a mathematician, and expressly thematizing Victorian mathematical developments. Among these novels it is also, a formalist might note, the shortest. And of course, readers will hasten to remark, it is the remotest from the mode of realism that this book is concerned to theorize. My argument here incorporates this brevity and this remoteness as themselves formal features, spinning a speculative line that far from realism's opposite, *Wonderland* distills realism to its essence. I have argued throughout this book for a formalist conception of realism as the projection of possible social space; I argue here that *Wonderland*'s enchantment of the bounds of reality reduces realism—it both concentrates and intensifies realism's world-projective, world-making faculty. Like *Wuthering Heights*, *Wonderland* foregrounds social antagonism and the inevitable baselessness of instantiated sociality. Like *Bleak House*, it mediates limits, affirming social structuration while estranging given structures. Like *Jude the Obscure*, as we will see in chapter 5, it conceives social form as the lineation of space. Realism's constitutive impulse to model social worlds finds its ultimate underlining in *Wonderland*'s concise query into the laws of the possible.

Spaces of Wonder

Before we get to the second proposition, a little visual detour is in order. *Wonderland* doesn't work linearly you know; and symbolic logic activates the imagistic matter of the letter—so let us make a short digression into images. The aestheticization of space and inquiry into space as medium of sociality that *The Order of Forms* first framed with the aid of early photography is central to *Wonderland*, and we might adjust our perception to that centrality by considering the photographs that Carroll worked on while also writing his book. These images might themselves have served as the book's illustrations, so shared are their interests. Take, for example, two images from Carroll's years with the Liddell family (whose daughter Alice is said to have been inspiration for the character in the story composed for her entertainment): *The Deanery* and *The Elopement.* Both of these images situate a child or children against the backdrop of an architectural structure.

In *The Deanery*, three children pose in an improbably small middle ground between an imposing building and an expanse of foreground. As with Tal-

FIGURE 4. Charles Dodgson, *The Deanery* (nineteenth century). Photograph: Department of Rare Books and Special Collections, Princeton University Library.

bot, the building in question is at an Oxford college (Christ Church), and the addition of children makes the question of institutional edification more pronounced. The composition is so innovatively distorted as to immediately evoke those precipitous transformations of scale that *Wonderland* takes for plot. Moreover, the foreground is captured at offset angle to reveal its highly manicured seams; this grass has been slavishly cultivated to follow curves like a carpet and limn pathways like a ruler. In turn this angling leaves the background building in inevitable partiality; the photograph encompasses the structure's façade with skill, but truncates the rear extent. The partiality merges the built form and the natural scape, an effect dramatically heightened by the building's open door, and by the plantings from which the building is framed to emerge, hedges whose edges are cropped out. As in *The Pencil of Nature*, an indeterminate hinge of architecture and nature compromises the subject, with the nascent life of three children perching at that foggy crease. Life, the photograph seems to suggest, rests precariously atop the jointure of nature and architecture, the product of provisional configurations of social space.

Such precarious perching becomes more transparently the subject in *The Elopement.* An overtly narrative photograph, it depicts a young girl in

FIGURE 5. Charles Dodgson, *The Elopement* (nineteenth century). Photograph: Department of Rare Books and Special Collections, Princeton University Library.

full white dress and dark-hooded cape stepping jauntily down a rope ladder hanging from the window of an upper-story window. No ground solidifies below her, and her posture preposterously ill suits climbing a ladder, posed as she is like a floating leaper. She is escaping, but she is also supported in her improbable endeavor by the window she grips and the architrave she treads. The camera surveys the diversity of building materials in appraisal of these ambivalent entrapping/supporting functions, focused in detail to render the palpable differences between brick, glass, stone, and slate textures and the wonder of their concert in one whole surface. The window from which the girl egresses is open, but so too is the window in the story beneath her, belying the need for elaborate escape technology. The slanted slate roof is an imposing top third of the picture, but is cropped so as to occlude its apex; the effect is of vertiginous momentum down. This is a story of the play that is made of evading form, and of the support forms offer nonetheless.

Carroll's photographs, we might say from just these two examples, natively converse in the idiolect William Henry Fox Talbot establishes, marking photography as a spatial medium and making spatial form the ultimate subject of the medium's mediation. Like Talbot's development of the *camera obscura* into architectural photography, Carroll develops the space of the camera, with its scalar experiments, variable size openings, shuttering walls, opaque curtains, and dynamic projections into the formal trappings of Wonderland as a space organized by tiny doors, sudden scalar shifts, and projective fantasy.[10] They illuminate other rooms of his endeavors, that we can better receive *Wonderland*, and its conspicuous enchantment of social space, as a project to deliberate structured relations. Political formalism can be articulated in multiple media.

Formalization in *Wonderland*

All the while that he was practicing the art of photography and composing several literary texts, Lewis Carroll was working as a mathematician, teaching, writing, and researching in geometry and algebra. Surprisingly, *Wonderland*'s energetic exploration of mathematical formalism has not played a strong role in the huge critical literature treating the text. Critics such as Helena Pycior and Elisabeth Throesch maintain that Carroll takes a "conservative" approach to developments in math, using his literary works to highlight epistemological pitfalls and ontological threats posed by formalism and speculative investigations of hyperspace.[11] Enthusiasts like Robin Wilson and Gillian Beer have produced whimsically toned catalogues of mathematical references in his letters and literary works, without assessing the interrelation of such references and literary texts as aesthetic enterprises.[12] I pull a rather different thread, trying to think through the ways that Carroll's formal techniques of literary world-making coarticulate mathematical formalism and political formalism. The novel's defamiliarizing of social normativity is continuous with its regard for mathematics as abstraction, a formalist procedure of simultaneous estrangement from and enchantment of the letter in "Reeling and Writhing . . . and then the different branches of Arithmetic—Ambition, Distraction, Uglification, and Derision."[13]

Political readings of *Wonderland* are even rarer than mathematical ones.[14]

Yet, as Kent Puckett notes, Carroll himself wrote a treatise on caucusing, and was keenly interested in political procedure. In his reading, Puckett shows how *Wonderland* tracks the rules of the game and then "reveals those rules *as* rules, as formal principles that order the matter of everyday life while standing in excess to that matter."[15] Forms in excess of matter is a good definition of the fundamental precept for both the revolution of mathematical formalism and the theory of political formalism: the rule is the rule, the form in abstraction is its own content.

Proposition B

This political formalism—this affirmative regard for the merely formal quality of sociation—is, I repeat, deeply at odds with our usual humanist platitudes. Oddity indeed: the ultimate genius of *Wonderland* is its making of aesthetic form out of this political formalism. Any novel might *present* the arbitrary character of the social. Indeed, writ large, this is perhaps the best definition of the novel as such, that thing long understood—since at least the Russian formalists defined literary language as the exposure of the artifice of convention, or since at least Lukács defined the novel as motivated by the existential irony that its confabulated totality is a mere shadow of a lost premodern immanence—that thing long understood to reveal that all modern worlds are confabulated. Any novel, every novel, tells the story of inventing the social, studies the frames that make worlds cohere. But only some novels make that story their discourse as well, arranging plot, imagery, point of view, characterization, setting, temporality into an interrelated mediation of the artificial infrastuctures that produce social space. *Wonderland*'s form amounts less to a book *about* symbolic logic's philosophy of sovereignty, death, and nonsense and more to a book that *performs* symbolic logic: fixing the signifier, lineating elementary relations, writing structure rather than relaying meaning. Not only a novel symbolic logic, but a novel *as* symbolic logic. Proposition B: the form of *Alice's Adventures in Wonderland* is symbolic logic. Down the rabbit hole, shall we?

The Graphic Novel

We began with symbolic logic's reductivism, its flattening of troubling semantic promiscuity into the austere signifier, a letter that means exactly what it means. *Alice's Adventures in Wonderland* builds its literary form from this tension between proliferating meaning and the stark contour of the letter, becoming the novel as symbolic logic through the incredible importance it places on the letter as such. Algebraic letters in symbolic logic function as de-semanticized empty marks, potentially full of meaning but powerful in their subtractivity. Where in arithmetical algebra the letter stands for a specific quantity, in symbolic logic this function of standing-for is replaced by standing-in, place-holding within a set of relationships that would itself be the horizon of any possible meaning of the letter. The letter's function within the order of relations preempts and precedes its individual content, and letterality itself comes into relief as the capacity to inscribe place-holding, to substantiate a spatiality. If the letter has been recognized in traditions from Saint Paul, political theology, deconstruction, and psychoanalysis as a material force constituting the law, the formalist revolution in mathematics enunciates such recognition in a different, more aleatory register. Letters institute the spaces they circumscribe, but they do not inherently signifiy any particular regime of space.

The text of *Wonderland* lures us first of all to this letter-ality with its print/illustration/diagrammatic hybrid, not only pictures everywhere, but Mallarmean typographic experiments in italics, centering and offsetting, blank space, asterisks, dinkuses, and outsize letters. Elementary subjects are homophoned into word pictures ("I only took the regular course . . . Reeling and Writhing . . . then the different branches of arithmetic: Ambition, Distraction, Uglification, and Derision"), the language of the book performing itself as "reeling" and "writhing"—setting-into-motion of the signifier, mobilizing material malleability. Not only does the text itself address the function of the material signifier in constituting worlds; that text is aestheticized in innovative ways that highlight the availability of the signifier for new formalizations.

Indeed, making and remaking the signifier was a huge part of composing this book. Carroll obsessed over the markings in the text—the punctuation, italics, section breaks, and illustrations—undertaking revisions consistently over thirty years, including an entire edition of the text whose revisions solely concerned the use of hyphens, dots, and commas. He originally made the illustrations himself, then sought out a famous illustrator to redo them. And he took the drastic steps of rejecting the first edition, and purchasing the entire run of the second edition, purely out of dissatisfaction with the illustration quality. Additional future revisions addressed the location of images on the page. The tenacity with which he finessed the graphic quality of the text suggests that this material of the letters matters seriously to the overall composition.

Even were the illustrations not subject to such perfectionist scrutiny, their presence, abundance, and charm are crucial to the work as a whole. A frontispiece stands portal to the work, presenting a markedly stratified panoptic social view of the domain of *Wonderland*: the King and Queen in court, attendants behind and beneath them, a gallery of spectators beneath the attendants, a table of guests beneath the gallery, and in the foreground a prisoner in chains, defiant of chin. We are entering a regulated kingdom of spatialized hierarchy, with freedom in the balance. An illustration rests atop the first page, above the text, and the very first sentence conveys Alice's disdain for books without pictures, her entailed desire for the visual becoming the impetus for the adventures themselves. Illustrations are on almost every page, and significant graphic experiments are launched within the first few chapters. The elevation of the illustrations produces a constant shuttle between the printed words on the page and the visual image, an effect that, I want to suggest, spatializes this narrative. This spatialization is akin to what Hillary Chute, in her landmark study of comics as literature, identifies as the "narrative architecture built on the establishment of or deviation from regular intervals of space"[16] consequent upon the "nonsynchronous" "blend of the verbal and the visual."[17] The shuttling between word and image aestheticizes in a new way both the graphic quality of the letter *and* the spatial dimension of the page.

The aestheticizing shuttling of reeling and writhing reaches an apex in mobilizing letters themselves into illustrations, as is vividly the case with "the mouse's tail," in chapter 3, "A Caucus-Race and a Long Tale." The previous chapter has engulfed Alice in a sudden pool of water, and she swims her way out in pursuit of a mouse; the next begins in crossing onto shore, the mouse leading "a whole party" of animals, endeavoring to "dry" them out by way of a dry tale—a recitation of political history. This tale has its intended effect, more or less, and soon Alice is alone with the Mouse, obliging him to go on drying and tell her his personal "history," which he disclaims is "a long and a sad tale." Alice punningly agrees: "'It *is* a long tail, certainly' said Alice, looking down with wonder at the Mouse's tail."[18]

While the Mouse speaks, she visualizes the tale as a tail, and with an extra-long dash the words on the page break off from standard block paragraphs, amassing below in the illustrative shape of a winding, s-curvy tail occupying seven-eighths of the page. Projects like this blur letter and line, word and picture, novel and spatial projection, adumbrating a sensibility that grasps the production of a world from out of the material of the letter.

Proposition C

If these exemplary fascinations with the very letter of its own discourse bespeak *Wonderland*'s technology of magnificent reduction, its absurdly joyful subtracting of semantic excess and aesthetic roundness to isolate flat letters

'Fury said to a
mouse, That he
met in the
house,
"Let us
both go to
law: *I* will
prosecute
you. – Come,
I'll take no
denial; We
must have a
trial: For
really this
morning I've
nothing
to do."
Said the
mouse to the
cur, "Such
a trial,
dear Sir,
With
no jury
or judge,
would be
wasting
our
breath."
"I'll be
judge, I'll
be jury"
Said
cunning
old Fury:'
"I'll
try the
whole
cause,
and
condemn
you
to
death."

FIGURE 6. "Mouse's Tail," in Lewis Carroll's *Alice's Adventures in Wonderland* (1865).

of social lineation and literary creation—and if, dear reader, our math lesson primed you to fathom that this letteralism *is* symbolic logic, we find ourselves holding a *novel as symbolic logic*, but begging the antecedent: Of what premise is *Wonderland* the algebraic abstraction? Proposition C: *Alice's Adventures in Wonderland* is the symbolic logic of literary realism.

Wonderland appeared in 1865 as an explosively popular but critically reviled alternative to the realist masterpieces that were its exact contemporaries: Trollope's *Can You Forgive Her?*, Gaskell's *Wives and Daughters*, Dickens's *Our Mutual Friend.* Nothing would seem plainer than that this nonsense novella is the opposite of realism, but I want to think this opposition formally—that *Wonderland* does not negate so much as simultaneously minimize and maximize the propensities of realism. Literary critical protocols so often reduce realism: in language more referential than other literary modes, it represents context and reifies reality, subsisting in a poverty of form. But *Wonderland*'s redux refracts realist form, through the looking glass.

The brute material of the signifier that we've seen to be the stuff of *Wonderland*'s form redacts realism's putative pragmatics of meaning, its language commonly taken to more felicitously *refer* than other literary modes. Little happens in this text other than the failure of reference: it is replete with bidirectional miscommunications of such frustrating sort and such circular repetitions that characters can scarcely be said to communicate with one another at all, a social milieu in which surely everyone, not merely Alice, "had never been so much contradicted in all her life before."[19] Even when characters intend their speech to be felicitously efficacious, they are dogged by inconsistencies and reversibilities:

> "Do you mean that you think you can find out the answer to it?" said the March Hare.
>
> "Exactly so," said Alice.
>
> "Then you should say what you mean," the March Hare went on.
>
> "I do," Alice hastily replied; "at least—at least I mean what I say—that's the same thing you know."
>
> "Not the same thing at bit!" said the Hatter. "Why, you might just as well say that 'I see what I eat' is the same thing as 'I eat what I see'!"
>
> "You might just as well say," added the March Hare, "that 'I like what I get' is the same thing as 'I get what I like'!"
>
> "You might just as well say," added the Dormouse, which seemed to be talking in its sleep, "that 'I breathe when I sleep' is the same thing as 'I sleep when I breathe'!"
>
> "It's the same thing with you," said the Hatter, and here the conversation dropped.[20]

However hard it is to say what one means, even if one has the intention to mean what they say, however wide the gap the Hare and the Hatter open, the Dormouse closes it by repeating with a difference, the difference of sameness, since his signature hibernations and outsize quantities of sleep minimize the qualitative alterity of the two. Words diverge, and converge again, but even when conversations peter out rather than intensify, the communication has been of a metasort. In these inflationary reductions, we can reperceive realism less as reference and more as inquiry into the possibility of reference; less as reification of reality and more as investigation into reality's constructions.

What holds reality together in *Wonderland* is not the everyday felicity of referential language, but the sovereign formalism of the signifier, its graphic inscription of material links. Words surrender to vertigo, to polysemous proliferation, falling and bouncing and thudding in confrontation with the gap between graphic, sensuous letters and the nonsense they beget. "Read me," the text exhorts, read me, in excess of, and in privation of, conventional reference, read me in graphemes and homophones, in pictures and puns. "While she was peering about anxiously among the trees, a little sharp bark just over her head made her look up in a great hurry. An enormous puppy was looking down at her"[21])—the imaginative turn of events seeming to materialize out of the very polysemy of "bark." Puns propel; such exchanges lay bare the material form of social relations in excess of meaningful content, the abstract link rather than concrete communication. In this propulsive movement from one sentence to the next via the contiguities of pun, *Wonderland* formalizes realism's archetypal metonymy—its distinction from the metaphoricity of poetry, allegory, romance, noted by critics from Roman Jakobson to Franco Moretti, contiguity rather than similarity, prosaic lineation.

Metonymy's peculiar causality—its encoding of an in-dwelling logic immanent to a structure, rather than making recourse to external elements; its immanent planarity in contrast to transcendent hierarchy—makes it the master trope of capitalism (though that is a lesson for another day when Althusser is teaching) but also the natural trope of mathematical logic, which prizes the internal cohesion of forms. As a logic novel, *Wonderland* operates not only metonymic syntax but also metonymic plot. Carroll celebrated in his Preface "the original line" of his arrangements, which indeed proceed purely as line.[22] Not cause and effect but spatial adjacency (going through hedges, opening doors, tumbling down holes) and spatial transit (new characters come on the scene en route elsewhere) stir Alice to new directions and new confrontations, and these new directions do not accumulate as bildung—character growth is literalized into spatial scale change, and as well cancels itself out (outsize growth, ridiculous shrinkage, normalcy again).

When the book lacks a spatial connection to what comes next, it corrals the space of the book itself, employing graphic transitions (deliberately set blank space or large phalanxes of asterisks) to dislocate causal ties.

On this spatial plane where plot becomes line, effect becomes cause, the consistency of the universe encompasses its infinite self-contrariness, and past also becomes present. *Wonderland* spatializes temporality ("It's always tea-time!"[23] the Mad Hatter confirms)—compressing what Nicholas Dames has called the "middle distance" of realism's narrative of the present's emergence from a near past into a map of the flats where monarchy and bourgeois, feudal estates and speculative railways, all swirlingly converge.[24] Wonderland is a terrain where footmen and duchesses live with their servants in one-room houses, a territory ruled by a sovereign queen, but equally ruled by upstart subjects demanding equal representation, children challenging authority, dormouses becoming protagonists, dodos designing caucuses, signifiers subverting fixity—its nonsense historicity a brilliant distillation of realism's spatial presentism. In projecting a political universe of variable possible governments equally subject to the charge of groundlessness, a mathematical hyperspace of insurgent logics, *Wonderland* embosses the realist endeavor to model possible social space, to study, in the abstract, what fabricated but internally consistent configurations of sociability might lodge.

In the end, *Wonderland*'s death sentence finally executes; an abrupt conclusion formalizing realist conventions of emphatic, resolute closure into total world dissolution:

> "Off with her head!" the Queen shouted.
>
> "Who cares for you! You're nothing but a pack of cards!"[25]

In the last words spoken inside the frame, Alice's flat reduction equates the something that is sovereignty with the nothing that is the material substrate of numerical values and ordered suits, the deliberately typeset paper blank space into which the Queen's domain disappears. The authority to make die and let live, or to make live and let die, whether gilded in hyperbolic excess or distilled in empty mediality, remains the minimally necessary normativity for a world to even cohere. What is realism but a practice of inscription become infrastructure, a theory of how words make worlds?

Each of these reductions (and at your next lesson we'll have time for more) brings forward conventionality as such, rendering thinkable both the rules of the game in all their artifice—the contingent designs of any social plane—and in all their indispensable function—the scaffolding of consistent worlds, the writing of consistent propositions. Decompleting and defamiliarizing the rules of world construction deployed by politics and the novel alike, *Wonder-*

land's aesthetic experiments formulate the political thought of the materiality of the signifier, the contrivedness of perspective and inevitability of ideological distortion, problems of causality, questions of social cohesion, and the contingent history of the present. *Wonderland* flashes the aesthetic qualities of the political, the contingent design of social space—and its pervasive, persistent threat of death makes clear how much this purely formal dispensation of the socius is simultaneously the ultimate content, how much recognizing the merely formal configuration of any world means affirming the mortal necessity for forms.

Wonderland is the novel of symbolic logic less because it refers to and thematizes logic as topic, and more because it equates novel form and logic. It thereby crystallizes, in every aesthetic dimension, the already abstract tendencies of the realist novel itself. *Wonderland* reduces the letter to bare form, emphasizing its constituting power, actuating the maxim of formalist mathematics—everything that can be consistently inscribed must be possible—and in so doing it reveals the formal aegis of realism, the production of possible worlds. Realism extrudes the world-making power of the signifier that symbolic logic ratifies; like formalist mathematics, realist novels model possible relations in accordance with limits; like the simultaneous constriction of the signifier and extension of the speculative practiced by the formal inscription of the possible, realism hews to convention to interrogate the constructedness of all social spaces; like the playful affirmation of political structuration in *Wonderland*'s form, realism in turn enchants the construct, making of every land a wonder.

I have made three propositions, and the clock ticks: What conclusion is consequent upon them? A Carrollian Dodgsonianism for the yearbooks, what they make is not a syllogism (it's good to advance beyond your first lesson) but a polysyllogism—since nothing, not even a ham sandwich, is better without poly. I leave it at this:

A Symbolic logic encodes a formalism of the political.

B *Alice's Adventures in Wonderland* is the symbolic logic of literary realism.

C Literary realism is political formalism.

5

Obscure Forms: The Social Geometry of *Jude the Obscure*

Before it begins, Thomas Hardy's *Jude the Obscure* distills its unforgettably searing critique of law into its three-word epigraph: "The Letter Killeth." Saint Paul's dictum famously divides law between spirit and letter, universal and particular, the unrepresentable and the all too representational.[1] The murderous agency of the letter follows from its debased particularity, its tyrannical enslavement of the idea in representation, and concomitant enslavement of the people in norms and prohibitions. Casting the mold of many a condemnation of law, the Pauline polemic emblematizes the conflict Hardy so poignantly stages between sex and civilization, desire and order. Any formalizing of social ordering, Hardy and Paul likely agree, will inevitably commit lethal violence, and thus the struggle of Hardy's protagonists to abide outside of extant orders for production and reproduction culminates in mass infanticide.

If the tragedy of *Jude the Obscure* is owing to law's domination as conceived by Paul, this would seem in advance to authorize readings of the novel in the vein of anarcho-vitalism. The very Pauline contrast drawn by, paradigmatically, Agamben, between "the simple fact of life" (vital spirit) and the "politicization of life" (lettering the conditions of and for life), names the drive of power formations to overexertion, the tendency of human institutions to subjugate humanity itself.[2] Commencing with Paul and making numerous judicious references to him throughout its text, *Jude the Obscure* bears out in its plot an indictment of law's totalizations and an interrogation of the value of life that position the text as a quintessentially biopolitical novel, as many recent readers agree.[3] What better exemplar of political pessimism and destituency could there be in all of English literature?

And yet the epigraph is far from the novel's last word on letter. As much as the plot of *Jude the Obscure* coheres to the antiformalist axis, its form, I argue, develops another theory of politics, rooted in another conception of letter—the theory *The Order of Forms* has deemed "political formalism."[4] In ways legible from the presentation of the epigraph onward, this novel's form is conspicuously experimental about typography, the lining and lettering of the letter. The form is also, as Hardy himself repeatedly maintained, "geometrically constructed," riveted by the study of lines and shapes.[5] Typography and geometry, this chapter asserts, betoken the mathematical formalism that proves crucial to the political imaginary of *Jude the Obscure*: tracing letters and calibrating shapes, the novel underlines the materiality of the letter irreducible to its normativity, the shape of the signifier irreducible to its signification. Aligning letterality with writing in excess of meaning, with the pure formality of marking, cutting, or lineating—the line within the letter—Hardy's typography instantiates a radicalization of geometry consistent with the revolutionary formalism of the non-Euclidean break. Like *Wonderland* before it, *Jude*'s mathematical formalism performs a surprising exuberance about the shape of letters, consequently projecting the malleability of social lineaments even as the novel tells the tale of lethally rigid norms.[6] Through its geometric structure and its typographic inventiveness, *Jude the Obscure* contemplates the obscurity of social forms, an ambiguity decisive for political formalism.

As the last of the chapters devoted to novel reading in *The Order of Forms*, this chapter reckons with what is often thought "the last Victorian" novel.[7] This finality is palpable in the text itself, in its abstraction from many of the conventions of the nineteenth-century novel, and such heightened abstraction poses our ultimate example of the novel medium's capacity for good abstraction, for thinking social structuration. Where the frame narratives and vacillating perspectives in *Wuthering Heights*, *Bleak House*, and *Alice's Adventures in Wonderland* mediate in the scaffolding of narration the question of the scaffolding of sociality, the pared omniscience of *Jude the Obscure* reflects the minimalist abstraction of sociality as such. As the sibling ending to our opening with *Wuthering Heights*, *Jude* retreads that threshold realism of antagonistically ungrounded sociality (and incestuous alliances), and it sublates these concerns from Gothic intensities into Spartan structures. Like *Bleak House*, it moves propulsively through close social spaces and beholds the law in its abstraction. On the same plane as *Alice's Adventures in Wonderland*, *Jude* pursues the letter of social formalization in its de-semanticized materiality. Among the novels I read here, *Jude* is also weighty in its articulation of social abstraction with architecture, the art of social projection, since Hardy worked as an architect and studded this novel with architectural tropes of social formation, and since it aggregates architectural projects into urban developments. I conclude the literary section of the book with this novel, in other words, because in it political formalism, mathematical formalism, and the formalism of realism are so tightly triangulated. The last Victorian novel condenses the affordances of that form with the affordances of social form itself.

Giving Ground: Geometry as Political Formalism

Before exploring the imagistic, discursive, and narratological rudiments of geometry within *Jude the Obscure*, it seems worth remarking, apropos Hardy's notion of geometric construction, that geometry is a strangely unintuitive model of literary composition. A novel makes its world out of words and letters, whereas geometry makes its cosmos out of lines and shapes. To take geometry as the structure or frame of literature posits the prior foundationality of the line to the letter, the component / or — prior to the composite **A**, foregrounding, as in a face–vase illusion, the contours of a letter before or in excess of its symbolism. When Hardy takes geometry as the frame of his novelistic form, the materiality of words and letters is percussed; shape and line are highlighted as elements with which to make a novel world.

Inside the world of *Jude*, varying resonances of "geometry" unfold both abstractly and concretely, conceptually and minutely—it is the most explicitly mathematical of all the novels I study in *The Order of Forms.* A Euclid primer provides the voraciously curious Jude with early intellectual success, and geometry provides the primer from which *Jude the Obscure* takes its rhetoric, tessellating circles and lines, squares and points, axes and asymptotes. Almost every page of the text is marked by "circuitous routes,"[8] "concave fields,"[9] "perpendicular scarps,"[10] "acute sorrows,"[11] "interstices,"[12] "conjectures,"[13] "convergences,"[14] "crooked and gentle declivities,"[15] and "curves of motion [that] had become subdued lines."[16] Adhering to the etymology of *geo-metry* ("the measure of earth"), the narrative conspicuously measures its own spatial organization, recurrently revisiting nodes like "the Fourways" (a perpendicular intersection) and partitioning its sections not as chapters with titles, but as "parts" with place names: "At Marygreen," "At Shaston," "At Melchester," and so on. The only Hardy novel to bear such a partitioned schema, *Jude the Obscure*'s topos is not only regional but punctual, a world made "at" discrete points.

While geometry informs the novel's rhetoric, it also orders the narration, whose mode might best be understood as *elliptical.* From the Greek *ellipsein* (to come short), an ellipse is formed when a cross section of a cone "comes short" of paralleling the base, and instead bisects the cone obliquely, yielding the oval rather than the circular shape. Interestingly, in nineteenth-century usage, according to the *OED*, "ellipse" also signified what we now deem "ellipsis," the grammatical connotation of "coming short": incomplete sentences driven by omission, and the typographical mark thereof, a dash (—) or dot dot dot (. . .). *Jude the Obscure* both practices and theorizes elliptical narration. There are standard syntactic moments (an abundance of sentences with ellipses, both in dialogue and in narration), but also moments of metacommentary self-consciously stressing the role of ellipses in constituting narrative as such. The discourse's jump cuts ("The last pages to which the chronicler of these lives would ask the reader's attention are concerned with the scene in and out of Jude's bedroom when leafy summer came round again"[17]), the story's redactions ("a shifting, nomadic life, which was not without its pleasures for a time. Two whole years and an half passed thus";[18] "that the twain were happy—between their times of sadness—was indubitable"[19]), and the narrator's abstentions ("The purpose of a chronicler of moods and deeds does not require him to express his personal views upon the grave controversy above given"[20]) are all pinpointed. Focusing the narrative in all its blind spots, these self-reflections illuminate the common ground of narrative and social formalization: to order relations means to make elisions—remainders of form's installation that become reminders of its incompleteness.

Elliptical narration thus gives shape to Hardy's geometric prescriptions for novel writing: "The novelist's talent is to see in half and quarter views the whole picture."[21] Angled portionality constitutes rather than diminishes the aesthetic whole: "Art is a disproportioning (i.e., distorting, throwing out of proportion)—of realities, to show more clearly the features that matter in those realities, which, if merely copied or reported inventorially, might possibly be observed, but would more probably be overlooked. Hence 'realism' is not Art."[22] In this realer realism, it is the shape of things, and not the "inventory" of their contents, where reality inheres. "The matter in those realities" can only be accessed by the twinge of defamiliarization in that "throwing out of proportion" and by the touch of vertigo in that subtraction from total. Quarter views, skewn proportions, angles and fractals, acute slices and obtuse scopes, disclose the pointed delimitation of reality, the way in which any given reality arbitrarily unifies the real disproportion. The halves and quarters that erect narrative distortion, Hardy's geometry suggests, realistically frame social distortion.

Geometry inflects the rhetoric and contours the narrative's realism, and also centers the novel's plot. One of the most basic shapes of geometry, the quadrilateral, patterns the movement of relations in the novel. A line connects every vertex to every other at least once: Jude and Phillotson share the

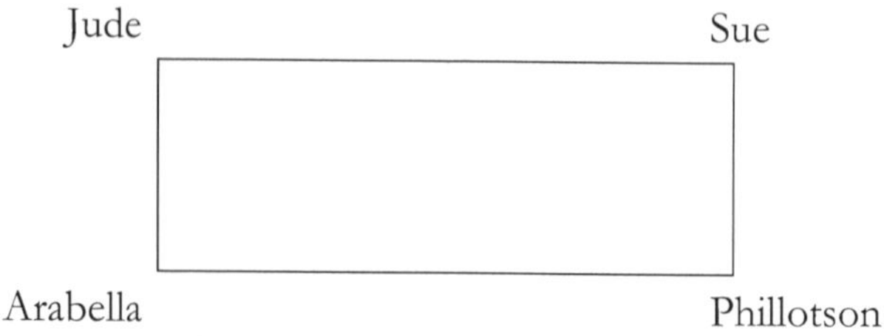

FIGURE 7. "Quadrangle."

special connection with which the novel begins, Jude and Arabella become sexually involved and married, Jude and Sue are lovers, Sue and Phillotson are married, and decisive plot turns emerge from the alliances and encounters of Sue with Arabella and Arabella with Phillotson. In this love rectangle, lines of connection extend, sever, and reconnect as couples come together, break up, and reunite; the repeated unions and estrangement of two of the couples (Jude and Arabella, Phillotson and Sue) verge on the rigid distantiation and passionate entangling of a third (Jude and Sue). These "rectangular lines" are named by *Jude*'s Preface as the tracks by which "the involutions of four lives must necessarily be a quadrille," a sad dance of alignment and realignment in which the stability of the rectangle is continually undercut. A destabilized rectangle undoes the constant perpendicularity of a pair of parallels, stressing the very idea of parallel: the narrator curiously repeats the phrase "They walked in parallel lines"[23] to chart Jude's first meeting with Arabella *and* his first meeting with Sue;[24] the double consonants in the names "Arabe**ll**a" and "Phi**ll**otson" graphically illustrate parallels; and poignant punctuations of the love story invoke ruptured parallels—Jude rebukes Sue in her effort to end their relationship for drafting "not a true parallel,"[25] and her parting words to him at one of their "divisions" bemoan his "unparalleled" love.[26]

Accorded pivotal importance, these negations of parallelism encode into the novel's figurative system the revolutionary formalist turn toward non-Euclidean geometry. Euclidean geometry derived theorems from postulates, studying pure shapes as reflections of actually existing shapes.[27] Held as the very paradigm of truth by philosophers like Descartes, Hobbes, and Spinoza (to whom there are several references in *Jude the Obscure*), and positioned as the cornerstone of Victorian education, revered equally for its beauty and its rigor, Euclidean geometry fused earthly intuition with celestial metaphysics, logic with truth. Splitting this fusion, the break with Euclid inaugurated by nineteenth-century European mathematicians—the first departure from his *Elements* in over two and a half millennia of intellectual history—was "the most consequential development" in a century widely recognized as supremely innovative in mathematics.[28] Likened by Victorians in many fields to both the Darwinian and the Copernican revolutions, the advent of non-Euclidean geometry amounted to a radical crack in the foundations of knowledge as such. As Andrea Henderson explains, "To have demonstrated that Euclidean space, so long regarded as the groundwork of knowledge, need not be taken as a given . . . was to have shown that absolute knowledge was not available even in the domain of geometry."[29] The undermining of the Euclidean premise—that the formalized laws of its ideal points and lines perfectly corresponded to real space—seismically relativized the absolute, creating a disjunction between the material universe and the laws supposed to self-evidently govern it. In the words of one historian of mathematics, "The introduction of . . . non-Euclidean geometry . . . forced the recognition of the artificiality of mathematics; by 1900 mathematics had broken away from reality . . . and had become the pursuit of necessary consequences of arbitrary axioms about meaningless things."[30] The very idea of geometry at the moment of *Jude the Obscure* thus refigures the novel's prominent critique of social and civilizational law by engaging foundational law in all its arbitrary axiomaticity, its sheerly posited, radically lineated shape.[31] Like Euclidean logic, social conventions derive force from their appearance of natural rightness; in non-Euclidean frames, the force becomes traceable as radical imposition, but creatively generative for all that. *Jude* is thus not only explicitly engaging formalist mathematics, but also quite emphatically educing the political imaginary of math, quite succinctly enunciating that formalism of the political that we have been keen to trace out.

At issue in the Victorian break with Euclid is the law of parallel lines, the fifth of five postulates comprising the *Elements of Geometry*. The first four postulates pertain, respectively, to the existence of straight lines connecting any two points, the indefinite extension of straight lines, the basis of a circle on any given straight line as its radius, and the congruency of right angles (this being a law of equivalence rather than a principle of construction like the other three). The fifth postulate combines indefinite extension and the law of congruency to assert that parallel lines of infinite length maintain constant right angles with their common perpendicular. Euclid postulated the infinite constancy of parallel lines—that they never intersect and that they share a perpendicular with a perfect right angle—whereas the non-Euclideans deduced the possibility that parallel lines of infinite length might, in their infinity, eventually curve away from each other, hyperbolically, or toward each other to meet, elliptically.

From the non-Euclidean perspective, if lines are infinitely long, their infinity accommodates rigidly maintained distances *and* their trespass, closer

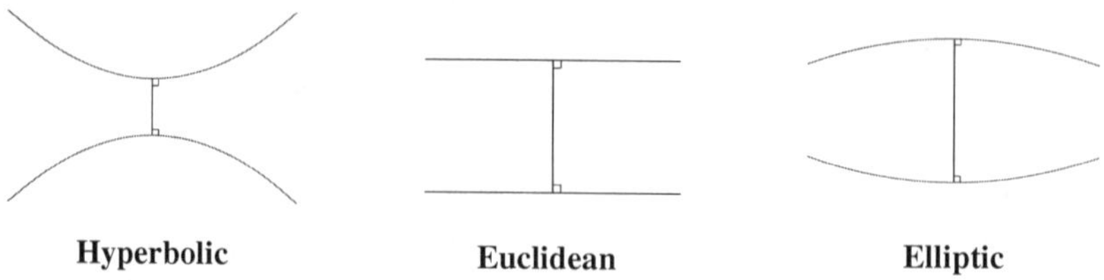

FIGURE 8. "Euclidean versus Non-Euclidean."

intimacies and further alienations. The novel expressly osculates Euclidean geometry to make it the arena of contest over absolute and relative laws when it pitches the conflicted and conflicting passions of Jude and Sue as a question of the possibility to, as Sue explains, "work everything out in Euclid problems."[32] In the course of dissuading themselves from their outlaw love, the narrative works out at least three times a veritable "proof" replete with three steps:

> He affected to think of her quite in the family way, since there were crushing reasons why he should not and could not think of her in any other.
>
> The first reason was that he was married, and it would be wrong. The second was that they were cousins. It was not well for cousins to fall in love, even when circumstances seemed to favor the passion. The third: even were he free, in a family like his own where marriage usually meant a tragic sadness, marriage with a blood-relation would duplicate the adverse conditions, and a tragic sadness might be intensified to a tragic horror.[33]

Within this proof, a cumulative force calculates romantic possibilities geometrically (by successive multiples of 2, rather than arithmetically by addition). The first reason pertains to Jude individually (a 1), the second to the twosome and its ill-advised mutuality (a 2), the third to the "duplicate" of the twoness by the weight of other generations, since Jude and Sue come from the same family that is marred by unhappy marriages (a 4). Like the geometric paradigm of "proof" deconsecrated by new discoveries, Jude and Sue's geometrically expressed normativity is repeatedly codified but ultimately overturned.

Outside of the proofs for which Euclid set the paradigm, Jude and Sue consummate an outlaw passion, resistant to marriage norms. Theirs is a bond despite expanding conceptions of incest and new restrictions on cousin relations, a bond despite their aging aunt's familial interdictions, a bond that wreaks two legal divorces and two aborted weddings (one at a clerk and one in a church). Their desperation to remain outside of marriage arises from multiple objections. One set of objections reflects Sue's feminism: she repeatedly deplores the "sordid contract"[34] of marriage, lamenting the exchange relations that reduce woman to "a she-ass or a she-goat"[35] and result in a "hopelessly vulgar institution."[36] Marriage is a debased business—rotten at the core even when unyoked from property ownership and the traffic in women. For the binding proscription to love, comfort, honor, and keep as long as life lasts intones a secular commandment, solemn injunction, formalized obligation entirely incompatible with fleeting desires and passionate attachments:

> Do you think that when you *must* have me with you by law, that we will be as happy as we are now? . . . Don't you dread the attitude that arises out of legal obligation? Don't you think it is destructive to a passion whose essence is its gratuitousness?[37]

By insisting that law is external to passion, Sue articulates what her aestheticized paganism has already implied—that she is "a woman with aberrant passions and unaccountable antipathies,"[38] and, as such, "the negation of civilization."[39]

Likewise Jude is her lover and partner in crime, repeatedly described as "a man of too many passions,"[40] "unbridled passion,"[41] and a misfit who heeds only his own "ruling passion."[42] The excess and aberrancy that characterize their essential natures prompt Jude and Sue to deem their relationship "nature's law."[43] That they use "law" to name their outlaw excess—and that Hardy's Postscript to the novel cites Diderot's sentiment "The civil law should only be the enunciation of the law of nature, which we bear in our hearts"[44]—is one indication of the novel's attention to the foundational ambiguity of law, its openness, its ideal shaping that elliptically eludes every real shape, the break with Euclid's parallels on another plane. Objecting to given law and lacking the legislation of nature's law, Jude and Sue look for new shapes. Hardy was acutely aware of law's shaping function, having served as a magistrate in cases of arson, bigamy, rape, incest, murder, divorce, and more in the County of Dorset for twenty-five years (longer than he wrote novels). When he avowed that his novel asks "the general question: whether civilization can escape the humiliating indictment that, while it has been able to cover itself with glory in the arts, in literatures, in religions, and in the sciences, it has never succeeded in creating that homely thing, a satisfactory scheme for the conjunction of the sexes," he elaborated "geometry" as a social science, a mode of thinking social congruency, the "scheme for the conjunction of the sexes," the matrix of relation.[45]

By the time of *Jude the Obscure*'s composition the revolutionary advent of non-Euclidean insights had complicated "geometry" as a grid of relation whose arbitrary or ungrounded character came into high relief. The break with Euclid is the most decisive initiation of the shift to mathematical formalism: Euclid's elements could no longer claim to correspond to real space; mathematicians and nonmathematicians alike reconceived geometry as a mode of representation, abstract and figurative. If the break makes the formalism of mathematics apparent as a matter of the autonomy of forms and formulae, it also engenders a new conceptualization of realms beyond experience—of the autonomy of, as it were, the concept. Specifically, "infinity" emerges as sundered from empirical experience but nonetheless *thinkable.* The internal consistency of infinity mandates that infinite parallel lines might be infinitely constant *and simultaneously* be inconstant, since infinity logically must encompass heterogeneous infinities, other infinities. Thus the break with Euclid's fifth postulate preliminarily expressed the idea codified by the discovery of set theory, that infinity is multiple.[46] Multiple infinities and even infinite infinities have as one implication, shared with the resonances of geometry we have been educing, that, as Ed Pluth puts it in his résumé of mathematician-philosopher Alain Badiou, "there is no one at the top, no possible overarching totality or unity of things: no big, all-embracing infinity, as a set of all things."[47] Unsettled, unintegratable "things" crucially repeat as a figure of social antagonism in the novel. From "the artificial system of things"[48] to "things in general, because they are so horrid and cruel,"[49] from "the humors of things"[50] to "the unfitness of things,"[51] the novel surmises "it is perfectly damnable how things are."[52] Sue is ultimately "driven out of my mind by things!"[53] and Jude, in one of the novel's many tautologies, quotes Aeschylus when he pronounces: "Things are as they are."[54] The narrator magisterially collects all these things into their most irrefutable, purest axiom: "the direct antagonism of things."[55]

The plural obduracy here is crucial: "things" diffusely alludes to the open condition of human life: while human being as such is defined by necessary relationality, no immanent structure for ordering that material interdependence exists. So much is at issue, to return to biopolitical theory, in competing conceptions about the jointure of life to forms of life. *The Order of Forms* has pitched this competition as between anarcho-vitalism and political formalism, between the repudiation of form/idealization of formlessness and the affirmation of form as essential but reformable. If biopolitical theory, as Ernesto Laclau has argued, propagates the fantasy that it is possible "to be beyond politics," political formalism, representatives of which might range from Hegel and Marx to Derrida, would hold human being at its most elemental, life at its barest, to be essentially political: "Man is political being" (*zoon politikon*).[56] In this view's closer reading of Aristotle, the difference between animals, men, and gods—the specificity that pertains to men, man's attribute—is that his life is qualifiedly political: there is no human life without politics, without the political interactions and designations of how to make life, of how to sustain human being in its desperate interdependence. In Agamben's "complete" biopolitical conception, then, "the direct antagonism of things" could be the conflict between politics and life (where the victor's name is "biopolitics"); in the other, materialist conception could be that irresolvable conflict among forms of life that is the stuff of politics.

Jude the Obscure's geometric form provides an opening onto its allegiances in the clash between formlessness and political formalism. The eerily repeated yet unspecifiable "things" that wreak antagonism testify to a conflict irreducible to the biopolitical paradigm's divide between politics and life, a conflict less measurable: between the order of things and their possible alternatives, between one order and infinite others. Activating a geometric imaginary in the shadow of the non-Euclidean break means confronting the infinity of antagonism as the ontological corollary to the epistemological relativization of law: "things" are nontotalizable; the realities erected atop them are necessary models rather than heavenly truths. In *Jude the Obscure*, geometry, the measure of ground, becomes a political theory, a method for thinking the ungroundedness of every social formation. At the limit, formalist geometry therefore appears as a vector of political formalism. Tropes of "geometry" thus enfold the critique of law the novel narrates, while also adding new dimensions: law in its particularity may be gruesome, but all law is particular—a fact that may be lamented or may be celebrated. *Jude the Obscure*'s geometry positions the novel as a formal investigation of the orders, properties, and relations of space demarcated in lines, surfaces, and solids—an investigation through which the novel embraces the fundament of universal particularity, the line within the letter of the law.

Making Ground: Typography as Geometry

The letter of the law returns us to Saint Paul and to *Jude*'s epigraph. The originating place the novel awards Paul's maxim must be understood as the introduction of a problem rather than its solution—for reasons at once practical (all the words that come after) and formal (the style of presenting the epigraph). Strikingly redacting the rejoinder "But the spirit giveth life," Hardy underlines the partiality and incompleteness of his epigraph, and his staging of it furthers this partiality: the epigraph is not solemnified in an autonomous inscription on its own page, but rather markedly embedded among

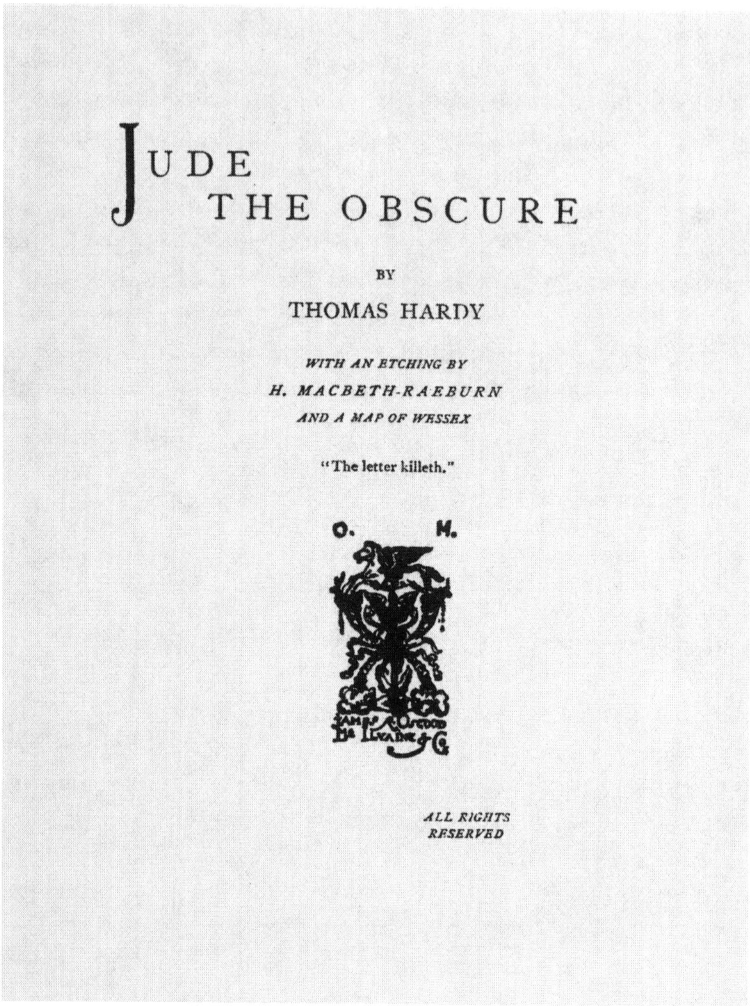

JUDE
THE OBSCURE

BY

THOMAS HARDY

WITH AN ETCHING BY
H. MACBETH-RAEBURN
AND A MAP OF WESSEX

"The letter killeth."

O. M.

ALL RIGHTS RESERVED

FIGURE 9. Title page, Thomas Hardy, *Jude the Obscure* (1895).

other inscriptions and other modes of inscription on the original title page he designed.

This staging engineers an encounter with typography: as the eye descends, that page bears the title, the author's name, the promissory note "with an etching by H. Macbeth-Raeburn and a Map of Wessex," the epigraph, the publisher's mark, and "all rights reserved." Cartographic projections, mordant impressions, literary fictions, proprietary attributions—these numerous technologies testify to modes of representation disjoint from the letter that kills. There is something of letter in writing, graphing, drawing, carving, the copresence of the epigraph and these other forms on the title page seems

THITHER

J. F. ☞

FIGURE 10. "Thither," from *Jude the Obscure* (1895).

A L L E L U J A

FIGURE 11. "Alleluja," from *Jude the Obscure* (1895).

to suggest, yet these arts of lining are exhibited while the letter is condemned. That there is no rejoinder to the letter, no alternative, no other, constitutes a performance of letter or letterality that proposes an alternative distinction—not the chasm between spirit and letter, but an almost imperceptible difference internal to the letter, between letter and line, the minimalest unit of signification and the sheer materiality of signifying. *Jude the Obscure* fathoms the letter beyond its bloodlust precisely by inscribing the distinction between letter and line within its very formal system, epigraphically problematizing "the letter" while graphically installing "the line" as its central principle. The fact that Jude and Sue both professionally work at what the novel calls "lettering" and "relettering" (carving gravestones, restoring engravings) reiterates in a different register that the primary opposition of interest here is not between letter and spirit, but letter and lettering, letter and itself.

Throughout the book, this design dynamism on the title page extends to additional experiments in typography, celebrations of the shape of the letter that highlight this distinction: an image of a road marker that Jude engraves at a crossways and repeatedly revisits; Gothicizations of religious language; epistolary facsimiles; and a map of a place that does not exist. Let us linger on just two such experiments, an early moment and the novel's climax. The early moment—not coincidentally, one of the text's several direct references to Paul—uses center-justified, boldface Koine Greek to dramatize the agency of letter. Jude's dedication to Paul's Greek compels him to devote his only weekly day of leisure to reading the New Testament. And yet, on the fateful day when his acquaintance with Arabella distracts him from his studies, the letters of the book instead read him:

> When he got back to the house . . . a general consciousness of his neglect seemed written on the face of all things confronting him. He went upstairs

> without a light, and the dim interior of his room accosted him with sad inquiry. There lay his book open, just as he had left it, and the capital letters on the title-page regarded him with fixed reproach in the grey starlight, like the unclosed eyes of a dead man:
>
> **Η ΚΑΙΝΗ ΔΙΑΘΗΚΗ**[57]

In its novelty, the successor covenant here emblematizes Jude's lapse into another pact, his succession from learned asceticism to "corrupt passions." His entanglement with Arabella spells the end of all his scholarly aspirations, as the "capital letters" themselves "regarded him with fixed reproach." In their fixity and their bold, capital, Koine opacity, the letters are at once "dead" and undead, paradoxically animated in their commanding agency, their galvanizing lure, their organizing center (as typographically illustrated by their centering). Via their gaze these letters operate as "point of view" (another of the novel's favorite concepts) or structural location, highlighting their formality rather than their content. Conversely, because it is not just any letter that reproaches Jude (his Greek textbook or Euclid primer might have served equally to remind him of forsaken studies), but the name of the letters that see themselves as spirit (Paul's new testament comes by way of epistles, after all), these letters actuate the spirit–letter opposition in all its ironic glory, undoing Paul's preference for spirit by yoking the word of Paul to "dead" "capital letters."[58]

Deadly letters evoke Hardy's overarching fixation on capital crimes, and recur at this novel's presentation of its murderous climax. Sue's realization "I said the world was against us, that it was better to be out of life than in it at this price; and he took it literally"[59] yokes the tragic mass infanticide to the letter, a reading prescribed by the novel's sole italicization, its freneticizing of the literal letter left as explanation for the murders:

> "*Done because we are too menny.*"[60]

The misspelling sadly underscores Father Time's youth, and punningly indicts "men" for their excessive sexual drive to be *in* life. Before and beyond these significations, however, it graphically performs the too-much of letter that is the murderer's literality—just as the recurrent subordinations in the sentence that introduces it overemphasize writing: "A piece of paper was found upon the floor, on which was written, in the boy's hand, with the bit of lead pencil that he carried."[61] The eerie present tense of the dead murderer's voice ("we *are* too menny") conjures an uncanny vitality of the letter that graphically inscribes itself in the doubling of the double letter, the literary indistinction of the correct "t**oo**" and the incorrect "me**nn**y," disclosing the duality of letter within and against itself, and further alluding to the ambiguity internal to the letter. The italicization portends all this excess, the letters straining at their own lines with duality, vitality, literality.

Road markers, remade books, Greek letters, Gothic letters, written letters, letters that read, letters that kill—in their sheer diffusion across the novel, these variations and creations attest to the impossibility of a world without letter. But the essentiality of letter does not prescribe its content; that there is letter does not entail signification. This is an elementary axiom of political formalism, the formalist regard for the force of the signifier, the force of social structuration, in excess of the weight of signification, the meaning or content of any particular dispensation of social space. Thus the novel's biggest typographic experiment of all is *Jude the Obscure*, the typewriting of obscurity, the paradox of delineating that which lacks an outline, the typological oxymoron of the distinctive individuality and illuminated interiority promised by the proper name and the novel genre undermined by the blur of the obscure. "Obscurity," from Latin roots meaning "away from the light," connotes darkness, unenlightenment, uncertainty, insignificance, indistinction, anonymity. A strange equivocation attends the putatively precise expression "the obscure"—not only the dramatic irony of presenting the character Jude as the very type of the obscure (useless, placeless, homeless), even as his fate is to be always too observed, too much in place, and too enlightened, but also the syntactical irony: How can something be a definite indefinite, a distinct indistinction, a type of no type?

The novel expressly poses this problem with respect to life, the life of Jude, but answers it with respect to forms, the infrastructure of life. As obscurity unfolds throughout *Jude the Obscure*, it signals less the essence of a character than the attribute of setting—the substantive in the title appears exclusively as the adjective in the text, almost always modifying place, especially built or designed places: "obscure field," "obscure public-house," "obscure alley," "obscure street," "obscure chamber," "obscure tavern," "obscure spot," "obscure nook," "obscure village," and an "obscure home." Streets laid upon the landscape, structures erected in the streets, shapes outlined betwixt and between, these alleys and spots and nooks are ways of delineating the physical space we inhabit and thus elementary forms of social organization. To repeatedly shade these fundamental, structuring lines is to insist on the residual indeterminacy of a determined form, to insist on the mereness of the forms of political existence. Like the gap between the letter and the line, such persistent unlining reminds us, in the way of all texts, that every particular representation—literary, mathematic, architectural, legal—also remains obscure. The obscurity of forms of life is the complement to their necessity: formally cardinal, but substantively variable. In its obscurity, a given social formalization may be lamentable, but it may also be open to new specifications.

The geometric scaffolding of the novel prioritizes the line within the letter, and, in parallel, Hardy's typographic experiments ultimately prioritize the malleability of lineations. The rhetoric of obscure forms graphs this malleability in multiple dimensions, emphasizing that shape is itself line. Indeed, the first shape derived in Euclid's *Elements*, the most elemental, is identical to a line: the circle. Even though circles require more complex maneuvers than other shapes when calculating their area or plotting their graph, compared to polygons, which are defined by the multiple lines that contain them, circles are essentially simple: defined by only one line, the curved line that circumscribes the boundary. Lines may be single or coupled at angles with others; they may be bold, italic, or Gothic; they may be parallel, perpendicular, and inconstant. The shape of things need not remain what was, and the necessity for shaping need not ossify into subjection.

This ambiguity of social forms capitalized by the novel's rhetoric of obscurity crystallizes in its keen depiction of cities. *Jude the Obscure* is Hardy's only urban Wessex novel, and the very idea of a city, across all the migrations in the text, seems to promise a dynamic of collective anonymity, liberty amid density, new, old, and re-constructions. The little boy Jude's first vision of a "far-off city," a radically distant and different lifeworld than his own village, comes in a sequence laden with geometric imagery.[62] With "the reflection that the higher he got, the further he could see," the boy climbs a ladder to look "at the point" where the city might emerge, praying "that the mist might rise."[63] "From the eastern horizon," the sun breaks through, "streaming out in visible lines" until the point finally acquires shape:

> Some way within the limits of the stretch of landscape, points of light like topaz gleamed. The air increased in transparency with the lapse of minutes, till the topaz points showed themselves to be the vanes, windows, wet roof slates, and other shining spots upon the spires, domes, freestone-work, and varied outlines that were faintly revealed. It was Christminster, unquestionably, either directly seen or mirage in the peculiar atmosphere.[64]

Points become lines, glints become buildings, "varied outlines" in mystifying mists and on distant horizons: the city emerges into sight as unseeable. Blind with desire for another way of life, obstructed by landscape and weather and the inexorable revolutions of the sun, Jude espies the city *as* mirage, "city of light."[65] Here, the angles of vision, the asymptotic sight, descry inextricable linkages of perspective to architecture, urbanism, and fantasy. The city comes into relief when "the sun is going down in a blaze of flame," when Jude's intense longing mounts "to wish himself out of the world."[66] Though "unquestionably" comprised of lines and points and shapes, the city has no particular shape, no discernable plan; at once formed and unformed, it is obscure.

Always holding the city in his sights, the young man later asks himself: "But how live in that city?"—a formulation weirdly devoid of modal verbs, decidedly subtracted of subjects.[67] Instead of "how might he live," only the minorest "how live," a grammatical oddity that accents the minimalism of life vis-à-vis the base environs, the rudiments appraised in political formalism: the polis precedes life. That his thought is presented as a question points to the open indeterminacy of the way of life, the necessity for intentional urban planning. And so his initial question begets another: "What was most required by citizens? Food, clothing, and shelter. . . . They built in a city; therefore he would learn to build."[68] In the little boy's Aristotelianism, the precondition of life is the city; to live is to partake in the life-construction of building a city, to live is to benefit from architecture as the first art. Building, forming, shaping, lettering: these are the essential processes through which Jude and Sue, not to mention Hardy the architect, earn their living, and they are the practices through which they fulfill their non-Euclidean ethos that "the social moulds civilization fits us into have no more relation to our actual shapes than the conventional shapes of the constellations have to the real star-patterns."[69] The investigation of elementary shapes, the interrogation of principles of lines, of properties of boundaries, of limits and frames—within these ways of knowing it is possible to design novel constellations. Like all realist blueprints, *Jude the Obscure* plots the undertaking of a geometrically informed project to design fitting shape: a marriage outside conventions, unsanctioned civilly and unsanctified religiously, a family of adopted children, bastard children, and elective affinities. Jude and Sue's commitment to reshaping makes their life's work: "relettering"[70] stonework, baking cakes of famous buildings, "windows, towers, pinnacles,"[71] renovating buildings, and erecting "model"[72] cities.

While their bond lies at the core of the text, they can neither find a place to live nor effectively agree on how to live—they cannot make a life in law—and thus chronically move and chronically revisit the question of whether to acquiesce to legal marriage, as well as regularly debate whether to look to the Bible or the Greeks in their quest for alternative political theologies. The bifurcation at the center of their union, the unamalgamable twoness of their "two-in-oneness"—and, it must be said, their final lack of reconciliation—is crucial to the novel's partisan response to the question of forms of life. Jude and Sue embody two different types of "desire which operated without regard of consequences,"[73] two different logics of the "social unrest that is purely the artificial product of civilization."[74] Sue wants, in her relationship with Jude at least, to remain "outside all laws except gravitation and germination,"[75] while Jude pursues a path "to make our natural marriage a legal one."[76] Sue asks the law to leave her alone; Jude asks the law for recognition. Sue imagines that there is a way outside of law; Jude assumes that there is law, and seeks reform. Sue indicts the universality of law and strives to be its exception; Jude insists on the nonuniversality of law, its incompleteness that also ensures no exception.[77] It is because she is thus an anarcho-vitalist and he a political formalist that we must remark the extent to which the novel is *his*: not only titularly, but narratologically, not only the total story of his life and death (whereas Sue remains living at the end) but the expulsion of Sue from focalization in the final part of the novel, the impossibility of concluding the narrative from her point of view.

Formalist geometry and its subset typography form the imagistic principle, narrative architecture, and tropological ground of *Jude the Obscure.* The novel's relationship to geometry is less one of interest or reflection than one of planar construction: *Jude the Obscure* draws its lines from geometric manifolds. On the whole, despite its biopolitical content, this construction poses a limit to any interpretation of the novel that would find a critique of institutions and rejection of particular laws akin to anarcho-vitalism's suspicion of all possible laws. In its ubiquity as infrastructure for the novel, the frame of the form, geometry queries the dispensability of law, and rejects the reduction of the political to the relations that obtain within any given polis.[78] The obscure forms of streets and cities, shelters and jurisdictions, lines and laws, necessitate the contingent emergence of alternative determinations. Through the premium it places on the line as the groundwork of the letter, *Jude the Obscure* maintains fidelity to the "antagonism of things" while sustaining hope for new shapes of relations. Passionate masons, experimental architects, and urban enthusiasts are the constituents of constructivism; in its abiding commitment to making forms, this novel charges political formalism with attentiveness to the labors and losses of making, and to keeping the promise of forms to shelter beyond harm.

6

States of Psychoanalysis: Formalization and the Space of the Political

In the first, larger part of this book, I have argued that literary realism's little-recognized faculty for abstraction produces unexpected affinities with formalist mathematics, and that this formalist synergy makes it possible to theorize a political ethos of formalist affirmation of social structuration. In this shorter concluding part, I take up works of political theory from the twentieth and twenty-first centuries that explicate these impulses of the nineteenth. I begin with the most explicit, Jacques Lacan's enthusiastic embrace of mathematical formalism as social practice.

On a Wednesday in 1972, the twentieth year of his seminars, Lacan made a rare statement of telos: "Mathematical formalization is our goal, our ideal. Why? Because it alone is matheme, in other words, because it alone is capable of being integrally transmitted."[1] What enables math to figure the end of psychoanalysis? Formalization as a goal of a clinical situation, a consummation of the work, suggests that letters and logic discharge a crucial function in concluding the treatment, in producing the transformative linkages by which analysands take up new relations to their symptoms and their desire, mobilizing a construction around a new signifier. But beyond the individual treatment, formalization as the ideal of transmitting integrally suggests that these letters and logic are the condition of possibility for generalizing treatment, for institutionalizing psychoanalysis. Formalization offered a mode of symbolization counter to word-writing, a kind of counter or para-writing that could somehow relay the kind of talking and para-talking at the center of the clinic. Such relay was always at issue for Lacan as for Freud, since they both thoroughly pursued the question of how to *institute* psychoanalysis, how to make spaces, forms, practices, and discourses to advance the cause, and both struggled profoundly with institutes, societies, organizations, associations, and groups, trying to find hospitable venues for affiliating around psychoanalysis. To take math for the "ideal" of psychoanalysis is therefore to enunciate subjectivization *and* institutionalization as the very purpose of the practice—to, in other words, cast psychoanalysis as an intervention distinctly concerned with building new social formations, as a project distinctly engaging *political* theory.[2]

Theorists of the political are quite accustomed to appreciating what psychoanalysis can do to account for domination, audit sovereignty, and critique ideology.[3] But less common is to think with psychoanalysis about politics as the question of elementary social links, about politics as the sphere of institutionalization, about politics as form, about the space of the political and the architectures that contour such space. Such thought would find itself profoundly at odds with today's hegemonic vitalist antiformalism, the tomes of twentieth- and twenty-first-century critical theory devoted to the anatomy of governmentality, the excision of the state, law, and form itself; to the lament of sovereignty, suspicion of organization, encomium of anarchy, and ecstasy of life; to the hypostasization of freedom as a messianic sublime beyond every institution, beyond every state, "beyond every idea of law."[4] Against this contemporary orthodoxy, psychoanalysis takes formalization as its goal: it uniquely prizes the instituting capacity of the material signifier, uniquely conceives and practices *institution*, uniquely affirms *structures* of and in political life, uniquely observes the *necessity of structuration.* Where other frameworks, both theoretical and practical, have become resoundingly antistatist, what psychoanalysis institutes is the thought and practice of a necessary but contingent *state*, that which stands, that which is formed, that which facilitates existence. "State" I propose here as the political topos of psychoanalytic attention to the irreducible symbolic dimension in social life.[5]

Formalization, as that which "alone is capable" of building a collective of psychoanalysts, is an aperture to psychoanalytic political theory more broadly because it delineates a procedure of symbolization whose counterintuitive and incomplete character actuates a reconstellation of socio-symbolic ordering, harkening a sociality premised upon the ineluctable openness and antagonism of the letter of the law, rather than the closed prescription of law's spirit. As an investigation of the letters that effectuate sociality, formalization engenders thinking and working upon the letter without guarantees, assuming responsibility for and toward the inevitability of incessant negotiation of the elementary forms of sociality. Social life will necessarily follow the dialectical movement of relation and disjunction, of makeshift meanings and their evacuation, provisional constitutions and their abolitions, fragile coalitions and their dissolutions. What remains the ultimate condition of such a dialectic is the implacable requirement *that there be form*, or, as Lacan puts it, that there is letter (*il y a de la lettre*).[6] Unlike other animals, the human being requires a collectivity for its very existence; this implacability prioritizes a minimally instituted socius as the precondition of the individual. Formalization is both theory and practice of this minimal installation. To make this case for formalization's importance to political theory, this chapter considers the backgrounds of formalization in Freud's work on institutionalization, in the formalist revolution of mathematics, and in Lévi-Straussian structuralism, then proceeds to reflections on some precepts of psychoanalytic political theory before concluding with speculations on the state.

Freud and Transmission

Lacan steadily advocates a "return to Freud," but to what in Freud is he returning with his ideal of formalization? In founding psychoanalysis, Freud struggled both with the regulations governing its practice, and with the tactical question of how to impart his findings to those who would undertake that practice. His late essay "The Question of Lay Analysis," which considers Austria's unique requirement that analysts be doctors, wrestles with three problematics that presage Lacan's demand for formalization as the practice of the incomplete symbolic that could constitute the training of analysts. First, Freud insists that psychoanalysis obliquely bisects existing academic and disciplinary divisions of knowledge. "If one had to found a college of psychoanalysis," then the faculty would necessarily draw from aspects of medicine and psychiatry, but also from "the history of civilization, mythology, the psychology of religion and the science of literature."[7] This is no simple interdisciplinarity, but rather the editing and curating of a new set of objects of concern, since "it must include elements from the mental sciences, from psychology, the history of civilization and sociology, as well as from anatomy, biology and the study of evolution. There is so much to be taught in all this that it is justifiable to omit from the curriculum anything which has no direct bearing on the practice of analysis and only serves indirectly (like any other study) as a training for the intellect and for the powers of observation."[8] Such a college would therefore deform all extant colleges, all currently constellated disciplines, with its new principles of breadth and depth and consequences, necessitating and amounting to a new discourse of the university. Moreover, a key to that discourse is its own mutability and propulsive proliferation of figures, for "in psychology we can only describe things by analogies . . . but we have to keep changing analogies, for none of them lasts long enough."[9] When descriptive images become reified or literalized, they expire; psychoanalysis circulates a kind of language that changes frequently in order to generate new intensities.

Second, Freud underscores that the validity of psychoanalysis cannot be tested or insured by standard disciplinary measures; the kind of knowledge produced in psychoanalysis is not subject to adjudications of, nor guarantees of, validity, but is rather irreducibly site-specific: only within the clinic, in the space between the analyst and analysand, can there be knowledge. Psychoanalytic knowledge transgresses disciplines but is simultaneously resistant to generalizability. It stands then that knowledge is not the basis of legislating relationships, but their product. Third, the very form in which Freud relays these essential thoughts on the "institutes" of psychoanalysis and codification of training is itself a *dialogue*, a long-form hypostasization of a skeptical interlocutor who poses questions, raises objections, makes concessions, and generally plays devil's advocate. The form here relays the content: there can be no programmatic statement on the training of analysts outside of the dialogic mode; interaction with an interlocutor who instantiates the field of the other is a structural requirement for psychoanalytic knowledge to develop. "Institutes" are fora that formalize these necessarily dyadic and dialogic relations, for there those who wish to be trained are themselves taken into analysis, as well as supervised while taking others into analysis.[10] The simultaneous relations of dialogue and of dialogue-about-dialogue that anchor institutes strategically underscore that training requires occupying multiple dialogic positions (the would-be analyst is herself analysand at the institute), that the way to learn to be analyst is to move between different discursive positions, move between different relations to an Other.

Freud's efforts to think through what could be regulated or codified in psychoanalysis, and his pioneering of the organizational form of the institute, are repeated by Lacan's contentious, career-long grappling with how to train analysts and thus how to form a movement of psychoanalysis. The ebb and flow of his political and institutional struggles comprised, as he put it in *Seminar XI*, "the base—in the topographical and even the military sense of the word—the base of my teaching."[11] *Seminar XI* is of course itself situated at an important juncture in the project of institutionalization, for its declaration of fundamentals comprised Lacan's first seminar at the École normale supérieure, arranged by Althusser after Lacan's excommunication from the International Psychoanalytic Association. Like Freud before him, tussling with various groups and society forms, Lacan founded three different official organizations (a society, a school, and an institute) dedicated to coordinating psychoanalysis—including a new one the year he died—and he was relieved of his post in as many more. What it meant to strategically organize, to collect under a sign, to elicit fidelity to a cause, to affiliate for the purpose of a praxis rather than a predetermined content, to install a society or a school or an institute—what it meant to take a body of texts, the Freudian oeuvre, and operationalize continued engagement with them, what it meant to transmit over time and outside of the clinic the unique experience of the clinic, what it meant to not give up on the desire for institution—all these intricacies animate the organically political theories of psychoanalysis.

The Analyst's Mathematics

How can math offer a solution to these political quandaries? Lacan's embrace of mathematical formalization as a strategy for questions of institution and organization powerfully instances the project of political formalism *The Order of Forms* elaborates. Prizing modeling over expression, Lacan highlights the performative power of mathematical formulae to bring into being that which they inscribe. This is precisely what Alain Badiou, the contemporary thinker most committed to formalization, celebrates in Lacan and in the nineteenth-century revolutions alike: the turn to formalism in mathematics amounts to nothing less than a metaphysical innovation, introducing a new kind of causality, an "anticipatory" or "retroactive" causality whereby a model creates the fact it fathoms.[12] As a goal of psychoanalysis, then, Lacan's mathemes inscribe this causality as proper to the political sphere of institutionalization, the making of arbitrary forms for making existence, and simultaneously the mathemes bring into being the kind of being that obtains in the letter, in the materiality of signification.[13] As Lacan puts it, formalization "is the most advanced elaboration we have by which to produce signifierness";[14] the formalized letter within the mathematical formula performs or precipitates letterness. Whereas classical mathematics posits letterness as a self-identical substance ("Mathematics is constructible only on the basis of the fact that the signifier is capable of signifying itself. The A . . . can be signified by its repetition A"[15]), formal mathematics, by contrast, discovers that "this position is strictly untenable, it constitutes a violation of the rules with respect to the function of the signifier, which can signify anything, except, surely, itself."[16] The revolution of mathematical formalization is a revolution in the status of the letter, a "throwing off" of the self-identity of the letter, actualizing instead the letter as self-differing, a difference that is the source of its power to unlock possibilities.

Far from an absolute signifier full of meaning, the letter of the matheme, the isolate signifierness, necessitates "a hundred and one different readings."[17] To return, then, to the question of how mathematics could provide resources for designing the training of analysts, we can note that formalized math instigates a special kind of *reading*: not intuitive reading, not hermeneutic reading, but reading that encounters the letter as surface and structure, reading that encounters the letter as nonsense and too much sense, reading that encounters symbolization otherwise than as significance or reference. Of his most major formalization, the formulae of the four discourses, Lacan says: "It is no accident if I have given only these little letters here. It's because I do not want to put things up that might give the appearance of signifying."[18] Confronted with mathematical formulae written on the board by a psychoanalyst, most readers, even mathematicians, are deprived of any experiential surety and intuitive footing; they are instead engaged in the pronounced and novel experience of the enigmas of symbolization. (Foreclosure of these enigmas is of course always an option: math is hard, and formalization inspired dismissals of Lacan as obscurantist, pseudo-scientific, non-sensical, and, in the notorious case of the Sokal Hoax, a fraud.) Attunement to these enigmas, awakening to their repetition at the entry into language, may comprise the best possible qualification for those who want to be analysts.

How can attunement of this sort be programmed or routinized? How can the training of analysts be specified without giving rise to the (always already widespread) illusion that psychoanalysis is a content, a hermeneutic, that it finds what it seeks? To pose the answer "formalization" to the question of training is to refuse the reification of concepts and contents, to insist that every psychoanalysis must invent itself, its practice in an actual clinic. This is no doubt why Lacan repeatedly defined psychoanalysis as nothing other than what is done by psychoanalysts: his trademark paradoxical metastatements and tautologies here profoundly convey that there is not a definition outside the exercise, that there is not a content outside the form of the clinic, that there is not a substance preexisting the relation.[19] The training of analysts is thus a question of how to ensure that a certain kind of relation, social linkage, or *form* is constructible, how to ensure that a certain interaction is enactable—it is a question of institutes, not a question of doctrines.

To invite those who are training to be analysts to receive their teaching from mathemes is to demand that analysts symbolize differently, surrendering fantasies of signification and intuition. To demand that analysts accept the position for which they ask without authoritative meaning bolstering it. To demand that analysts subjectively assume the contingency of the signifier. There is no exit from the negotiations of the word, nor ever, even in formalization, an arrest of the movement of the signifier. In this respect, formalization aims not at an abyssally fundamental content of the signifier, but at registering the abyss of the signifier. What would be an institution organized around this abyss?

Structure's Formalization

Lacan's friend Claude Lévi-Strauss's writing of structure made fundamental strides in mapping institutions of the abyss, and crucially inspired formalization.[20] Lacan's very first formalization, in his essay "The Instance of the Letter in the Unconscious, or, Reason since Freud" (1957) draws heavily on Lévi-Strauss's reading of Saussure.[21] Where Saussure had conveyed, with his graphic, the importance of two aspects of the sign,

$$\frac{\text{Signified}}{\text{Signifier}}$$

Lacan highlighted the asymmetries between these aspects:

$$\frac{\text{S}}{\text{s}}$$

He isolated the letter within the matheme, relocating the signifier to the top of the matheme, above the bar, removing the arrows implying connection across the bar, and reducing the signified to a small *s*. In thus inscribing the primacy of the signifier and the ineradicability of the bar between sound-image and meaning, Lacan set out to punctuate the structuralist insight into the function of the signifier in instituting the elementary forms of sociality, yoking this insight to its Freudian parallel about the function of the signifier in organizing the unconscious. Early on, he indicates that "the signifier, with its own action and insistence, intervenes in all of the human being's interests—however profound, primitive, elementary we suppose them to be"; later he notoriously pronounces, "The unconscious is structured as a language."[22] The "unconscious is structured" conveys for him a truth of structure: that structure, far from a subject-less form, is that which, in its language-ness, in its systematic but contingent knitting of signifiers, retroactively precipitates the subject.

Thus for Lacan, as for Lévi-Strauss, a structure "ha[s] to be defined as the order of the effects of language."[23] Lacan explicitly attributes to Lévi-Strauss his conviction that "before strictly human relations are established, certain relations have already been determined,"[24] and goes on to locate language not as culture but as nature: "Nature provides—I must use the word—signifiers, and these signifiers organize human relations in a creative way, providing them with structures and shaping them."[25] What are these preestablished, predetermined relations of the signifier, and what resources might they provide for articulating that which psychoanalysis affirms in its fundamental political formalism, that which psychoanalysis affirms as the formalism of relations, the priority of relationality?

For Lévi-Strauss, this fundamental signifier at the base of the social link is finally less a letter and more a line, a purely formal inscription, akin to the bar between signifier and signified. He identifies this bar through an activity of formalization: he ethnographically solicits graphs of social relations from two different strata of a single society, and receives two different sets of graphs that nonetheless share a common feature—an axis that at once relates and splits the village, a bar that universally establishes the very possibility of regulatory schema for society. His name for this purely formal bar that originates structure is "zero value institution," an institution that installs not any particular institution, but the form of institutionality as such. Lévi-Strauss writes, "These institutions have no intrinsic property other than that of establishing the necessary preconditions for the existence of the social system to which they belong; their presence—in itself devoid of significance—enables the social system to exist as a whole."[26] The logical symbols, letters, and diagrams of structuralism endeavor to minimally represent this minimalism of the zero institution. That is, although structuralism is often associated with a totalizing mania for full representation, the thought of structure therein actually operates a hole in representation.[27] Structure is not identical to itself even as it is self-referential; this nonidentity necessitates that no social order can ever be represented instantaneously, that neither diagram nor formula will tell the truth of a social relation. Formalization is the graph of structure, the writing of incompleteness.

As its precursors, mathematics and structuralism ignite in Lacanian formalization a drive toward the performative power of purely formal minimalism. In upholding this kind of symbolization as the ideal of psychoanalysis, Lacan specifies analysis as a distinct kind of writing and a distinct kind of speech. The analyst, as the other side of the master, is one who has heard that "language speaks us," that "when I say, 'the use of language,' I do not mean that we use it. It is language that uses us. Language employs us."[28] The "product" of the analyst's discourse is a new S_1, an S_1 under the bar, an S_1 subjectivized as contingent and produced. This production is both writing and speech, both formalization and the clinical relation within which the contingency and emptiness of formalization are deliberated. Formalization is a goal, an ideal, but an incomplete ideal—the ideal of incompletion. Indeed, immediately after Lacan's statement that formalization is the goal, he himself decompletes this ideal:

> Mathematical formalization consists of what is written, but it only subsists if I employ, in presenting it, the language I make use of. Therein lies the objection: no formalization of language is transmissible without the use of language itself. It is in the very act of speaking that I make this formalization, this ideal metalanguage, ex-sist.[29]

Writing must be activated in speech if it is to function as transmission; mathemes must be spoken of to be situated as the transmission of psychoanalysis, and they must be spoken of to be received as the transmission of psychoanalysis—the students must mull the letters. All this is to say that at the very core of the analyst's discourse is an insistence on a hole in language, a hole that formalization effectuates rather than plugs. Formalization isolates signifierness, not as the essence of meaning, but as the irreducible nonmeaning that incites interpretation (both reading and analytical interpretation). This is the dimension in which Lacan's mathemes are not figurative but literal, not analogies but inscriptions.[30] His mathemes are inscriptions *as form* rather than *of content*; his mathematics is not a metaphor but a practice of symbolization otherwise.[31]

Formalization and the Space of the Political

It is precisely this practice of symbolization that offers a psychoanalytic theory of the state: through these various valences, "formalization" emerges as the topos not only by which psychoanalysis thinks through the conjunction of language and institution, but also through which it aims to reorder social linkage. An operation of minimalization—of isolating signifiers from signs, of inciting encounter with the signifier as such—formalization is also an operation of institutionalization, of transmission, of codification. This dynamic combination of minimalization and institutionalization, of subtraction and stasis, is where we can locate the very basis of a psychoanalytic theory of the state: not the canonical state of political theory, but a primal site of formalizing the space of the political. In his remarkable essay "Freud and the Political," Mladen Dolar broaches this space, focusing on the way that the corpus of Freud's political metapsychology (*Group Psychology and the Analysis of the Ego, Totem and Taboo, Moses and Monotheism, Civilization and Its Discontents*) consistently underscores that a political whole is impossible, that, indeed, "political" is the nomination in Freud of the impossibility of a self-identical, unconflicted socio-symbolic order.[32] "The point has been variously named as conflictuality, antagonism, rift, a crack in the social tissue, an excess, the point of ambivalence, untying of social bonds, negativity. This point runs through all Freud's works.... A core around which they turn as their common ground . . . has to be conceived as the site of the political, ubiquitously inherent in Freud's work—as a site."[33] Dolar emphasizes that psychoanalysis outlines this site, but stops short of intervening in it. But what if the demarcation of the site actually itself constitutes an intervention? What if the writing of a fundamental antagonism is a political act, an act of symbolization that limns "that which resists symbolization absolutely," an act of formalizing that performs the contingent structuration of the rift?

Lacan's project of formalization helps us to think the political intervention of forming in/around/as antagonism: the bar, the zero value institution, in all its radical arbitrariness, is a writing that makes sociality possible. I am wagering that this practice of writing can invigorate our understanding of "the state"—instead of the state as a loose assemblage of institutions, communities, and bodies that it paradoxically centrally controls, or of the state as the orthodox regulatory disciplinarian overseeing those more organic organizations, we would have simply the state as zero value institution.

This prospect of "the state" as elementary structuration can be read in Lacan's schema of the four discourses, his most substantive formalization. There he encodes the possibility of historical shifts in discourse (such as from the master to the university), and emergence of new signifiers, even as the schema also observes certain axiomatic limits, certain insuperable structuring factors. Recall that Lacan offers formulae of modalities of social linkage—the master's discourse, the university discourse, the hysteric's discourse, and the analyst's discourse. Each formula is predicated upon the fundamental linguistic premise of Lacan's theory of the subject—that the signifier represents the subject for another signifier:

$$\frac{S_1}{\$} \rightarrow S_2$$

From this basis, Lacan specifies that the different discourses are in a certain established relation with one another—that, for instance, the psychoanalyst's discourse is "the other side" or "inverse" of the master's discourse—and that the movement from one discourse to another is the product of rotational quarter turns. Each of the four variations is formally represented as a matheme. Here is the master's discourse:

$$\frac{S_1}{\$} \qquad \frac{S_2}{a}$$

When he lays out his theory of four discourses in *Seminar XVII*, Lacan is explicit that while he is not pronouncing on "origins," he can nonetheless locate the discourse he presents first, the master's discourse, as historically first, or historically primary in recorded history and recorded knowledge: in Plato and Aristotle, in the pinnacle of classical democracy and its attendant slavery, in the birth of philosophy.[34] He goes on to assert that today's discourse is different, the university discourse rather than the master's,[35] and to cite Descartes as the progenitor of this historical shift. And he explicitly pronounces the shifts or transitions from one discourse to another as "what deserves, strictly speaking, to be designated by the term 'revolution.'"[36] If the formalization of the four discourses appears to side with structure against history, the very principle of the structure—the principle of shifting—encodes historical transformations.

Constructing History

Just such a history is relayed by a centerpiece of Freud's political metapsychology, *Moses and Monotheism*: Moses worked to install a new world order by means of the new monotheistic signifier, radically reconfiguring the precedent socio-symbolic field. Likewise, Lacan looks with a structuralist eye at the generality of the social function. Defining the signifier as "distinct from meaning"[37] and as that "without which the order of human meanings would be unable to establish itself"[38]—as, thus, a kind of precondition of meaning—Lacan goes on to underscore the immense rupture that is the advent of a new signifier:

> The emergence of a new signifier, with all the consequences, down to one's most personal conduct and thoughts, that this may entail, the appearance of a register such as that of a new religion, for example, isn't something that is easily manipulated—experience proves it. Meanings shift, common sentiments and socially conditioned relations change, but there are also all sorts of so-called revelatory phenomena that can appear in a sufficiently disturbing mode for the terms we use in the psychoses not to be entirely inappropriate for them. The appearance of a new structure in the relations between basic signifiers and the creation of a new term in the order of the signifier are devastating in character.[39]

Such devastation is not necessarily wrought by acts of the will—it is difficult to engineer, "not easily manipulated." This is not only to say that revolutions are ruptures, that the installation of a new sociality is unshakably excessive, as *Totem and Taboo* attests, but also that the very subject of the political envisioned by psychoanalysis may be terrifying: the psychoses pose a specter of suffering, even though they might also be the best incarnation, in this reality, of a possible alternative political subjectivity.[40]

The traumatic history that is the advent of new signifiers has a more liberatory instantiation in the psychoanalytic cure, which chiefly entails the subjective assumption of the contingency of enjoyment and the subjective establishment of a "construction." Of course, since the rise of social constructionism and Foucault's notion of a construction of the self via *ascesis*, we are all familiar with "construction" as a project of efficacious fabrication, a project with the insidious quality of manufacturing reality and its avenues of domination, but also a project with the liberatory quality of offering new possibilities for performance and actualization. In psychoanalysis, however, the term "construction" is at once more technical than this colloquial usage and more ambiguous. As Freud developed the notion in *Constructions in Analysis* (written at the very end of his career simultaneously with his political theory *Moses and Monotheism*), a "construction" is an image or narrative "divined" in the course of analysis by the analyst and analysand together, which assembles "fragments of historical truth" within a framework of a "primal scene" or fantastical origin of fantasy. The key dynamic for a construction, Freud insists, is not its representative value, but its performative function, its "outcome."[41] The construction therefore, as Kenneth Reinhard insightfully argues, amounts to an "act" in and of psychoanalysis, an event in the clinic that transforms the analysand by mobilizing "shards of language that don't signify a semiotic content but embody a strange jouissance."[42] The transformative power derives not from the revelation imparted by the construction (the analyst tells the analysand his secret history) but rather from the striking effect of the words of the construction themselves upon the course of treatment ("The analyst finishes a piece of construction and communicates it to the subject of analysis so that it may work upon him"[43]). Freud was emphatic that this "work" differed from interpretation. Reinhard captures the stakes: "The construction is not an interpretation of the complex of unconscious significations in the symbolic order, but more like a re-citation or re-quotation of some element in the analysand's phonetic patterns and signifiers, a narratival confection that aims not at understanding the real, but at *materializing* it."[44] This materialization might be thought of as the elemental reordering of discourse, since Lacan suggests that "perhaps it is from the analyst's discourse that there can emerge another style of master signifier."[45]

In his final seminar, Lacan advances this other style as a new being of the signifier; formalization represents the possible writing of or toward a new signifier, *vers un signifiant nouveau*. I would suggest, then, that construction is equivalent to *un signifiant nouveau*, that construction is a modality of formalization, mobilizing a cluster of signifiers for their performative rather than semantic effect.[46] And it is of central importance for my purposes in extrapolating a psychoanalytic political theory from the practice of formalization that for Freud a construction is possible and is efficacious at two levels: for an individual in the clinic, and for a society. He could only have authored *Constructions in Analysis* while he was also authoring what he repeatedly presented as a "construction," *Moses and Monotheism*; a construction as a transformative act may change the subject's symptoms or suffering, and/or may change the organization of the social. The "symbolic" register encompasses not only language but social consistency, ideology, meaning, and the assignation of locations within the social field. A new or different symbolic, right down to its grammar, would therefore seem to be a condition of a new or different set of social relations. For psychoanalysis, in other words, social transformation and symbolic transformation are inextricable and equivalent; for most of his career, formal mathematics models Lacan's best bet as to what a different society looks like: not intuitive, not meaningful, not transmissible without dialogue, only a repeated, formalist encounter with the letter of structuration.

We now come to a crucial point. As it writes these possibilities of transformation and revolution, the schema of the four discourses also instantiates a crucial limit: while there are four elements and four positions, Lacan inscribes only four possible variations (not twenty-four). The elements may move into a new position but only by maintaining their same relative position: moving clockwise, S_2 will always be to the right of S_1, and so on. Moreover, the positions are unchangeable: the first position, occupied by S1 in the master's discourse, is always the agent, "the place from which the discourse is ordered."[47] The second position, the other, is the addressee of the agent's discourse. The third position, the product, is what the discourse produces as remainder, and the fourth position, the truth, is what the discourse produces as effect. From these positions, we can glean certain axioms of the social link as conceived by psychoanalysis: every discourse has intended and unintended products. Every discourse is a structure. Every structure inscribes ambiguity. The position of the agent of discourse is always the position of the law; there is the law within any particular structure (the agent orders the discourse), but then there is the general law of structure (that the positions are invariable).[48] Such internal law of the discourses suggests a sine qua non structuration of social linkage itself. Formalization condenses this fact of structuration; formalization is the writing degree zero of the function that is the zero institution.

The Letter of the Law

Within the political metapsychology, this zero institution more regularly appears as "the law." Psychoanalysis generally does not address laws, but the law, a register or concept or abstraction rather than a particular instantiation; a field of structuration of sociality. This law is neither the juridical administration nor discursive incursion of statute into the hearth, but rather a transcendental condition for human sociality whose concrete installations will always be contingent, as are the desires it inspires. This law, as Freud defines it in his speculative masterpiece *Totem and Taboo*, is the paradoxical chaos of order, the ungroundedness of any sociality, the antagonism that insuperably determines structure. Freud famously invents a myth of a primal horde governed by a terrifying father to whom accrue exclusive rights of enjoyment of women; a band of brothers rebel against him; their guilt at their murderous deed impels them to formulate a ban on future killing articulated with and as a scheme for the distribution of enjoyment of women. Two brief remarks about this elaborate text are necessary here. First, as Joan Copjec observes, the extravagance of the text is not beside the point but the point itself: the law is not something to be transcended but itself a transcendent structure, outlandish and unaccountable yet also an extraordinary mundanity, a stupid facticity.[49] Second, the scheme that Freud drafts is organized by the repetition of the law. The law of the father is law at the order of obscenely groundless primordial installation; the law of the brother is law at the order of the obscenely grounded primary institution; the law of *Totem and Taboo*, the law Freud speculatively assesses, is the law of the repetition of obscene excess. This unshakable excess is not the violence that other traditions view as the imposing of the law, nor even the supplement of enjoyment that supports the law, but *the rift in the law itself*, its own impossibility, its nonimmanence and nonidentity, its negativity.

The psychoanalytic theory of the state must stem from this fundamental axis of the negative in psychoanalysis, consistent with the study of the negative we read in *Wuthering Heights*.[50] Less an apotheosized lack than an active and agential void, "the negative" inheres in the galvanizing force of constitutive incompletion for both the enjoying subject and the social field; this incompletion is not an obstacle to subjectivity or sociality, but rather the condition of possibility for it. Formalization negatively represents this central negation, this operating of negativity: there is no letteral relation; what the letter relays is without guarantees. This would be a strict corollary to the maxim that "there is no sexual relation" and the insight that there is no social relation (that social antagonism is insuperable). Formalization prompts a theory of the politics of negation, a theory of the possibility of institutions of the negative.

In attending to this radical negativity, this constitutive antagonism and constitutively senseless, nonsensical character of the law, psychoanalysis underscores what we saw in *Bleak House* as law's fundamental formalism. Law *is*. Subjects are subject to the law, and perhaps enjoy the law, and generally obey the law, not because it represents ("the just," "the good"), but because it fails to represent, it simply structurally exudes. Where this nonsensical quality of the law—its nonsignifying core, its nonsignifying function—is repressed by most theories of the law, which seek to yoke it to ideals or fill in its void with content, psychoanalysis directly reveres the void or split of the law. So I am suggesting that formalization as a decompletion of the signifier presages the theory and practice of the law as form, as reductio ad absurdum. Only a theory that holds that signification is itself antagonistic can envision a sociality whose structuring principle is the openly incomplete signifier; only this sort of theory of the state can encounter the state as radically minimal form. Ultimately, then, the project of formalization is the kind of representation adequate to this ontology of law. Formalization is an operation of minimalization—of isolating signifiers (in the case of algebra) from signs, of inciting encounter with the signifier as such. Formalization is also an operation of institutionalization—of transmission, of codification. As the goal of psychoanalysis, this dynamic combination of minimalization and institutionalization, of subtraction and stasis, isolates the state as the positivization *within* sociality of the very stain of sociality. The minimal material institution of being, the psychoanalytic state is nothing other than the statehood of signifierness.

Infrastructures of the Signifier

Todd McGowan's recent bold endeavor to positively specify the political project of psychoanalysis, a positivity of the aggregation of traversed subjects "enjoying what we don't have," provides an important avenue by which to conclude. Whereas the traditions of ideology critique and of social cohesion theories that I mentioned at the beginning of this chapter mobilize psychoanalysis as a purely descriptive exercise (in which Freud and Lacan uncover the unconscious, including the unconscious of a specific society, but they do not articulate programs for an alternate society), McGowan shrewdly perceives the transcendental tenor of the psychoanalytic insight (that "antagonism between the subject and the social order is irreducible"[51]) and thus concludes that a positive psychoanalytic politics fundamentally embraces this antagonism. McGowan underscores the futility of pursuit of a good life or a good polis, and instead commends that "rather than trying to progress toward overcoming the barrier that separates us from the good society, we begin to view identification with the barrier as the paradoxical aim of progress."[52] Such an identification, a fundamentally psychic process, opens onto "an emancipatory politics of the limit,"[53] and may succeed in establishing a "society of the death drive,"[54] of repetition and negation and the inheritance of loss. In rejecting the possibility of legislating the good life, a society of the death drive elevates as its core principle the enjoyment that cannot be legislated, but only accrues indirectly, circuitously, through the encounter with limits.

McGowan directly proposes that this society can only obtain indirectly; installing such relations "would not involve a radical transformation of society: in one sense, it would leave everything as it is."[55] It is nevertheless my contention that something more programmatic and more collective—more formalizable—is indeed possible, that "identification with the barrier" and assuming rather than repressing social antagonism are psychic states that also have infrastructural correlates. Psychoanalytic political theory, in other words, can usefully illuminate modes of social linkage as much as modes of subjectivization. That statehood of the signifier precisely so illuminated by formalization, enacted by a horde of sisters who subjectivize the death drive, is not a state full of content (democracy and the market), but one whose empty, purely formal character is directly avowed, whose tautological inscription is axiomatic rather than lamentable—avowed perhaps in a positive position on the a priori character of law; avowed perhaps in a positive practice of the party or proletarian dictatorship as political formation; avowed perhaps in a positive practice of *la passe* as citizenship rite; avowed perhaps in a positive practice of unfounded authority (such as a rotational seat of power); avowed perhaps in ways unforeseeable in political theory; but operationalizable in struggle over the readings of the letter of installation. Formalization as ideal gives us to think the formal state, the forms of sociality that underscore their own antagonistic character.

We are everywhere, right and left, exhorted to oppose and transcend the state. But the materialism of the signifier, the formalism of the political, offer a counter to this orthodoxy, a path to embracing the state as limit, embracing the space of the political as the only and proper sphere of life (and death), a path to embracing limits as the condition of freedom. What would be an institution that subjectively assumed its zero value? What would be a letter of the law that openly entailed the deliberation pursuant to its incompletion, a party that openly courted the other sides of its discursive formation?

What would be a form of institute that hosted rather than repressed the ungroundedness of all forms? What would be a law not against but *of* antagonism? What would be a state that traversed the fantasies both of its groundedness and of its ancillarity? What would be a state whose goal, whose ideal, was relentless withering? In these manifold forms and their manifold negations, in the dialectics of their actualization, these would be the states of psychoanalysis, ideals that matter.

Conclusion

Sustaining Forms

We live in destructive times, on an incinerating planet, over institutional embers, around prodigious redundancy between the plunder of the commons and the compulsive echolalia "Burn it all down." Theory must prepare to build things up, and literature models that building. *The Order of Forms* outlines a way of reading and thinking conducive to the affirmative project of revaluing the structuration of sociality by reappraising aesthetic form's capacity to mediate that structuration. This political formalism orients itself first and foremost to composed relationality. How is a work put together, what is it made of, what gives it internal consistency? How does the form-work of novels in particular disclose elementary structures of worldly sociality, and practice the mediations that enable the ongoing construction of those structures? In turn these observations of literary order found new esteem for social order: a political formalism beholds how relations are aesthetically made, and reciprocally a formalism of the political affirms madeness, marking out the essentiality of form to collective existence. It embraces the constituting of forms above and beyond the destituent paradigm's desire for formlessness. Our skills of understanding the composition of made things must be turned to the work of celebrating making. Humanists, too, are makers, equipped for the task of constructing new togethernesses, new compositions, new orders, and to sustaining those formations in time and space.

Political formalism approaches literary works like the realist novel as utopian models of possible socialities configured to project and integrate elementary structures of spontaneous organization. Such models theorize this structuration as a basis of, rather than obstacle to, political freedom itself. A formalism of the political encounters the forms that comprise our social interdependence as mere forms, ungroundable yet indispensable, promoting a core idea of form as something purposeful but simultaneously emergent, something conspicuously constructed and efficacious, something spontaneous and malleable. This core idea encompasses the dialectic of form rejected or otherwise suppressed amid the proliferation of theoretical and practical antiformalisms—from Adorno and Agamben to Foucault, Said, Edelman, Latour, Hardt and Negri, and Moten—since those so thoroughly contest the exclusions of any given construction, so persuasively audit the reifications that occlude reformability.

The allergy to form in the humanities has had very deleterious effects in both practice and theory. In practice, intellectuals based in the humanities have often had trouble constituting collective bodies. We can count that in the failure to mass unionize or otherwise politically collectively respond to the massive restructuring of labor in higher education in the past four decades. We can count that in automatic disdain for the important means of power in official politics (institutions, elections, legislation) as irredeemably tainted. But we can also count it in a more broad failure of humanists, experts with an incomparably strong aptitude for articulating values, to impart constructive visions of cultural production, equality, and flourishing that could guide the elocution of concrete political demands such as debt-free education and art for all. In many ways, these failures align: lacking a robust positive representation of what the study of literature, art, and culture offers beyond historic preservation or cautionary catalogues of domination, humanists have been unable to think their own faculties for composition—for making ideas of public goods, for making institutions that uphold the *universitas* in the university, for making spaces adequate for human beings, for making equipment for living, for making forms of and for sustained collectivity—and have consequently misperceived their own position in an ever-intensifying class war.

The ensuals of reflexive antiformalism extend beyond this realm of tactics and strategy. Theory itself, the fraught practice of situated abstraction, has been diminished. Theorists have consigned themselves to immanentizing domination, to the lamenting of institutionality, normativity, and the state, and recently to abjuring critique in favor of empiricizing description. Forfending theory's wonderful openings for wild norms, conducive institutions, and emancipatory syntheses, we have constrained theory's projective capacity to the minimal axes of ethical hospitality for provisional encounters, ephemeral affects of oceanic connectivity, and fleeting specters of whatever being. We have indicted art's complicities, not elaborated its moxie. We have prophylactically refused reification, messianized revolution, forestalled agency, and thus impeded most theorizing of sustainability, effectivity, re-forming. In thrall to these subtractions, we have forsworn the bigness, velocity, and liberating abstraction of theory itself.

As an alternative to these practical and theoretical legacies, political formalism commits to structuration as such, tracing the radically essential, radically ungroundable installation of social order and pivoting that formal recognition into the opportunity for constructing new socialities, new constitutions, new orders of forms. Although thus at odds with many theoretical hegemonies of the recent past, political formalism as I draft it can indeed claim theoretical legacies from the art and thought of the more distant past. My readings of *The German Ideology*, *The Manifesto of the Communist Party*, and Lacan's mathematics all suggest that Marxism and psychoanalysis together provide very astute frameworks for fathoming the groundless essentiality of social relations, and in this respect their own contributions to political theory are incredibly valuable. Where canonical political theory across millennia endeavors to ground the state successively in divine right, contract, consent, theological seduction, or the justness of democracy, Marxism and psychoanalysis directly avow the impossibility of grounding forms of political collectivity. Such avowal opposes not only contemporary theory adages but also those crucial arcs of critique that would seek to dismiss social forms on these grounds of ungrounds—emblematized in Walter Benjamin's conflation of abyssal constitution with "violence."[1] Instead, Marx's emphasis on spontaneously emergent social forms and on the liberatory dimension of normativity, along with Freud's and Lacan's emphasis on the socio-symbolic field as the condition of possibility for the subject's existence and its enjoyment, helps to illuminate a path for theory that would embrace the affordances of form while conceding its arbitrary character.

The readings of novels in *The Order of Forms* similarly stress this approbative regard for structuration, bearing out the argument that literary realism rates understanding as a productive abstraction, a projection of possible social space that defamiliarizes lineaments and enchants the construct. Attending to the singular blueprints of each of the texts in question here, I analyze the intercalating resonations of different formal elements into synthetic form. The resulting formalist practice draws upon long traditions of formalism while more firmly articulating ontological connections between the built form, literary mediation, and infrastructures of the political. Human beings make the forms in which their interdependence holds; artistic forms refract these making practices; the form of the novel in particular mediates and theorizes the making of worlds.

Political formalism combines close analysis of the composition and agency of forms with a willingness to admit the ontological quality of social structuration. At once a method of reading and a commitment to regard dialectically the faculties of such frameworks for relationality as household, the city, law, and the state, it also instills wonder for the myriadism of social space. Literary realism acutely mediates these ballasting frameworks, especially in their minimalism and their malleability. Thus, across the chapters here, "household" encompasses elementary interrelationality for the making of life, foundational shelter, replicable connections, room at the inn, and contested hearths; "the city" encompasses zones of multiple collectivities and possibilities, jostling clusters of households, occasions for manifold building, and surprisingly small fields of interdependence; "the law" encompasses the *nomos* of the *oikos*, the force of social normativity, tautological facticity, contrived axiomaticity, and that which arbitrarily sutures any given social space; and "the state" encompasses formalized relationality, monarchy, democracy, bureaucracy, the dictatorship of the proletariat, and that which stands. In their innate dialectic, novel venues for exploring these goods of social forms also keep pace with remainders of formalization and obstacles to installation: that objective register at which economic, scalar, governmental, and sexual antagonisms hold open questions that any sociality can only provisionally answer. Yet the very generativity of these literary efforts to contemplate worldly integuments—the very beauty wrought in their novel forms—complements this astute awareness of implacable antagonism with sensuous enthusiasm for provisional make-dos.

The maxims, ideas, and wagers of political formalism derive largely from realist aesthetics, with seminal inspiration from formalist mathematics, and in abiding resonance with the unsurpassed nineteenth-century matrices of Marxism and psychoanalysis. While not providing a full history of why a tension exists, I have pitched the book on a profound tension between this earlier center of gravity (1848–1972) and the more recent fifty years to suggest repeatedly that literature and theory of the past can intervene in our present deadlocks. Something like what Giovanni Arrighi calls the long twentieth century—the period between the Springtime of the Peoples and the advent of neoliberalism—this earlier center continues to offer resources for mitigating the antiformalist, anti-institutional, antistatist bias of cultural theory in our present.

Nascent Political Formalisms Today

The present thus beckons. At the moment, a few unwoven strands of contemporary theory strike me as tacitly promising for the braiding of political formalism. This conclusion therefore broaches recent resources for reactivating a dialectic of form, for reanimating in the twenty-first century that nineteenth-century dynamism of form emblematized in formalist mathematics and realist aesthetics. I point to the speculative experiments with form in Jodi Dean's militant advocacy for the party and Fredric Jameson's dialectical utopia of the military. In books published in 2016, Dean and Jameson both implicitly turn to a concept and practice of form as a way out of deadlocks in contemporary activism and dead ends in contemporary thought.[2] Although these projects don't label themselves "formalist," their precise willingness to regard formalized relationality as formal, available for ends of liberation as much as domination, stations some posts of political formalism.

Jodi Dean's advocacy for and embrace of "the party" in political struggle hinges on the need for an organization to advance mobilization, for an infrastructure to sustain the libidinal energies that surge in moments of crowds, and for an aegis to coordinate the inchoate political imaginaries of spontaneously assembled actors. She comes to this meditation on form at the summit of a large body of impressive works assessing the internet and the ideologies of communicative connection it begets, persistent blind spots in the political theory of democracy, the role of the psyche in political struggle, and disarticulation of the project of communism from Soviet history. Dean identifies the dynamic I have called anarcho-vitalism as a pervasive horizontalism and resistance to synthesis. If these are the habits and tendencies that have dominated democratic, liberal, and left political action for the past fifty years, it is no coincidence that during the same period the Right has profoundly consolidated institutional and cultural power, and done so through vehicles like party loyalty, extremist caucus, and quick uptake of institutional modality by insurgent interests like "the Tea Party." All the while that this divergence of tactics has been taking place, the fervent advocates of horizontalism have ignored its substantial overlap with the ethos of corporate governance in the open-office team-player era, the ideology of neoliberalism in the antistatist, antiunion, deregulated libertarianism of action, and the consumerist hegemony of individual choice. The party appeals to Dean as an antidote to horizontalism not because of its content—not in a capacity as transmitter of knowledge or representation of interests—but in its *form*, its ability to abstractly "hold open a gap in our setting so as to enable a collective desire for collectivity."[3] This holding open, this exhortation to a subjectified people to emerge, is a faculty of the party as form, in its features as a "mode of association" spanning "multiple levels and domains" and scaling "local, regional, national, and sometimes international"[4] contexts, and its coalescence around a platform. The party affords span and scale, depth and breadth, *and* the intercalation of these extents, the articulation of pathways for their interrelation. The party lays minimal planks, fundamentals held in common. While Dean works in the spirit of communism, her party remains formal to such an extent that she subtracts it of any content other than collated collective sovereignty. That is, her regard for the party achieves *formalism*: attuned to the party's infrastructural function as collective power, beyond or before its particular platform. Dean's approach to the party form, her insistence on it as a form, and her thinking dialectically about the virtues of that form as an occasion for experimentation and opportunity for change profoundly illustrate formalist regard for the agency and composition of forms. Taking form as technique rather than obstruction, Dean underscores how formalized relationality stands essential and malleable, ready for reform and redeployment.

"Redeployment" becomes one of the most pointed themes in Fredric Jameson's recent dialectical venture, *An American Utopia*. Jameson engages in a speculative experiment to project the utopian potential in decadent capitalism by looking for existing infrastructure that could be scaled into a whole new collectivist society, and finding his answer, scandalously, in the military. Jameson proposes that the military, with its articulated hierarchies, universal provision of needs, variability of functions, and spatial network, provides a practicable model of utopian sociality, a form appropriable away from its hitherto existing content and mobilizable for new ends, ends of formal coalition rather than contentful missions. An available arrangement of coordinated infrastructure exists, so why not repurpose it? Jameson's outlandish wager rings only dialectical: the future is with us in the present. What is more, the wager collects an audacious willingness to regard form as model, as emergent agency that exceeds intentional design, as configuration open to alternative mobilization. Such dialecticity clasps the most essential dimension of political formalism's opposition to the idealized formlessness of anarcho-vitalism: instead of confronting forms with undesirable aegises and clamoring for form's abolition, it acknowledges the merely formal register of the form so as to begin appropriation for new purpose. The explicit, unrepentant, committed utopianism of Jameson's argument resounds the projective ethos of political formalism: better socialities can be built; humanist expertise in formal composition, counterfactuality, artifice, and speculative projections can be brought to bear in such building. Infrastructure is sexy.

Important commonalities in this recent work of Dean and Jameson bring political formalism into relief. Their premise of infrastructure and organization and formation as not just sites of struggle but *techniques* for struggle spotlights prospects of political formalism. Their commitment to study what forms make in the abstract generates imaginative reuse and conjectural social spaces. Dean espouses the form of the party, Jameson the form of the military; Dean sees the party as the form that can bring about a communist horizon, and Jameson sees the military as the form that can effectuate that horizon; for both thinkers, form is the answer rather than the problem. The core commitment to thinking in formal terms about different possible instantiations of the collective reflects an unstated affirmation of the order of forms, of form as framework for the political rather than that against which politics must rebel. Beautifully, these arguments on behalf of form distinctively take shape in unusual genres for theory: Dean writes a stump speech that provocatively promotes positive positions; Jameson creates a generic utopia that details alternate social formation. These very unusual modalities of positive persuasion and of creative genre reveal in their stylistic verve the limitations of business as usual in negative dissolution and aesthetic suspicion. In making a new rhetorical form for theory, both of these works perform in their own composition that affirmative attitude toward composed relationality that distinguishes political formalism.

Reception of these works has thus far been hostile, scandalized, dismissive—a reception that surely protests too much, betraying the antiformalist truisms gluing together the present hegemony. In these highly inventive theoretical departures, these heretical trajectories toward something utterly unsayable in current circles, Dean and Jameson both illustrate that form as such has been forgone in the ecstasy for destituent power, and that approving form as inherently, indispensably political, and politics as inherently, indispensably formal, is the necessary starting point for building new collectives now. The lesson of dual power and of the party—that institutional infrastructures suitable for the future are already available in the present, that institutions must be redeployed for a different politics to take place, that organizations and forms are not the liberal suppression against which all radicals must rebel but the tools of transition to a less iniquitous constellation—composes the most urgent curriculum for today, a curriculum hinging on the study of forms. Experiments in thinking the formal infrastructure of utopia and the formal infrastructure of sustained collective constituent power point to concrete practices of the state: providing housing, transportation, education, and health care while addressing climate crisis; providing collective determination of these provisions. These are elementals that must be elevated to universals, actualized in the infrastructural relation of a formal state, a state that admits itself as the indispensable support of social space.

Formalizing Psychic Politics

It is because I am so keen to advance this formalism to the point of its most liberating abstractions that I would pause to point out how Jameson's experiment in particular is limited by the ultimately insufficient actualization of its formalist impulses: after outlining the refunctioning of the military, his utopia elaborates psychic retrenchment. Making extensive appeal to Freud and Lacan, Jameson puts forward realities of jealousy and envy and greed, transcendentalizing psychological traits in the grand tradition of the worst capitalist apologists. Regularly credited as the author of a statement that he himself refers elsewhere—"[Someone once said] it is easier to imagine the end of the world than the end of capitalism"—Jameson ultimately evinces a corollary in his experiment: it is easier to imagine an infrastructural end to capitalism than an end to capitalist psychic economy.

This limit to the imaginable amounts to a psychologism, recurring to essentializing claims about the human that naturalize a particular order of things.[5] In an effort to register that even a revolutionary formalist reconstitution of the military as a collective state does not permanently solve social antagonism, *An American Utopia* limns the abiding antagonism that we have seen to preoccupy realist novels of world-making. Limns—but does not formulate or formalize. As the brilliant political theory of *Wuthering Heights* shows us, this error can be avoided if the essentializing claim remains objective rather than subjective, confined to the facticity of the negativity at the seam of the social, the absent immanent form of our constitutive interdependence. Insisting on the human's abidingly capitalist psyche fails the bar of thinking this antagonism formalistically, a failure pronounced in political theory from Thomas Hobbes to Chantal Mouffe. Strikingly, psychoanalysis, the very asset Jameson deputes for his concerns, actually repeatedly elevates the formal composition of the psyche. The tense contrast between psychologism and avowing social antagonism already animates psychoanalysis from the beginning, since Sigmund Freud wrote numerous works of political theory—*Totem and Taboo, Thoughts for the Times on War and Death, Group Psychology and the Analysis of the Ego, Civilization and Its Discontents*, and *Moses and Monotheism*—works whose career-spanning arc and repetitive gestures bespeak a perpetual emphasis on the intrinsically social character of psychoanalysis, what Alenka Zupančič has called the "objective" register that complements its "subjective" focus.[6]

In the most comprehensive of these works, Freud directly faced the idea of utopian socialism and of the communist horizon with a stark reminder of antagonisms that exceed capitalism. *Civilization and Its Discontents*, his master thesis on the disturbance inherent in culture, the impossibility of social relations suturing themselves into a conflict-free immanence, houses Freud's pleading a certain agnosticism on economic matters, claiming "no concern with any of the economic criticisms of communism" but underscoring that any communism that mistakes the abolition of private property for the abolition of social antagonism is "based on an untenable illusion."[7] Even after the abolition of private property, and even, Freud says, after the abolition of the family, and even after "new paths the development of culture could take," dissatisfaction will remain an indisputable feature of social existence; sociability itself will reckon with its ungivenness. Freud formulates a fine line: absolutizing antagonism objectively versus subjectively. This very line separates psychologism from psychoanalysis, idealism from materialism: recycling platitudes hypostasizing the irredeemable aggressivity of human nature versus improvising a vocabulary for registering structural antagonism, the gap in the social, its nonimmanence. No civilization without discontent. Freud sustains and repeats this objective social lack across his lifelong project of speculative political theory, formulating the psychoanalytic contribution to the critique of political economy—every economy, every *nomos* of the *oikos*, law for the dispensation of life, is riven by its ungroundedness. Every world lacks immanent social relation. Every state is merely formal.

Any analysis of social transformation must address psychic transformation. But the key to so doing is not presuming in advance that we know what the psyche is; it is necessary to be formalist rather than substantive about ourselves. The ultimate lesson of the maxim "It is easier to imagine the end of the world than the end of capitalism" is the importance of holding open the difference between capitalism and the world. When we are certain that the psychic formations that obtain in the present will also be those of the future, we close this rift. When we insist that our current psychic organizations chain us to capitalism, we repress this difference. When we know that libidinal production secures commodity chains, underwrites financial instruments, and commissions boundless drive, we collapse this chasm. There are worlds beyond capitalism, worlds of other desires, other drives, other antagonisms. They are not more satisfying, but they are more just. It is the task of psychoanalysis, in representing the contingency of the unconscious and the insuperability of social antagonism, to keep projecting the horizon of those worlds, and it is the original practical politics of psychoanalysis to ceaselessly design clinics and institutes, forms that provide the space and time for a new social link to arise.

Ordering Forms

Just as stagnatingly dangerous as psychologism is the absolutization of the dissent from formed relationality—institutions, standing formations, the state—into the messianic horizon of destituency that forestalls the constitution of new futures. Dean's positive, projective focus on the party as infrastructural form and Jameson's positive, projective utopianization of the military form directly combat the fantasy of ceaseless, immanentist hypostasized formlessness. The abstract and formalist character of this type of argument is precisely its strength. Existing forms of sociality do not exhaust all possible socialities; confronting the grave wrongs—violence, subjugation, racialization—perpetrated by hitherto existing state formations need not culminate in wholesale indictments of all possible formalizations. It can rather culminate in speculative constructions, the galvanized modeling of social spaces wrought of aestheticized materials, in a world that proffers no grounded archetypes. Exercises in theory, these are also the office of novels, which in their enormous, beautiful, abstract syntheses teach us not to rest too long with undoing the world, but to originate other buildings.

From Dean's and Jameson's fascinating willingness to regard form as technique, we can educe a new imagining of the political entailments of composition—of making arrangements and holding them in formation. Although the politics of forms has usually been reduced to the politics of containment or closure, this new imagining makes space to insist on the contrary that the politics of forms inhere in the ways forms emergently, integrally blend and then make sustenance and equality possible, and in turn in the way that aestheticizations therefore mediate principles of order, arrangement, interdependence, and distribution that structure human collectivities. Literary and artistic works exist in dialectical relation to their contexts of production, working with available materials but ontologically disposed to exceed what already exists. In their composed relationality, they mediate the making of social form.

As opposed to the methods inspired by anarcho-vitalism, formalist method attends to these integralities, mediations, and structurations, and to opportunities for alternative forms. Literary critics who spurn formalism for historicism consign their analyses to audits of what certain forms have done, rather than effectively projecting what forms in general can do. Humanists who offer only attacks on institutionality resign the prospect of building standing formations that sustain more just orders. Theorists who deify de-reification foreclose the construction of collective signifiers, collective ideas, collective infrastructures. An ability to vividly account for generalities often differentiates humanistic thought from more calculative paradigms, and abstractly appraising the potential agency of forms predicates any constructed justice. Particular significations do not exhaust the structuring power of the signifier. Social forms admit reform and new formalizations, but socially oriented theory can only notice this availability if it grants simultaneously the force of determinations (not everything is flow; causality exists) and the essentiality of forms (no freedom in formlessness). Formalized sociability—order, organization, institution, law, the state—extends support, benefits, and efficacy beyond those reifications and suppressions of particularities so often cited in antiformalist antinominanism. Formalist critics can deploy their intellectual expertise in the service of public goods by promoting that interpretation of order and sensitivity to ordering that can enable actors and collectives to valorize order and build better orders. Humanists who project these affordances of social form neither refuse political horizons for criticism nor conflate the practices of formal analysis with the acts of political organization, but rather stake out an organic resonance and common concern between the study of form and the construction of social space.

Literary critics, especially readers of novels, skillfully interpret blueprints for other social spaces. They can be ambassadors for architecture, advocates and strategists for building, for operationalizing off-page all the world-making of on-page models. The arts of social building exceed engineering, to encompass imaginative projection, enabling abstraction, compelling storytelling, and creative synthesis. Formalist method honors these arts as the ontology of literature; committed to this ontology, literary formalists can adroitly affirm sustained construction. Too often and for too long, dismantling has dominated literary critical protocols, but the terrain of our field should also host creation. Accentuating this intricacy of aesthetic and social form at once results in and requires a different political orientation than destituency. To confirm composed relationality opens the prospect of formalistically ratifying mere form, of embracing formedness rather than formlessness as political ideal. Political formalism gives a name to this orientation and its ensuing practice of constructive criticism, that study of relations as part of shaping them, that appreciation of the order of forms as prelude to better building.

Notes

Introduction

1. Paradigmatically, Rita Felski, *The Limits of Critique* (Chicago: University of Chicago Press, 2015), along with Stephen Best and Sharon Marcus, "Surface Reading: An Introduction," *Representations* 108, no. 1 (2009): 1–21.

2. Bruno Latour, *We Have Never Been Modern*, trans. Catherine Porter (Cambridge, MA: Harvard University Press, 1993), 113.

3. Giorgio Agamben, *The Use of Bodies*, trans. Adam Kotsko (Stanford: Stanford University Press, 2016), 263–67.

4. Walter Benjamin, "The Work of Art in the Age of Mechanical Reproduction," in *Illuminations*, ed. Hannah Arendt and trans. Harry Zohn (New York: Harcourt Brace, 2007), 217–51.

5. Jacques Rancière, *The Politics of Aesthetics* (London: Bloomsbury, 2006).

6. Caroline Levine, *Forms: Whole, Rhythm, Hierarchy, Network* (Princeton: Princeton University Press, 2017), 17. (emphasis original).

7. Levine, *Forms*, 3.

8. Levine, *Forms*, 47.

9. Levine, *Forms*, 150.

10. Ernst Bloch, "Building in Empty Spaces," in *The Utopian Function of Art and Literature: Selected Essays*, trans. Jack Zipes and Frank Mecklenberg (Cambridge, MA: MIT Press, 1989), 198.

11. Karl Marx and Friedrich Engels, *The German Ideology* (Amherst, NY: Prometheus Books, 1998), 57.

12. Karl Marx, *The Manifesto of the Communist Party*, https://www.marxists.org/archive/marx/works/1848/communist-manifesto/.

13. Readers who hear in "the order of forms" an echo of Levine's succinct claim that "it is the work of forms to make order" will correctly note that I place great emphasis upon this constitutive function of forms, and that I find her work enormously generative. For this very reason, I will state at the outset that I push for a more consistently Marxist approach to the aesthetics of politics, and that I consequently differ from Levine in three key respects. First, I accord to forms not only a widespread operativity from the skillet to the sonnet, sex to the socius, but also an *essence*—they are essential for human life, they pertain to the ontology of the human. This ontological dimension, no matter how unpopular in humanist inquiry, should be a serious component of a

robust formalism. Second, where for Levine the ubiquity of forms occasions the indispensability of formalism as "the recognition of the many different patterns and shapes that constitute political, cultural and social experience" (Levine, *Forms*, 17), there is no order among forms; Levine countenances no hierarchy in which some forms reveal, theorize, or mediate others. For Levine, aesthetic forms have no distinction from cultural or political forms; representation does not work to render phenomena thinkable but rather just comprises another instance of phenomena, and thus, something like the lived experience of a temporal pattern (catching a train on time) would be equivalent to the production of temporality in a historical novel in terms of their wholly comparable occasioning of critical reflection. Art, in other words, is not required to help us to think about experience, because experience itself already reveals its own formed-ness. Levine presents this nonprivileging of art as an eminently practical dispelling of the aura of autonomy that has attended the past formalisms she surpasses, and as a tenet of formalism's nondisciplinarity. But to my mind it forecloses the dimension of mediation that I argue is intrinsic to forms. As I asserted above, forms are composed relations that reveal their composition, their madeness. A tree, is not, therefore, a form (Sandra Macpherson argues otherwise). Among forms, some exhibit greater capacity for inciting formalist regard: a novel engaged with a phenomenon stands a better chance of provoking thought of the phenomenon's contingency and design than does the phenomenon itself. This is the privilege of art. Third, as part and parcel of my insistence on the faculty of mediation as a crucial dimension of form, I also maintain a commitment to the baseline Marxian concepts of mediation, determination, and causality—concepts that are all explicitly disregarded by the Latourian catholicism that compels Levine. Just as art is a privileged vehicle of mediation, it is also a privileged site of revealing the dialectic of determination, for it works with available materials and emerges in specific context, but it radically detaches itself from context, building something new. In every situation, there are limits to how much can be made new; tactics are of utmost importance, and purity cannot be the enemy of the strategic, but at a certain point a critical mass of tactics will confront the structural limits of the situation; reconfiguring a situation is radical and eventual, exceeding the pragmatic and the tactical.

14. Tom Bottomore provides the most comprehensive overview of this philosophical lineage in Bottomore et al., *A Dictionary of Marxist Thought* (Cambridge, MA: Harvard University Press, 1983), 373–75.

15. Raymond Williams, *Marxism and Literature* (Oxford: Oxford University Press, 1977), 97–98.

16. Foremost among them is Levine, seconded by Tom Eyers's *Speculative Formalism* (2017), and Susan Wolfson's edited volume *Reading for Form* along with her *Formal Charges.* George Levine's edited volume *Aesthetics and Ideology* (1994) also styles itself a reclamation. Curiously, most of the work that has given the impression of critical energies around this topic takes the shape of essays cataloging existent formalisms and the history of formalisms, rather than theorizing or even practicing formalist method. In this vein would be the much cited Marjorie Levinson piece "What Is New Formalism?," *PMLA* 122, no. 2 (2007): 558–69, along with Sandra Macpherson's "A Little Formalism," *ELH* 82, no. 2 (2015): 385–405, and Jonathan Kramnick and Anahid Nersessian's "Form and Explanation," *Critical Inquiry* 43, no. 3 (2017): 650–69.

17. The very most contemporary mathematical debates do involve the ability to resuture signs to things.

18. Andrea Henderson, "Math for Math's Sake: Non-Euclidean Geometry, Aestheticism, and *Flatland*," *PMLA* 124, no. 2 (2009): 455–71; and Henderson, "Symbolic Logic and the Logic of Symbolism," *Critical Inquiry* 41, no. 1 (2014): 78–101.

19. Morris Kline, *Mathematics for the Nonmathematician* (New York: Dover, 1985), 577.

20. Clarence Irving Lewis, *A Survey of Symbolic Logic* (Berkeley: University of California Press, 1918), 335.

21. Cited in Jeremy Gray's *Plato's Ghost: The Modernist Transformation of Mathematics* (Princeton: Princeton University Press, 2008), 223.

22. Catarina Dutilh Novaes, *Formal Languages in Logic: A Philosophical and Cognitive Analysis* (Cambridge: Cambridge University Press, 2014), 13.

23. Jacques Lacan, *Écrits: The First Complete Edition in English*, trans. Bruce Fink (New York: W.W. Norton, 2006), 147.

24. One good overview is provided by Michael Detlefsen's "Formalism," in *The Oxford Handbook of Philosophy of Mathematics and Logic*, ed. Steward Shapiro (Oxford: Oxford University Press, 2007), 236–317.

25. Existing work on math and literature almost exclusively follows this tack. This approach I reject out of hand as ceding too much to the positivist factish episteme. Fact: a mathematician lived. Fact: a poet studied his work. Finding: there are references to the mathematician in the poet's poems.

Probability is the most common topic taken up, especially in studies of the eighteenth-century novel and the evolution of plot. Recently emphasis has turned toward number, demography, and statistics, often blending Foucauldian analysis with digital humanities (https://www.rc.umd.edu/praxis/numbers or Audrey Jaffe, *Affective Life of the Average Man* [2010]). Occasional essays recognize that certain very special literary objects, such as Lewis Carroll's works or the Oulipo group, would seem to demand recognition of mathematics, and even formal mathematics (when it comes to Oulipo's notions of constraints upon which to scaffold a literary world). And modernism has an entire subfield devoted to logic and literature, where logic is sometimes taken as formal mathematics. See, for instance, Ann Banfield's *The Phantom Table* (2007).

26. This dialectic of the model is, I think, kin to the enterprise Fredric Jameson has famously deemed "cognitive mapping"—though only if we consider his actual presentation of the notion rather than the way it has been taken up. For Jameson a cognitive map is art that "instructs . . . about the true economic and social forms of existence" but does not yet exist in any known art form and can only be understood if we "dismiss all figures of maps and mapping from your mind and try to imagine something else." Fredric Jameson, *Postmodernism, or, the Cultural Logic of Late Capitalism* (Durham: Duke University Press, 1992), 409. A cognitive map is a map that isn't a map, a map that helps us to learn about "true" forms, where "true" must signify, with paradoxical equivocity, the accuracy of what is and the adequacy of what could be. Jameson has consistently been taken to be calling for referential, didactic art, for documentary and cartography that depict current conditions, for art that minimizes its mediating function. While such misperceptions have therefore been generative for a wide variety of critics in a wide variety of fields, this has reduced Jameson's innovation to merely another example of the long-standing debates in Marxist aesthetic theory over art's referential capacities. Rather than reproduce these polarities (art should be allegorical/art should be referential), Jameson has actually devoted his career to sublating this opposition, in ways quite different from, say, Paul de Man. And he has suggested, in his work on spatiality that follows the call for cognitive mapping—especially his work on utopias—that cognitive mapping must be a dynamic, two-pronged operation, fully synonymous with "critique"—assessment of social relations in the utopian pursuit of those relations' potential. To my mind, "model" as a term has the advantage of dispelling some of these pervasive literalisms of "map."

27. Alain Badiou, *The Concept of Model: An Introduction to the Materialist Epistemology of Mathematics*, trans. Zachary Luke Fraser and Tzuchien Tho (Melbourne: re-press, 2007).

28. Jean Baudrillard, "Simulacra and Simulations," in *Selected Writings*, ed. Mark Poster (Stanford: Stanford University Press, 1988), 166.

29. On the Victorian fascinations with phantasmagoria, Isobel Armstrong, *Victorian Glassworlds: Glass Culture and the Imagination, 1830–1880* (Oxford: Oxford University Press, 2008), 256–67. A book about forms of political configuration in the Victorian era as they may speak to the limits of the thought thereof in our own must of necessity engage with the political form that links that past to our present: empire. I consider empire one of several overlapping constitutive logics and practices of the political in the Victorian era (alongside financial capitalism, liberalism, and secularism). However, in keeping with my insistence on the faculty of art to exceed the determinations of its conditions of production, I maintain that the novels of the period are capable of critically projecting socialities that repudiate imperial violence, imperial resource extraction, and imperial dichotomies of metropole/colony, self/other, governing/governed. More pressingly, my study is aimed at how novels deliberate and conjure the fundamental unit of the socius—the minimal bonds and infrastructures of social relationality necessary for human existence—and is *not* therefore aimed at empire, which I take to be a wholly maximal distortion of connectivity for the sake of violently racialized value accumulation. I consider works that theorize and perform the hearth, shelter, the family, and the law, and do so in active conjunction with mathematical tropes, redoubling their interest in elementality. Empire has often been understood as a cultural rubric atop or even prior to its economic framework. But in keeping with the Marxian methods this book practices, I approach empire as an essentially economic force, taking heart from recent work by Nathan Hensley, Nasser Mufti, and Zarena Aslami. The elementary structures of sociality that my book considers include the most fundamental possible assignations of norms and forms for making life, which are of course economic questions of the provision of materials and support for existence. When my arguments grapple with what are fundamental to such relations and what are epiphenomenal contingencies, I consider that such questions are questions about empire, even if they do not take the more recognizable shape of questions about cultural bias and racialization. Similarly, I consider that novels not readily considered "about" social problems nor readily in the mode of realism nonetheless figuratively engage with the questions of sociality at issue there. If *Wuthering Heights* seems improbably far and hermetically domestically sealed from the depictions of colonies we expect in imperial fiction, I will nevertheless show how its theorization of the antagonisms inherent in any possible economic relation critically mediate imperial power. For a helpful critique of "aboutness" in political criticism, see Hensley, *Forms of Empire* (2017).

30. Clifford Geertz, "Religion as a Cultural System," in *The Interpretation of Cultures: Selected Essays* (New York: Basic Books, 1973), 87–125; cited in Willard McCarty, "Modeling: A Study in Words and Meanings," in *A Companion to Digital Humanities*, ed. Susan Schreibman, Ray Siemens, and John Unsworth (Oxford: Blackwell, 2004), http://www.digitalhumanities.org/companion/.

31. Henri Lefebvre, *The Production of Space*, trans. Donald Nicholson-Smith (Malden, MA: Wiley-Blackwell, 1992), 27.

32. Lefebvre, *The Production of Space*, 11.

33. Lefebvre, *The Production of Space*, 12.

34. Lefebvre, *The Production of Space*, 85.

35. Lefebvre, *The Production of Space*, 33.

36. Lefebvre, *The Production of Space*, 42.

37. Lefebvre, *The Production of Space*, 83.

38. Lefebvre, *The Production of Space*, 86.

39. See John Crowe Ransom, "The Concrete Universal," *Kenyon Review* 16, no. 4 (1954): 554–64. In *Literature and Revolution*, ed. William Keach (Chicago: Haymarket Books, 2005), Leon Trotsky argued that the Russian formalists were too much in the sway of Kant; see Ewa Thompson, *Russian Formalism and Anglo-American New Criticism: A Comparative Study* (Berlin: De Gruyter Mouton, 1971). This nonbridge is also evinced in Gerald Graff's definitive history of literary criticism, *Professing Literature* (1987). Anne H. Stevens's *Literary Theory and Criticism* (2015) also offers a good schematic of the differences.

40. Jonathan Culler, "The Most Interesting Thing in the World," *diacritics* 38, nos. 1–2 (2008): 14.

41. Contemporary Shklovskyites in this vein would include Michael Clune, *Writing against Time* (2013), Elissa Marder, *Dead Time* (2002), and Martin Hägglund, *Dying for Time* (2012).

42. Victor Shklovsky, "Art as Device," *Poetics Today* 36, no. 3 (2015): 162.

43. Victor Shklovsky, *Theory of Prose* (Elmwood Park, IL: Dalkey Archive Press, 1990), 62.

44. Shklovsky, "Art as Device," 161.

45. Alan Bishop, "Western Mathematics: The Secret Weapon of Cultural Imperialism," in *The Postcolonial Studies Reader*, ed. Bill Ashcroft, Gareth Griffiths, and Helen Tiffin, 2nd ed. (New York: Routledge, 2006), 71–76.

46. Robert Kaufman, Review of *Formal Charges: The Shaping of Poetry in British Romanticism*, by Susan J. Wolfson, Romantic Circles, 15 January 2001, https://www.rc.umd.edu/reviews-blog/susan-j-wolfson-formal-charges-shaping-poetry-british-romanticism (emphasis mine).

47. Sianne Ngai, *Our Aesthetic Categories: Zany, Cute, Interesting* (Cambridge, MA: Harvard University Press, 2012), 44.

48. From the avant-garde of twenty-first century studies, like Alison Shonkwiler and Leigh Claire La Berge, who argue that "realism expresses a desire for the most thorough possible indexing of capitalism," to theorists of the postmodern, like Catherine Belsey and Linda Hutcheon, who declaim the referential naivete and ideological "intelligibility" of the bygone era, and even to renowned scholars of the nineteenth century, like Edward Said, Patrick Brantlinger, and Catherine Gallagher, who present novels as univocal references to dominant values, "always connected to the stuff of the real," prevailing conceptions of realism cohere around this conviction that it is first and foremost the indexical reiteration of the extant world. Alison Shonkwiler and Leigh Claire La Berge, eds., *Reading Capitalist Realism* (Iowa City: University of Iowa Press, 2014), 8; Catherine Gallagher, "George Eliot, Immanent Victorian," *Representations* 90, no. 1 (2005): 63.

49. In this respect, it is no accident that Franco Moretti, prince of digital humanities and distant reading, is rightly a scholar of literary realism: the illusion that realism refers necessarily begets the delusion that it is counting, and not reading, which will yield "better" knowledge of the world of the novel.

50. Eric Hayot's admirably ambitious theorizing in *On Literary Worlds* (2012) in prioritizing world-making as literary ontology is a companion piece here. Creatively arguing that "world" be expanded from its usual notions in literary studies as "a marker of scale" (40), Hayot sketches a notion of world as "the unity of form, diegesis, and feeling composed by the rough totality of a work" (42); "aesthetic worldedness is the form of the relation a work establishes between the world inside the work and the world outside the work" (45). Hayot does not refer to his method

as formalist, though he does at one point call it structuralist (165), and his book is admittedly schematic, so it remains somewhat to be seen whether his reading methods effectuate what I hope mine will, but I appreciate immensely his speculative spirit and effort to reorient literary studies wholesale. In the course of redefining literature as world-making, Hayot, a modernist, has occasion to implicitly challenge conventional distinctions between modernism and realism, by deeming realism less a stage in literary history and more a transhistorical "mode" identifiable primarily by its elevation of the "empirical" and its attitude of "world affirming" (124). Within his schema, this distinction of realism is relative to the world outside the work, to its context—realism affirms whence it comes.

51. Marx and Engels, *The German Ideology*, 37.

52. Marx and Engels, *The German Ideology*, 37.

53. Marx and Engels, *The German Ideology*, 37.

54. Marx and Engels, "Introduction to the Critique of Political Economy," in *The German Ideology*, 2.

55. Marx and Engels, *The German Ideology*, 37 (translation modified: *Geschictsschreibung*).

56. Marx and Engels, *The German Ideology*, 42.

57. W. J. T. Mitchell, *Iconology: Image, Text, Ideology* (Chicago: University of Chicago Press, 1986), 173.

58. Louis Althusser, "Ideology and Ideological State Apparatuses," in *On the Reproduction of Capitalism* (New York: Verso, 2014), 254 (emphasis original).

59. For his explanations of his early prioritization of nature, see William Henry Fox Talbot, "Some Account of the Art of Photogenic Drawing," in *London and Edinburgh Philosophical Magazine and Journal of Science* 14 (March 1839), reprinted in *Photography into Print*, ed. Vicki Goldberg (New York: Simon and Schuster, 1981), 36–48.

60. This conception of space as fundamentally political is adjacent to the notion of social space developed by Henri Lefebvre and Kristin Ross, a notion in which space is not the ground atop which society is built, but rather the very medium of society. But I also mean it in the more strictly political sense that I develop below.

61. Roland Barthes, *Camera Lucida: Reflections on Photography*, trans. Richard Howard (New York: Hill and Wang, 1982).

62. For more discussion of this point, see Cervin Robinson and Joel Herschman, *Architecture Transformed: A History of the Photography of Buildings from 1839 to the Present* (Cambridge, MA: MIT Press/Architectural League of New York, 1987); Robert Elwall, *Building with Light: An International History of Architectural Photography* (New York: Merrell Publishers, 2004).

63. William Henry Fox Talbot to William Jerdan, 30 January 1839, *Literary Gazette and Journal of Belles Lettres, Science, and Art*, 2 February 1839, 73, http://foxtalbot.dmu.ac.uk/letters/ftbh.php?docnum=03782.

64. G. W. F. Hegel, *Hegel's Aesthetics: Lectures on Fine Art*, vol. 1, trans. T. M. Knox (repr., Oxford: Oxford University Press, 1998).

65. Both Andrea Henderson and Irene Tucker have commented upon this theory of writing.

66. Marx and Engels, *The German Ideology*, 37.

67. Marx and Engels, *The German Ideology*, 37. Raymond Williams's meditations on language in *Marxism and Literature* develop these tendencies: "Language is in fact a special kind of material practice: that of human sociality" (165).

68. Marx and Engels, *The German Ideology*, 49.

69. Michel Foucault, *The Order of Things: An Archaeology of the Human Sciences* (New York: Vintage Books, 1973), 299.

70. In *Read My Desire: Lacan against the Historicists* (Cambridge, MA: MIT Press, 1994), Joan Copjec formidably frames this immanentization as "the reduction of society to its indwelling network of relations" (6).

71. Timothy Brennan's *Wars of Position* (2006), Alex Woloch's *Or Orwell* (2016), Joseph North's *Literary Criticism* (2017), Amanda Anderson's *The Way We Argue Now* (2006), and Tracy McNulty's *Wrestling with the Angel* (2014) have all been inspirational to me in their accounting of this hegemony from various perspectives.

72. Hannah Arendt, *The Human Condition* (Chicago: University of Chicago Press, 1998).

73. Michel Foucault, *The History of Sexuality*, vol. 1 (New York: Pantheon Books, 1986), 143.

74. Jacques Derrida, *The Beast and the Sovereign*, vol. 1 (Chicago: University of Chicago Press, 2009), 349. I was fortunate to take these seminars as a student at UC Irvine.

75. Karl Marx, *A Contribution to the Critique of Political Economy* (New York: International Publications, 1979), 189.

76. One could also find resources for this position in the work of scholars of the nineteenth century like Bruce Robbins and Amanda Anderson, who counter Foucault's paradigm-defining view of institutions and the state. See especially Robbins's *Upward Mobility and the Common Good* (2007), and Anderson's *Bleak Liberalism* (2016).

77. This interventionist approach to the humanities is one guise of what the V21 Collective deems "strategic presentism"—engaging the past so as to engage the present—where engagement means more than accumulating knowledge or edifying the knower; where engagement signifies activating frameworks, concepts, and insights from the past to produce new ways of intervening in the present. Strategic presentism is an approach to making arguments—arguments with consequences; arguments about how things in the present (whether ways of thinking or ways or ordering socialities) should be different; arguments about how past formulations can reform the present. The argumentative ethos invests in *critique*, the investigation of social relations, including epistemic relations, for the purpose of opening onto new relations. Presentism beholds the proper history of the Victorian period, when the capitalist exploitation, anthropogenic climate change, financial speculation, dramatic income inequality, criminalization of debt, institutional misogyny, and imperial war that overdetermine twenty-first-century experience were first actualized. Strategic presentism also draws on the historically specific fact that the project of critique is a nineteenth-century project, and that many of the most noted Victorian thinkers themselves practiced a presentist historiography. Friedrich Nietzsche, Karl Marx, and Sigmund Freud, the three thinkers commonly associated with the origins of critique as a social enterprise elaborating the epistemological enterprise of Immanuel Kant, each came of age in nineteenth-century contexts, and each avowed profound inspiration by Victorian intellectual milieus. Novelists like Charles Dickens, George Eliot, George Gissing, William Thackeray, and Anthony Trollope frequently and systematically employed the present tense to produce connections between their literary worlds and their extant worlds, and wrote eloquently about their transitions from journalistic to novelistic careers as motivated by strong social reformist ambitions. Essayists like Matthew Arnold, Thomas Carlyle, William Morris, and John Ruskin all addressed works, practices, and ideas from past moments (ancient Greece, medieval England, Gothic Europe) for the explicit purpose of criticizing conditions of labor, achievements of art, and quality of life in their presents. For more discussion of presentism as Victorian historicity and as critical tool for Victorian studies, see V21 Collective, "Forum on Strategic Presentism," *Victorian Studies* 59, no. 1 (2016): 87–116.

Chapter One

1. Previous critics have of course noted James's interest in architecture, but they have often been rather literally focused on where James lived, how he shared his companion Edith Wharton's commitment to interior design, and how he depicted the cities he visited while writing. When less referential, as in the work of Ellen Frank, the argument is made that architectural imagery portends the mental constructions and spaces of consciousness that we are to take as James's true subject—the opaque facades and inaccessible interiors of the psychological other. I will be taking James as rather more deliberately social than this. Closest to my interests here is Mark McGurl's *The Novel Art* (2001), which, in the course of attending to the class politics of James's distinction of the novel as fine art, remarks the ways that *The Princess Cassamassima*, the most overtly political of James's works, employs a few key architectural analogies in characterization and in crafting the social hierarchies in the text (82). McGurl's readings emphasize that these spatial formations are instruments of social distinction: James crafts multidimensional social space to put a finer point upon the stratifications that back his elevation of the novel from mass good to high art. I want to follow this suggestion that James engages in a specifically spatial thinking of the social, and that his doing so is intricately bound up with his metaliterary projects, to see not only what rarifications of the novel are consequent, but also what general theory of the realist novel in particular might dwell in those social volumes.

2. Henry James, *Literary Criticism: French Writers, Other European Writer, the Prefaces to the New York Edition* (New York: Library of America, 1984), 1130 (emphasis original).

3. Henry James, *The Art of Fiction and Other Essays*, ed. Morris Roberts (New York: Oxford University Press, 1948, 324–38.

4. Dorothy Hale, *Social Formalism: The Novel in Theory from Henry James to the Present* (Palo Alto: Stanford University Press, 1998), 25.

5. David Kurnick, *Empty Houses: Theatrical Failure and the Novel* (Princeton: Princeton University Press, 2012), 113.

6. Sharon Cameron, *Thinking in Henry James* (Chicago: University of Chicago Press, 1989), 174.

7. Seymour Chatman, *Later Style of Henry James* (Oxford: Blackwell Publishers, 1972), 27.

8. Henry James, *The Portrait of a Lady* (New York: Penguin, 2011), 606.

9. Henry James, *The Wings of the Dove* (New York: Penguin, 2008), 345.

10. Henry James, *The Golden Bowl* (New York: Penguin, 2009), 327–28.

11. James, *Literary Criticism*, 1075.

12. James, *Literary Criticism*, 1170.

13. James, *Literary Criticism*, 1080; see also 1094–95: "Proper fusion . . . resides in some such measure of these things as may consort with the fine measure of other things too."

14. James, *Literary Criticism*, 1135.

15. James, *Literary Criticism*, 1041.

16. James, *Literary Criticism*, 1327.

17. The environs of *Roderick Hudson*, for instance, rank "a peaceful, rural New England community *quelconque*—It was not, it was under no necessity of being, Northampton Mass" (James, *Literary Criticism*, 1044). London in all its riches must nonetheless be enhanced imaginatively: "We use our material up, we use up even the thick tribute of the London streets—if perception and attention but sufficiently light our steps" (1086). More generally, James recommends, with erotic tinge, making imaginative forays in place of literal visits: "I recall pulling no

wires, knocking at no closed doors, applying for no 'authentic' information . . . to haunt the great city and by this habit to penetrate it, imaginatively, in as many places as possible—*that* was to be informed, *that* was to pull wires, *that* was to open doors, *that* positively was to groan at times under the weight of one's accumulations" (1101). See also 1328: "of the mind, of the author's projected world, in which objects are primarily related to each other, and therefore not 'taken from' a particular establishment anywhere."

18. Richard Blackmur, introduction to Henry James, *The Art of the Novel* (Chicago: University of Chicago Press, 2011), xxxviii.

19. Peter Brooks takes a decidedly nonspatial turn in arguing that the later connotation of "a secret plan to accomplish a hostile or illegal purpose" "nearly always attaches itself to the others: the organizing line of plot is more often or not some scheme or machination, a concerted plan for the accomplishment of some purpose" and that, therefore, "plots are not simply organizing structures, they are also intentional structures" (*Reading for the Plot: Design and Intention in Narrative* [Cambridge, MA: Harvard University Press, 1992], 12). His study of desire in narrative is magisterial, but this intentionalist strain rather subsumes the spatial qualities of narrative to the temporal.

20. Michel de Certeau, *The Practice of Everyday Life* (Berkeley: University of California Press, 1988), 115.

21. Mikhail Bakhtin, *The Dialogic Imagination* (Austin: University of Texas Press, 1981), 84.

22. Morson and Emerson comment on this mathematical origin as well. See Gary Morson and Caryl Emerson, *Mikhail Bakhtin: Creation of a Prosaics* (Stanford: Stanford University Press, 1990), 368.

23. The essay is even called "Forms of Time and Chronotope in the Novel," and he asserts: "In literature the primary category in the chronotope is time,"; Bakhtin, *The Dialogic Imagination.*

24. Joseph Frank, "Spatial Form in Modern Literature," *Sewanee Review* 53 (1945): 225.

25. Even more recently, Rosa Mucignat has argued for the importance of space to realism, focusing on the affinities of realist procedure with the evolving nineteenth-century science of archaeology; realism for her is a primarily "visual" "recognition of . . . complexity, the mutual influence of the different and coexisting levels of reality, which produces an image of space that is stratigraphic as well as topographic" (*Realism and Space in the Novel, 1795–1869: Imagined Geographies* [New York: Routledge, 2016], 21–22). Mucignat explicitly opposes this archaeology to what she calls the "homogeneous space of mathematics." In underscoring the infinitization of space in mathematics, I want to emphasize how untethered realism's spatial productions are from any referent, even one requiring archaeological excavation to index.

26. Alex Woloch, *The One vs. the Many: Minor Characters and the Space of the Protagonist in the Novel* (Princeton: Princeton University Press, 2003), 13.

27. Woloch, *The One vs. the Many*, 14.

28. Roman Jakobson, "Two Types of Aphasic Disturbances," in Roman Jakobson and Moris Halle, *Fundamentals of Language* (The Hague: Mouton, 1956).

29. Jonathan Culler, *Structuralist Poetics: Structuralism, Linguistics, and the Study of Literature* (1975; New York: Routledge, 2002), 201.

30. Audrey Jaffe, *Vanishing Points: Dickens, Narrative, and the Subject of Omniscience* (Berkeley: University of California Press, 1991), n.p. (digital version).

31. Catherine Gallagher, "Formalism and Time," *Modern Language Quarterly* 61, no. 1 (2000): 229–51.

32. Lefebvre, *The Production of Space*, 15.

33. See Hegel, "Architecture," in *Hegel's Aesthetics*, 1:630–700.

34. Jacques Derrida, "Architecture: Where the Desire May Live," in *Rethinking Architecture: A Reader in Cultural Theory*, ed. Neil Leach (London: Routledge, 1997), 303. See also Jacques Derrida, *Chora L Works: Jacques Derrida and Peter Eisenman*, ed. Jeffrey Kipnis and Thomas Leeser (New York: Monacelli Press, 1997), 8: "All other arts have a telos of representation, but architecture seems not to depend on it."

35. Gérard Genette, "La literatur et l'espace," in *Figures 2* (Paris: Seuil, 1969), 43–44 (translation mine).

36. See Bernard Tschumi, *Architecture and Disjunction* (Cambridge, MA: MIT Press, 1994), 207–15.

37. Fredric Jameson, "Architecture and the Critique of Ideology," in *Architecture, Criticism, and Ideology*, ed. Joan Ockmanm (Princeton: Princeton Architectural Press, 1985), 53.

38. Jameson, "Architecture and the Critique of Ideology," 71.

39. Foucault launches his theory of carcerality from the decks of Bentham's panopticon, the architectural tower at the center of modern prison design. Michel Foucault, *Discipline and Punish, The Birth of the Prison*, trans. Alan Sheridan (1975; New York: Vintage Books, 1995).

40. Henri Lefebvre, *Toward an Architecture of Enjoyment*, ed. Lukasz Stanek and trans. Robert Bononno (Minneapolis: University of Minnesota Press, 2014), 147–48.

41. Regarding this essentially architectural quality of utopia, it is interesting to note the historical fact that Renaissance architectural utopias precede the literary crystallization by Thomas More in 1516.

42. Patrick Brantlinger, *Fictions of State: Culture and Credit in Britain, 1694–1994* (Ithaca: Cornell University Press, 1996), 146.

43. James, *Literary Criticism*, 1041.

44. In "Victorian Realism," in *The Cambridge Companion to the Victorian Novel*, ed. Deirdre David, 2nd ed. (Cambridge: Cambridge University Press, 2012), Caroline Levine writes, "Amanda Claybaugh has recently argued that realism is best understood as a 'syndrome,' a motley assortment of characteristics—'such as contemporaneous subject matter, events and characters understood as types, and a thick description of the social world'—that developed independently but were imitated so often that eventually they came together to create a recognizable kind of novel" (85). Levine cites from Claybaugh's *The Novel of Purpose: Literature and Social Reform in the Anglo-American World* (Ithaca: Cornell University Press, 2007). See also Fredric Jameson, *The Antinomies of Realism* (New York, Verso, 2013).

45. Take, for instance, one of the most prominently lauded products of the Stanford Literary Lab, Pamphlet #4, "A Quantitative Literary History of 2,958 Nineteenth-Century British Novels: The Semantic Cohort Method," May 2012, by Ryan Heuser and Long Le-Khac, which set out to evaluate two transformations in the novel: "a systematic concretization in language and fundamental change in the social spaces of the novel" (2)—transformations seminally identified by Raymond Williams. In the study, Heuser and Le-Khac outpace prior quantitative studies in striving "to move beyond investigating single words or small groups of words to a more systemic investigation of linguistic changes" (4). If the enabling principle of word frequency studies is that individual words in literary texts can be assigned an unmistakable referential function, Heuser and Le-Khac acknowledge some limitations of this principle: "Given the semantic richness of language and the diffuseness of cultural trends, it's unlikely that such trends could be isolated by tracking the behavior of a few words" (4), yet their excision of the limit is not to temper quantification with uncountable richness, but to scale up the units of their counting so as

to register "semantic cohorts" (groups of words used synonymously or contiguously with some consistency through history), and thus "isolate linguistic objects large enough to approach the scale of cultural change" (10), to prove with "quantitative evidence" what generations of readers of Williams have already known, that there were "pervasive and fundamental transformations in the language of the British novel over a crucial period of its development, 1785–1900." In finding that "abstractions related to "social normativity" significantly declined over the period, while "hard" words related to materials and the body significantly increased, Heuser and Le-Khac conclude that "social space" in the novel is broadening while "social restraint" is lessening (novels become more urban and adventurous, less provincial), and that there is "a dissolution of stable social schema organizing relations as social spaces become wider and more complex" (44). The entirety of the contrast of abstract nouns and concrete verbs, "telling and showing" is taken here as referential index of lessening social stability, but at the precise moment in history, it must be said, that the novel has long been said to be most involved in stabilization and restraint at a grander scale: empire. Because the quantitative, even when the counted is a cohort rather than an individual word, correlates word to meaning, rich meanings that attach more figuratively to language—such as the concrete pragmatics of empire, the ideological contrast of British rationality and Indian unruliness, the universalization of particular abstractions as concrete facts—these uncountables go completely overlooked. An iterative notion of language—hard, descriptive words signify less moralizing, a more open social field—applied to hundreds of titles of hundreds of pages of noniterative language cements the concept that literary language is referential and that we can know something by amassing its references.

46. The protocols of new historicism pay lip service to rhetoric in social life, but effectively subtract rhetoric from literature by equating literary language with social discourse. A novel or poem holds the same fascination as a political pamphlet, conduct manual, or mercantile ledger, and is to be explained as continuous with those other types and genres of discourse, emanating from the same cause. As Gallagher and Greenblatt put it in their manual for the practice, "The mutual embeddedness of art and history underlies our fascination with the possibility of treating all of the written and visual traces of a particular culture as a mutually intelligible network of signs"; Catherine Gallagher and Stephen Greenblatt, *Practicing New Historicism* (Chicago: University of Chicago Press, 2000), 7. It is this mutual intelligibility that I am calling reductive. If you want to understand what the vacuum in church leadership hierarchy means in an Anthony Trollope novel, you should turn to the explanatory acreage of the news archive and organizational records of the Church of England. Trollope couldn't possibly be theorizing "churchness" as institutional form, meditating on vacuums and hierarchies and the relations and stories they engender, querying the infrastructures for bridging the immanent and the transcendent—he could only be documenting a precedent reality. His language is taken to be indexical, iterative, referential, and the referent is taken to be a putatively real ground. Readers of Trollope read to accumulate information about "the Victorians"; critics of Trollope read to broker this accumulation. Literariness—the agency of displacement, condensation, distortion, figuration, defiguration, formalization—is nowhere at issue, and the job of the critic is to confirm, in scientific fashion, that context determines text.

47. Ian Watt, *The Rise of the Novel: Studies in Defoe, Richardson, and Fielding* (Berkeley: University of California Press, 2001), 18.

48. Watt, *The Rise of the Novel*, 26.

49. Watt, *The Rise of the Novel*, 29.

50. Watt, *The Rise of the Novel*, 13.

51. Erich Auerbach, *Mimesis: The Representation of Reality in Western Thought* (Princeton: Princeton University Press, 2003), 22.

52. René Wellek, "The Concept of Realism in Literary Scholarship," *Neophilologus* 45, no. 1 (1961): 10.

53. Wellek, "The Concept of Realism," 17.

54. Wellek, "The Concept of Realism," 17.

55. George Levine, *The Realistic Imagination: English Fiction from Frankenstein to Lady Chatterley* (Chicago: University of Chicago Press, 1981), 6.

56. Paul de Man writes intermittently on the novel (most notably his section on Proust in "Semiology and Rhetoric") and novel theory; see also his essay "Georg Lukács' *The Theory of the Novel*," in *Blindness and Insight* (Minneapolis: University of Minnesota Press, 1983), 51–59. Derrida's engagement with "realism" often aligns itself with a discussion of philosophical empiricism—see Jacques Derrida, *Positions*, trans. Alan Bass (Chicago: University of Chicago Press, 1982), 64–65; Derrida, *Dissemination*, trans. Barbara Johnson (Chicago: University of Chicago Press, 1983), 25. In addition to Hillis Miller, perhaps the most engaged thinker of deconstruction and the novel is Barbara Johnson; see especially "My Monster/My Self," in *A World of Difference* (Baltimore: Johns Hopkins University Press, 1989), 144–54.

57. J. Hillis Miller, *Ariadne's Thread: Story Lines* (New Haven: Yale University Press, 1995), 102.

58. Friedrich Engels, "Letter: Engels to Margaret Harkness in London," April 1888, https://www.marxists.org/archive/marx/works/1888/letters/88_04_15.htm.

59. Fredric Jameson, *Ideologies of Theory* (1988; New York: Verso, 2009), 26.

60. Jameson, *The Antinomies of Realism*, 5.

61. Georg Lukács, *The Theory of the Novel*, trans. Anna Bostock (Cambridge, MA: MIT Press, 1971), 38.

62. Lukács, *The Theory of the Novel*, 67.

63. Lukács, *The Theory of the Novel*, 76.

64. Lukács, *The Theory of the Novel*, 71.

65. Georg Lukács, "Marx and Engels on Aesthetics," in *Writer and Critic, and Other Essays*, trans. Arthur Kahn (Lincoln: iUniverse, 2005), 78.

66. Lukács, *Writer and Critic*, 17.

67. Lukács, *Writer and Critic*, 19.

68. Lukács, *Writer and Critic*, 19.

69. Lukács, *Writer and Critic*, 20.

70. Lukács, *Writer and Critic*, 37.

71. Lukács, *Writer and Critic*, 46.

72. Jameson, *The Antinomies of Realism*, 215.

73. Fredric Jameson, *The Political Unconscious: Narrative as a Socially Symbolic Act* (Ithaca: Cornell University Press, 1981), 104.

74. Jameson, *The Political Unconscious*, 104.

75. Jameson, *The Political Unconscious*, 152.

76. Jameson, *The Political Unconscious*, 151.

77. Fredric Jameson, "Postmodernism, or the Cultural Logic of Late Capitalism," *New Left Review* 146 (1984): 71.

78. Jameson, "Postmodernism," 84.

79. Jameson, "Postmodernism," 88.

80. Jameson, "Postmodernism," 89.

81. Jameson, "Postmodernism," 89; see also 91–92.

82. See, notably, Alberto Toscano and Jeff Kinkle, *Cartographies of the Absolute* (London: Zero Books, 2015); but also, exemplarily, Ian Baucom, "Hydrographies," *Geographical Review* 89, no. 2 (1999): 307; Patrick Jagoda, "I Wired," *Critical Inquiry* 38, no. 1 (2011): 193; Bill Brown, "The Dark Wood of Postmodernity (Space, Faith, Allegory)," *PMLA* 120, no. 3 (2005): 737; and even, disappointingly, Phillip Wegner, "Things as They Were or Are: On Russell Banks's Global Realisms," in *Reading Capitalist Realism*, ed. Alison Shonkwiler and Leigh Claire La Berge (Iowa City: University of Iowa Press, 2014), 94.

83. Jameson, "Postmodernism," 90.

84. In *The Geopolitical Aesthetic: Cinema and Space in the World System* (Bloomington: Indiana University Press, 1995), Jameson zoomed in on film's propensities to "think a system so vast that it cannot be encompassed by the natural and historically developed categories of perception with which human beings normally orient themselves" (2). These propensities derive not only from film's obvious emphasis on the visual, but also its tendency toward self-consciousness about mediation and medium history, its collective conditions of production, and, most importantly, the inherently *spatial* quality of film—its reliance on the pro-filmic event, its projection of exteriority, its integral set-design. Where the question is how to think space—the integrated world system of global capitalism—cinema is thus a uniquely useful medium, a use-value intensified in those particular films expressly committed to the project of "trying to figure out where we are and what landscapes and forces confront us in a late twentieth century whose abominations are heightened by their concealment and their bureaucratic impersonality" (3). The hyperspatial aesthetic of such films—shots and plots galvanized by space, setting, landscape, transportation, telecommunication—is demonstrably prevalent in the 1970s, after the end of Bretton Woods and the beginning of neoliberal crisis, and signals for Jameson a desire for fortifying the orienting categories of perception strained by systematized world-history, "a desire called cognitive mapping" (3).

85. Jameson, *Postmodernism*, 112. We could add, so many years on, that Gehry's signature aesthetics of liminality—his career trajectory toward making the wrapping of a building evermore fluidly sculptural—delves into the depths of surface, probing brave new dimension.

86. Jameson, *Postmodernism*, 162.

87. Fredric Jameson, *The Seeds of Time* (New York: Columbia University Press, 1996), 136–37 (emphasis original).

88. Fredric Jameson and Michael Speaks, "Envelopes and Enclaves: The Space of Post-Civil Society (An Architectural Conversation)," *Assemblage* 17 (1992): 337.

89. Jameson, *Postmodernism*, 51.

90. Fredric Jameson, *Archaeologies of the Future: The Desire Called Utopia and Other Science Fictions* (New York: Verso, 2007), 5.

91. Jameson, *The Antinomies of Realism*, 5. His only direct treatment of realism and utopia symptomatically concerns not literature but television, and, even more symptomatically, content and not form. The instances of utopianism he identifies in David Simon's *The Wire* pertain to plot points and characterological idiosyncracies—to creativity and collectivity, craftsmanship and agency—whereas the form of the thing—its multiplotted, multifocal, integrative, network, its figurations of interdependence and causation, its structures of parallelism and concentricity, lieutenancy and repetition, and its scaling of totalization and mapping—seems to me a far more striking utopian site.

92. Fredric Jameson, "Utopia as Replication," in *Valences of the Dialectic* (New York: Verso, 2010), 410–34.

93. Lukács, *The Theory of the Novel*, 67.

94. Lukács, *The Theory of the Novel*, 76.

95. Lukács, *The Theory of the Novel*, 38.

96. Jameson, *The Seeds of Time*, 141.

97. The realist novel, Hillis Miller seminally opines, "is a structure not supported by anything outside itself . . . a structure in which the elements are not detachable pieces . . . every element draws its meaning from the others so that the novel must be described as a self-generating and self-sustaining system." J. Hillis Miller, *The Form of Victorian Fiction* (South Bend: University of Notre Dame Press, 1970), 29–30.

98. Jameson, "Architecture and the Critique of Ideology" 72–73.

99. Jameson, "The Realist Floorplan," in *On Signs*, ed. Marshall Blonsky (Baltimore: Johns Hopkins University Press, 1985), 374.

100. Jameson, "The Realist Floorplan" 374.

101. "Relative autonomy" is Althusser's phrase. Here it is necessary to contravert Jameson. He writes of "the structural and inherent conservatism and anti-politicality of the realist novel as such . . . ontological realism, absolutely committed to the density and solidity of what is—whether in the realm of psychology and feelings, institutions, objects or space— . . . the very choice of the form itself is a professional endorsement of the status quo" (*The Antinomies of Realism*, 215).

Chapter Two

1. Karl Marx, *The Communist Manifesto* (New York: Penguin, 2002), 2. The Penguin edition I cite prints the title as the more familiar *The Communist Manifesto*, but in the text here I preserve the stricter German in the translated title *The Manifesto of the Communist Party* because of its reference to the indispensable form of "the party" (which I take up in the conclusion).

2. Marx, *The Communist Manifesto*, 3.

3. "History is what hurts" is Jameson's phrase from *The Political Unconscious*, 102.

4. See Carolyn Lesjak, "1750 to the Present: Acts of Enclosure and Their Afterlife," *BRANCH: Britain, Representation, and Nineteenth-Century History*, ed. Dino Franco Felluga. Extension of Romanticism and Victorianism on the Net, http://www.branchcollective.org/?ps_articles=carolyn-lesjak-1750-to-the-present-acts-of-enclosure-and-their-afterlife.

5. Karl Marx, *Capital*, vol. 1 (New York: Penguin, 1992), 880.

6. For elaboration of this formalist dimension of Marx's thought, see the introduction.

7. See, for example, Fredric Jameson, "The Dialectic of Utopia and Ideology" in *The Political Unconscious*, 281–300.

8. Jameson, *The Political Unconscious*, 10.

9. See Georg Lukács, *The Historical Novel*, trans. Hannah Mitchell and Stanley Mitchell (Lincoln: University of Nebraska Press, 1983).

10. Emily Brontë, *Wuthering Heights* (1847; New York: Penguin Classics, 2002), 4.

11. Brontë, *Wuthering Heights*, 4.

12. Brontë, *Wuthering Heights*, 4.

13. Brontë, *Wuthering Heights*, 4–5.

14. Brontë, *Wuthering Heights*, 4.

15. Brontë, *Wuthering Heights*, 7.

16. Dorothy Van Ghent is among the first to note this obsession in *The English Novel: Form and Function* (New York: Harper, 1953). The obvious importance of boundary imagery has inspired a panoply of scholarly interpretations dedicated to one or another side—that the novel polices divisions, that the novel undermines divisions. It seems at least possible to say that the very problematizing of boundaries while maintaining their desirability, the deconstructing that is also a remarkable project at institution, encodes in literary themes and imagery the question of the possibility and necessity of limits—the question of counting the infinite.

17. Brontë, *Wuthering Heights*, 28.

18. Isabella's lengthy first-person account, nested at the center of the frame narratives, dwells, as Lockwood's comparable narrative does, upon the floor plan of Wuthering Heights and its irregularity.

19. Brontë, *Wuthering Heights*, 307.

20. Brontë, *Wuthering Heights*, 7. I point to this numerical fact of usage frequency in the interest of describing the form of the text, not in the interest of the sorts of indexicality often at issue in computational humanities. Themes are built out of repetitions; to describe how a text thematizes may involve referring to these repetitions, but such reference does not presume that word usages are themselves referential.

21. Brontë, *Wuthering Heights*, 82.

22. The hearth is where Nelly narrates to Lockwood, who describes himself as riveted to the story, "incapable of moving from the hearth" (chapter 7); the hearth is where Heathcliff and Catherine spend their rare, peaceful times together (chapter 7); the hearth is where Catherine and Nelly climactically debate Catherine's love for Heathcliff (chapter 9); the hearth is where Heathcliff and Nelly have numerous tête-à-têtes; it is where Heathcliff and Earnshaw physically battle "locked together on the hearth" (chapter 17); where little Catherine first meets Hareton (chapter 18) and first encounters the grown-up Linton (chapter 21) and where all their subsequent encounters in their directed courtship transpire; where Hareton and Catherine make their first peace (chapter 32).

23. Aristotle, *The Politics* (New York: Penguin, 1981), 59.

24. See, for example, Nicole Loraux, *The Divided City: On Memory and Forgetting in Ancient Athens* (New York: Zone Books, 2006); D. Brendan Nagle, *The Household as the Foundation of Aristotle's Polis* (Cambridge: Cambridge University Press, 2006); and Vincent Pecora, *Households of the Soul* (Baltimore: Johns Hopkins University Press, 1997).

25. Marx and Engels, "The Contribution to the Critique of Political Economy," 2.

26. Quoted in Robert Perceval Graves, *Life of Sir William Rowan Hamilton*, vol. 3 (London: Longmans, Green, 1889), 219.

27. Augustus De Morgan, *Formal Logic* (London: Taylor and Walton, 1847); George Boole, *The Mathematical Analysis of Logic* (New York: Macmillan, 1847); in 1848 Janos Bolyai and Nikolai Lobachevsky determined that their works together amounted to a hyperbolic geometry that disproved Euclid's fifth postulate. All of these developments in geometry and algebra opened onto a field of radically new conceptualizations of rational versus real numbers and of the possibility of enumerating infinity. The advent of non-Euclidean formulations essentially underlined the possibility that infinity was itself multiple: two parallel lines could infinitely maintain a constant right angle with their perpendicular intersector *and* they could, in an additional infinity, eventually curve toward or away from one another. That is, infinity strictly thought, must accommodate a law of infinite constancy and the possibility of its trespass. On a different

plane, Boolean algebra established the conditions of possibility for Cantorian set theory (the theory of actual infinity) by elaborating the relationships and functions between sets, including empty sets.

28. Peter Hallward, "Appendix," in *Badiou: A Subject to Truth* (Minneapolis: University of Minnesota Press, 2003), 327.

29. Georg Cantor, *Contributions to the Founding of the Theory of Transfinite Numbers* (1887), quoted in Michael Hallett, *Cantorian Set Theory and Limitation of Size* (Oxford: Oxford University Press, 1996), 131.

30. For Foucault this shift happens in other human sciences in the seventeenth century; we can either say that mathematics is a latecomer or a holdout of resemblance, or note that the shifts that interest Foucault are not themselves diachronically delimited so much as cyclically instantiated.

31. Brontë, *Wuthering Heights*, 56.

32. Brontë, *Wuthering Heights*, 16.

33. Brontë, *Wuthering Heights*, 95.

34. Among others, "wild, confused, disjointed, and improbable"; *The Examiner* 8 January 1848; Miriam Allott, ed., *The Brontës: The Critical Heritage* (New York: Routledge, 2010), 220.

35. Some examples of framing, exile, and containment include "complete exile from the world" (Brontë, *Wuthering Heights*, 13); "buried alive: she has thrown herself away upon that boor, from sheer ignorance that better individuals existed" (13); "she was the queen of the country-side; she had no peer" (66); there are several other handsome, rich young men. . . . If there be any, they are out of my way (79); "What were the use of my creation if I were entirely contained here?" (82); Catherine's illness (88); "Tell her what Heathcliff is—an unreclaimed creature, without refinement—without cultivation; an arid wilderness of furze and whinestone" (102); Catherine's eyes "gaze beyond, and far beyond—you would have said out of this world" (158); this shattered prison . . . I'm tired, tired of being enclosed here" (162); "and the whole extent of landscape besides lay in shadow" (190).

36. Alain Badiou, *Being and Event* (New York: Continuum, 2007), 23.

37. Brontë, *Wuthering Heights*, 251.

38. Brontë, *Wuthering Heights*, 19.

39. Brontë, *Wuthering Heights*, 35.

40. Brontë, *Wuthering Heights*, 34.

41. See Terry Eagleton, *Heathcliff and the Great Hunger: Studies in Irish Culture* (New York: Verso, 1996); and Susan Gillman, "Remembering Slavery, Again," *Los Angeles Review of Books*, 7 February 2016, https://lareviewofbooks.org/article/remembering-slavery-again/. We should note also, as Ivan Kreilkamp strongly does, that Heathcliff is "so forcefully associated with animals; *species* seems as salient as race as a category by which to consider Bronte's depiction of the character, and should not be reduced to or considered as a subcategory of race." Ivan Kreilkamp, "Petted Things: *Wuthering Heights* and the Animal," *Yale Journal of Criticism* 18, no. 1 (2005): 98.

42. Jameson, *The Political Unconscious*, 127.

43. There is some fascination, surely, in the biographical fact of house-ness here. What we know of Emily Brontë pertains almost exclusively to her house. The few walls within which she dreamed up innumerable permeable boundaries, the limited sphere from which she contemplated wide worlds—Haworth was a cherished enclosure that conditioned imaginative openings. Emily invented languages, contrived other astronomies, and inscribed a universe of pain in her one single book, and she did it all while preferring never to leave her house. She went to

school for only eighteen months of her twenty-nine-year life; she tolerated her only job away from home for just six months.

44. Karl Marx, *Critique of Hegel's Philosophy of Right* (Cambridge: Cambridge University Press, 1970), 141.

45. Hallward, *Badiou*, 35.

46. Marx and Engels, *The German Ideology*, 57 (emphasis original).

47. Brontë, *Wuthering Heights*, 337.

Chapter Three

1. Apologies to George Eliot's "every limit is a beginning as well as an ending," the opening line of *Middlemarch*'s finale.

2. Charles Dickens, *Bleak House* (1853; New York: Penguin Classics, 2003), 455.

3. Edgar Johnson, *Charles Dickens: His Tragedy and Triumph* (New York: Simon and Schuster, 1952). See also Joseph Gold, *Charles Dickens: Radical Moralist* (Minneapolis: University of Minnesota Press, 1972).

4. Caroline Levine, "Narrative Networks: *Bleak House* and the Affordances of Form," *Novel: A Forum on Fiction* 42, no. 3 (2009): 517.

5. Levine, "Narrative Networks," 519.

6. Emily Steinlight, "Dickens's 'Supernumeraries' and the Biopolitical Imagination of Victorian Fiction," *Novel: A Forum on Fiction* 43, no. 2 (2010): 229.

7. Dickens, *Bleak House*, 20.

8. James Buzard, "'Anywhere's Nowhere': *Bleak House* as Autoethnography," *Yale Journal of Criticism* 12, no. 1 (1999): 13 (emphasis original). His reasons are to highlight the "trope of dissociation" (14) that he reads beneath the motifs of connection, to appreciate how "Dickens's point is that culture constitutes not only the moral oneness of the nation but the system of internal differences that delineates meaningful roles and identities" (31).

9. In recent years, "scale" has become a buzzword in literary criticism, evoking as it does the historical span of the Anthropocene, the closeness or distance of reading methods, the status of man amid a cosmos of "objects," and the legend of literary purchase on "the" world (1:1; allegory; metonymy; typicality, etc.). Strong interventions in this trend include Julie Orlemanski, "Scales of Reading" (2014); Mark McGurl, "The Posthuman Comedy" (2012); Franco Moretti, *Graphs, Maps, Trees* (2007); Susan Stanford Friedman, *Planetary Modernisms* (2015); and Wai-Chee Dimock, *Through Other Continents* (2008).

10. See Victor Turner, "Liminal to Liminoid, in Play, Flow, and Ritual: An Essay in Comparative Symbology," *Rice University Studies* 60, no. 3 (1974): 61; Paolo Freire, *Pedagogy of the Oppressed* (London: Continuum, 2000), chap. 3; Tracy McNulty, *Wrestling with the Angel: Experiments in Symbolic Life* (New York: Columbia University Press, 2014), 26.

11. Dickens, *Bleak House*, 16.

12. Dickens, *Bleak House*, 118.

13. See, for example, Dickens, *Bleak House*, 197–98: "Twice lately there has been a crash and a cloud of dust, like the springing of a mine, in Tom-all-Alone's; and each time a house has fallen. These accidents have made a paragraph in the newspapers and have filled a bed or two in the nearest hospital. The gaps remain, and there are not unpopular lodgings among the rubbish. As several more houses are nearly ready to go, the next crash in Tom-all-Alone's may be expected to be a good one."

14. Dickens, *Bleak House*, 251.

15. Some readers may hear in this suggestion that *Bleak House* effects a "political formalism" toward the law an echo of the term more proper to theories of the law within the discipline of the law, "legal formalism." Generally contrasted with "legal realism," legal formalism in that discourse would indicate little of the ontological commitment to social structuration in variable forms that I have centered in political formalism, and rather that position that the law can in general be thought to guarantee its own applicability and sufficiency in every circumstance, whereas legal realism evokes the extralegal factors (like norms) that contribute to the law's function. For an endogenous discussion of these terms, see Brian Leiter, "Legal Formalism and Legal Realism: What Is the Issue?," *Legal Theory* 16, no. 2 (2010): 111–33.

16. See D. A. Miller, *The Novel and the Police* (Berkeley: University of California Press, 1988).

17. Karl Marx, *Mathematical Manuscripts of Karl Marx* (London: New Park Publications, 1983), 3.

18. Marx, *Mathematical Manuscripts*, 10.

19. Marx, *Mathematical Manuscripts*, 21.

20. Nancy Armstrong, *Desire and Domestic Fiction: A Political History of the Novel* (Oxford: Oxford University Press, 1990); Miller, *The Novel and the Police*; Mary Poovey, *Making of a Social Body* (Chicago: University of Chicago Press, 1995). In regard to Poovey, I specifically have in mind chapter 6, "Domesticity and Class Formation: Chadwick's 1842; Sanitary Report."

21. Pierre Bourdieu, *Outline of a Theory of Practice*, trans. Richard Nice (1977; Cambridge: Cambridge University Press, 2013), 89.

22. The whole edifice of *The Practice of Everyday Life* rests on this analogy between reading and inhabiting, dwelling, moving.

23. For the preeminent treatment of problems of domesticity, see Armstrong's *Desire and Domestic Fiction.*

24. Dickens, *Bleak House*, 856.

25. Dickens, *Bleak House*, 66.

26. Dickens, *Bleak House*, 66.

27. Dickens, *Bleak House*, 904.

28. Dickens, *Bleak House*, 256.

29. Dickens, *Bleak House*, 257.

30. Dickens, *Bleak House*, 261.

31. Dickens, *Bleak House*, 256.

32. See, for example, Caroline Levine's "Network," in *Forms*, 112–31.

33. Dickens, *Bleak House*, 483.

34. Dickens, *Bleak House*, 772.

35. See Bruce Robbins, "Telescopic Philanthropy: Professionalism and Responsibility in *Bleak House*," in *Nation and Narration*, ed. Homi K. Bhabha (New York: Routledge, 1990), 213–30.

36. Dickens, *Bleak House*, 227.

37. Dickens, *Bleak House*, 228.

38. Dickens, *Bleak House*, 648.

39. Dickens, *Bleak House*, 450.

40. Marx, *The Communist Manifesto*, 223.

41. Dickens, *Bleak House*, 455.

42. Dickens, *Bleak House*, 119–20.

43. Dickens, *Bleak House*, 67–68, 75–76.

44. Dickens, *Bleak House*, 82.

45. Dickens, *Bleak House*, 86.

46. Benjamin Joseph Bishop, "Metonymy and the Dense Cosmos of *Bleak House*," *SEL Studies in English Literature 1500–1900* 54, no. 4 (2014): 804.

47. Matthew Beaumont, "Beginnings, Endings, Births, Deaths: Sterne, Dickens, and *Bleak House*," *Textual Practice* 26, no. 5 (2012): 821.

48. Alex Woloch, "*Bleak House* 19, 20, 21," *boundary2online*, 4 October 2016, https://www.boundary2.org/2016/10/alex-woloch-bleak-house-19-20-21/.

49. Audrey Jaffe notes that Esther too has little interior insight, insofar as she is a character made "self-effacing" to blend with the perspectival features of omniscience. See Audrey Jaffe, "*David Copperfield* and *Bleak House*: On Dividing the Responsibility of Knowing," in *Vanishing Points.*

50. Dickens, *Bleak House*, 237.

51. Dickens, *Bleak House*, 989.

52. Though perhaps no ending would be satisfactory, Barbara Hardy finds the ending the place where Bleak House becomes small. "The book's total exposure leaves the reminder of scars uneffaced, the bleakness of the slums, the terribly bad housekeeping of England. The conclusion is only partially responsive to the rest of the novel, squeezes its solace through too narrow an exit. The reconciliation is a part that will not stand for the whole." Barbara Hardy, *Moral Art of Dickens*, 2nd ed. (London: Athlone Press, 2002), 13.

53. See, for instance, Hillis Miller on the third-person narrator as "everywhere in London and its environs"; J. Hillis Miller, *Charles Dickens: The World of His Novels* (Cambridge, MA: Harvard University Press, 1958), 160.

54. Dickens, *Bleak House*, 20.

55. Dickens, *Bleak House*, 20.

56. Dickens, *Bleak House*, 158.

57. Dickens, *Bleak House*, 159–60.

58. Dickens, *Bleak House*, 256.

59. Levine, "Narrative Networks," 518.

60. Dickens, *Bleak House*, 27.

61. For James Buzard in "'Anywhere's Nowhere,'" this nongoing means that the novel opposes "place-less, unrepresented, external spaces of unmeaning or unvalue" (15) to British "consequential ground" (14).

Chapter Four

1. See Henderson, "Symbolic Logic and the Logic of Symbolism."

2. See the discussion of *Las Meninas* in Foucault, *The Order of Things.*

3. Anonymous review of Michael Faraday's *Experimental Researches in Chemistry and Physics* published in the *Athenaeum*, 12 March 1859, cited in Gillian Beer, *Alice in Space: The Sideways Victorian World of Lewis Carroll* (Chicago: University of Chicago Press, 2016), 48.

4. Paul Livingston, *The Politics of Logic: Badiou, Wittgenstein, and the Consequences of Formalism* (New York: Routledge, 2014).

5. See, for example, Derrida, *The Beast and the Sovereign*; and, Michel Foucault, *The Birth of Biopolitics: Lectures at the Collège de France, 1978–1979* (New York: Picador, 2008).

6. Lewis Carroll, *Alice's Adventures in Wonderland and Through the Looking-Glass*, ed. Hugh Haughton (New York: Penguin Classics, 2003), 76.

7. Carroll, *Alice's Adventures in Wonderland and Through the Looking-Glass*, 74.

8. Carroll, *Alice's Adventures in Wonderland and Through the Looking-Glass*, 74.

9. Carroll, *Alice's Adventures in Wonderland and Through the Looking-Glass*, 104.

10. For more on how Carroll's play with mirrors and doors in his books evokes his photographic practice, see Brassai, "Carroll the Photographer" in *Lewis Carroll: Photos and Letters to His Child Friends*, trans. Warren Weaver, ed. Guido Almansi (Parma, Italy: Franco Maria Ricci, 1975), 188–98.

11. See, for example, Elizabeth Throesch, "Nonsense in the Fourth Dimension of Literature: Hyperspace Philosophy, the 'New' Mathematics, and the *Alice* Books," in *Alice beyond Wonderland: Essays for the Twenty-First Century*, ed. Cristopher Hollingsworth (Iowa City: University of Iowa Press, 2009), 37–52; Helena M. Pycior, "At the Intersection of Mathematics and Humor: Lewis Carroll's 'Alices' and Symbolical Algebra," *Victorian Studies* 28, no. 1 (1984): 149–70.

12. See Beer, *Alice in Space* (2016), and Robin Wilson, *Lewis Carroll in Numberland: His Fantastical Mathematical Logical Life* (New York: W. W. Norton, 2010), which is quite literally a list of mathematical scenes.

13. Carroll, *Alice's Adventures in Wonderland and Through the Looking-Glass*, 85.

14. Nancy Armstrong's interpretation of *Wonderland* as part of an industrial complex disseminating images of women as consumers and centralizing the female body in the economic relations of empire is the most notable political reading. See Nancy Armstrong, "Sexuality in the Age of Racism: Hungry Alice," in *Fiction in the Age of Photography* (Cambridge, MA: Harvard University Press, 2002), 201–43.

15. Kent Puckett, "Caucus-Racing," *Novel: A Forum on Fiction* 47, no. 1 (2014): 13.

16. Hillary Chute, "Comics as Literature? Reading Graphic Narrative," *PMLA* 123, no. 2 (2008): 454.

17. Chute, "Comics as Literature?," 452.

18. Carroll, *Alice's Adventures in Wonderland and Through the Looking-Glass*, 28.

19. Carroll, *Alice's Adventures in Wonderland and Through the Looking-Glass*, 45.

20. Carroll, *Alice's Adventures in Wonderland and Through the Looking-Glass*, 61.

21. Carroll, *Alice's Adventures in Wonderland and Through the Looking-Glass*, 37.

22. He uses the phrase in reference to *Wonderland* in the Preface to *Sylvie and Bruno* (New York: Dover, 1988), xxxvi.

23. Carroll, *Alice's Adventures in Wonderland and Through the Looking-Glass*, 64.

24. Nicholas Dames, "'The People v. O. J. Simpson' as Historical Fiction," *Public Books*, 1 April 2016, http://www.publicbooks.org/the-people-v-o-j-simpson-as-historical-fiction/.

25. Carroll, *Alice's Adventures in Wonderland and Through the Looking-Glass*, 108.

Chapter Five

1. On this bias against writing as the Pauline legacy, see Tracy McNulty, "The Event of the Letter: Two Approaches to the Law and Its Real," *Cardozo Law Review* 29, no. 5 (2008): 2209–38.

2. In Agamben's by now familiar terms, this opposition first occurs in Aristotle, between *zoe*, the natural life "common to all living beings (animals, men, gods)," and *bios*, the qualified life of an individual or group. Jacques Derrida, among others, finds Agamben's interpretation a misreading of Aristotle.

3. This critical consensus focuses on the ways that *Jude*'s interrogation of the value of life shares an idiom with the biopolitical imperative to maximize human capital, and on the novel's climactic elimination of excessive life as a "Malthusian" proposition, Malthus being a pivotal figure in Foucault's history of biopolitics. See Gillian Beer, *Darwin's Plots: Evolutionary Narrative in Darwin, George Eliot, and Nineteenth-Century Fiction* (Cambridge: Cambridge University Press, 2000); Regenia Gagnier, *The Insatiability of Human Wants: Economics and Aesthetics in Market Society* (Chicago: University of Chicago Press, 2000); Catherine Gallagher, *The Body Economic: Life, Death, and Sensation in Political Economy and the Victorian Novel* (Princeton: Princeton University Press, 2006); Aaron Matz, "Terminal Satire and *Jude the Obscure*," *ELH* 73 (2006): 519–47. The idea that *Jude the Obscure* is quintessentially biopolitical also seems supported by the fact that it is the only novel by Hardy to treat a character from childhood until death. Edward Said finds it a type of narrative "coeval with the very process of life itself; . . . biological self-perpetuation and unfolding genealogy based on the creative urge, marriage, and family." Edward Said, *Beginnings: Intention and Method* (New York: Basic Books, 1975), 138. To anticipate our discussion of geometry, it seems worth noting that Malthusianism might comprise another resonance of the novel's geometry, since Malthus's notorious *Essay on the Principle of Population* operated on the model of geometry: "Sexual passion may always be considered in algebraic language, as a given quantity. . . . Population, when unchecked, increases in a geometrical ratio. Subsistence increases only in an arithmetical ratio." Thomas Malthus, *An Essay on the Principle of Population* (New York: Oxford World Classics, 1999), 291.

4. For this notion of a "structural function" of letter as operative in the thought of Jacques Lacan, Sigmund Freud, Walter Benjamin, and Jacques Derrida, see Tracy McNulty, "The Commandment against the Law: Writing and Divine Justice in Walter Benjamin's 'Critique of Violence,'" *Diacritics* 37, nos. 2–3 (2007): 34–60; McNulty, "The Event of the Letter."

5. Thomas Hardy, *The Collected Letters*, vol. 1, *1840–1892*, ed. Richard Little Purdy and Michael Millgate (Oxford: Clarendon Press, 1979), 93.

6. As against Agamben and Paul, this other conception of letter has been formulated by Lacan, Freud, Benjamin, and Derrida.

7. Jahan Ramazani, *Poetry of Mourning: The Modern Elegy from Hardy to Heaney* (Chicago: University of Chicago Press, 1994), xi. For more thoughts on this finality, see Anna Kornbluh, "Thomas Hardy's End of Prose," in *BRANCH: Britain, Representation, and Nineteenth-Century History*, ed. Dino Franco Felluga, Extension of Romanticism and Victorianism on the Net, http://www.branchcollective.org/?ps_articles=anna-kornbluh-thomas-hardys-end-of-prose.

8. Thomas Hardy, *Jude the Obscure*, ed. Dennis Taylor (New York: Penguin Classics, 1998), 118.

9. Hardy, *Jude the Obscure*, 190, 208.

10. Hardy, *Jude the Obscure*, 199.

11. Hardy, *Jude the Obscure*, 341.

12. Hardy, *Jude the Obscure*, 18, 30.

13. Hardy, *Jude the Obscure*, 106, 141, 153, 156, 239, 291, 336, 348, 387, 445.

14. Hardy, *Jude the Obscure*, 82, 100, 337.

15. Hardy, *Jude the Obscure*, 78.

16. Hardy, *Jude the Obscure*, 132.

17. Hardy, *Jude the Obscure*, 401.

18. Hardy, *Jude the Obscure*, 309.

19. Hardy, *Jude the Obscure*, 288.

20. Hardy, *Jude the Obscure*, 288.

21. Thomas Hardy, "The Science of Fiction," *New Review* 4 (1891): 315–19.

22. Florence Hardy, *The Early Life of Thomas Hardy, 1840–1891* (New York: Macmillan, 1928), 229.

23. Hardy, *Jude the Obscure*, 39.

24. During his first meeting with Sue, we find a similar construction: "They walked on in parallel lines." Hardy, *Jude the Obscure*, 100.

25. Hardy, *Jude the Obscure*, 351.

26. Hardy, *Jude the Obscure*, 361.

27. Joan L. Richards, *Mathematical Visions: The Pursuit of Geometry in Victorian England* (New York: Academic Press, 1988), 5.

28. Among others, see Morris Kline, *Mathematics for the Nonmathematician* (New York: Dover, 1985), 476: "No system of thought has ever been so widely and completely accepted as Euclidean geometry. To preceding generations it was the 'rock of ages' in the realm of truth. Tradition buttressed self-evidence, and experience bolstered common sense. Men such as Plato and Descartes were convinced that mathematical truths were innate in human beings. Kant based his entire philosophy on the existence of mathematical truths. But now philosophy is haunted by the specter that the search for truths may be a search for phantoms"; also Kline, *Mathematical Thought from Ancient to Modern Times* (Oxford: Oxford University Press, 1972), 1023: "most consequential development."

29. Henderson, "Math for Math's Sake," 456.

30. Kline, quoted in Hallward, *Badiou*, 77. Set theory and the foundations of mathematics are the branches of mathematics today in which this question of the ontological status of mathematical objects remains unsettled.

31. This is a place to remark again on the novel's unusual organization: the "parts" are not enumerated (Part One, Part Two) but ordinated (Part First, Part Second), attesting to the novel's commitment to relativity and the order of things, rather than absolute essences.

32. Hardy, *Jude the Obscure*, 153.

33. Hardy, *Jude the Obscure*, 90.

34. Hardy, *Jude the Obscure*, 170.

35. Hardy, *Jude the Obscure*, 209.

36. Hardy, *Jude the Obscure*, 271.

37. Hardy, *Jude the Obscure*, 272.

38. Hardy, *Jude the Obscure*, 205.

39. Hardy, *Jude the Obscure*, 147.

40. Hardy, *Jude the Obscure*, 193.

41. Hardy, *Jude the Obscure*, 353.

42. Hardy, *Jude the Obscure*, 313, 332.

43. Hardy, *Jude the Obscure*, 308, 333, 339.

44. Hardy, *Jude the Obscure*, 467.

45. Thomas Hardy, "The Tree of Knowledge," *New Review* 10 (1894): 681. Hardy served as magistrate from 1894 to 1919. For a biographical account of Hardy's professional and intellectual engagement with law, see William A. Davis, *Thomas Hardy and the Law: Legal Presences in Hardy's Life and Fiction* (Newark: University of Delaware Press, 2003).

46. Felix Klein synthesized the non-Euclideanisms into the theory of hyperbolic and elliptic geometry in 1871; Georg Cantor produced set theory in the later 1870s.

47. Ed Pluth, *Badiou: A Philosophy of the New* (Cambridge: Polity, 2010), 87.

48. Hardy, *Jude the Obscure*, 217.

49. Hardy, *Jude the Obscure*, 221.

50. Hardy, *Jude the Obscure*, 118.

51. Hardy, *Jude the Obscure*, 277.

52. Hardy, *Jude the Obscure*, 166.

53. Hardy, *Jude the Obscure*, 339.

54. Hardy, *Jude the Obscure*, 339.

55. Hardy, *Jude the Obscure*, 342.

56. Ernesto Laclau, "Bare Life or Social Indeterminacy?," in *Giorgio Agamben: Sovereignty and Life*, ed. Matthew Calarco and Steven DeCaroli (Stanford: Stanford University Press, 2007), 22. In his final seminar, dedicated to exploring the perennial cofiguration of the beast and the sovereign, Derrida criticized Agamben's misreading of Aristotle: "But precisely, what Aristotle says—is that man is that living being who is taken by politics: he is a political living being, and essentially so. In other words, he is zoo-political, that's his essential definition, that's what is proper to him, *idion*; what is proper to man is politics; what is proper to this living being that man is, is politics, and therefore man is immediately zoo-political, in his very life, and the distinction between bio-politics and zoo-politics doesn't work at all here" (*The Beast and the Sovereign*, 349). Derrida points up Agamben's misprision of Aristotle in the course of considering the persistent coappearance of beast and sovereign as an outgrowth or symptom of man's political animality. If the agent of political power par excellence often appears in the image of a wolf or beast, this is owing to the intractable fact that politics define the human not against the animal but *as* animal; politics is the sphere of human animality. Albeit for a different purpose than Derrida's, this definition of human being—this formulation of politics not as an additive to life but as precondition of life in its very material animality—fundamentally interests additional thinkers we could counterpose to Agamben, namely, Hegel and Marx. Keen to dispel the individualist delusions of bourgeois political economy, Marx always insisted on the "larger whole" on which the individual depends: "Man is *zoon politikon* in the most literal sense: he is not only a social animal, but an animal that can be individualized only within society" (*The German Ideology*, 84). And before him, Hegel similarly avouched the "universal sustaining medium" of the collective, the dependence of the life of the individual on the "life of a people" *for its very existence* (G. W. F. Hegel, *Phenomenology of Spirit*, trans. A. V. Miller [Oxford: Oxford University Press, 1979], 212). In his gloss on Hegel, Warren Montag achieves a wonderful distillation: "It is thus only the 'power of the whole people' (*die Macht des ganzen Volks*) that confers upon the individual sufficient power to exist. In the universal there is life; in the particular only death"; Warren Montag, "Necro-Economics: Adam Smith and Death in the Life of the Universal." *Radical Philosophy* 134 (2005).

57. Hardy, *Jude the Obscure*, 48–49.

58. The possibility of severing the letter of the new testament from its content, of severing the letter–spirit distinction from itself, is reinforced by Sue's typographic project, her "*new* New Testament": "I altered my old one by cutting up all the Epistles and Gospels into separate *brochures*, and rearranging them in chronological order as written, beginning with Romans, following on with the early Epistles, and putting the Gospels much further on. Then I had the volume rebound" (Hardy, *Jude the Obscure*, 152, emphasis original). Sue makes it new, collaging the brochures of the book, collating to her liking, contracting an artisan to bind them. Along with her other arts (Greek statuary and inexpensive photographs), the new New Testament

testifies to her free thinking, her thinking it possible to free the word from its binding, to craft new representations—and even new laws—from the matter of the old.

59. Hardy, *Jude the Obscure*, 338.

60. Hardy, *Jude the Obscure*, 336 (quotation marks in original).

61. Hardy, *Jude the Obscure*, 336.

62. Hardy, *Jude the Obscure*, 20.

63. Hardy, *Jude the Obscure*, 21.

64. Hardy, *Jude the Obscure*, 21.

65. Hardy, *Jude the Obscure*, 25, 34, 112.

66. Hardy, *Jude the Obscure*, 31.

67. Hardy, *Jude the Obscure*, 34.

68. Hardy, *Jude the Obscure*, 35. Hardy, the only architect among the major Victorian novelists, knew intimately the process of learning to build. The son and grandson of masons, he trained for five years in London, assuming a post as restorer when returning to Dorset in 1867 and continuing to practice, including designing buildings from the ground up, throughout his writing career. His architectural notebooks are curio cabinets of sketches, tracings, and enclosures, fastidious and repetitive studies of shapes and lines: there are pages and pages of drawings of arches and of Corinthian capital columns, for instance. While architects feature in *A Pair of Blue Eyes* and *A Laodicean*, architecture preoccupies the passages of description in numerous novels. Yet, as Tomas Monterrey has remarked, despite the expertise that would enable him to embellish architectural imagery with technical and specialized visual language, he inclined toward "simple, unusual, startling elements, such as geometrical shapes (the ring, the oblong and rectangular stone, the octagonal tower), peripheral/non-architectonic elements (portraits built on the walls, ruins, inscriptions, board with letters)"; Tomas Monterrey, "Architecture in Hardy's Narrative Technique," in *Traditions and Innovations: Commemorating Forty Years of English Studies at ULL (1963–2003)* (Tenerife: RCEI, 2004), 332. Architecture appears to have signified to Hardy "rambl[ing] under the walls and doorways, feeling with his fingers the contours of their mouldings and carving" (*Jude the Obscure*, 79)—a way of limning the lines of all those traced and retraced arches and capitals, a way of being with geometry.

69. Hardy, *Jude the Obscure*, 205.

70. Hardy, *Jude the Obscure*, 300.

71. Hardy, *Jude the Obscure*, 312.

72. Hardy, *Jude the Obscure*, 295.

73. Hardy, *Jude the Obscure*, 104.

74. Hardy, *Jude the Obscure*, 129.

75. Hardy, *Jude the Obscure*, 139.

76. Hardy, *Jude the Obscure*, 270.

77. The narrator calls this opposition "the antagonism of sex to sex" (Hardy, *Jude the Obscure*, 166). In this they embody the two logics of sexuation as mapped by Lacan onto the Kantian antinomies of reason: the masculine, dynamic antinomy expressing the contradiction between universality and its exception, the feminine, mathematic antinomy posing the opposition of no universality and no exception. The fact that Jude is feminine and Sue masculine reinforces the structural-logical, rather than gendered, nature of sexuation for Lacan; Jacques Lacan, *On Feminine Sexuality, the Limits of Love and Knowledge: The Seminar of Jacques Lacan, Book XX, Encore*, ed. Jacques Alain-Miller, trans. Bruce Fink (New York: W. W. Norton, 1999).

78. Copjec, *Read My Desire*, 5.

Chapter Six

1. Lacan, *On Feminine Sexuality*, 119.

2. The possibilities of psychoanalytic political theory have been most strategically advanced by Slavoj Žižek, in works spanning his career, from *For They Know Not What They Do: Enjoyment as a Political Factor* (1991; New York: Verso, 2007) to *Living in the End Times* (New York: Verso, 2010). This book is indebted to his work throughout, while also trying to focus narrowly on the question of institutionality that formalization poses and the question of the state which I argue it can illuminate, neither of which have particularly been a subject of Žižek's sustained analysis.

3. Formidable examples include, of course, Freud's political metapsychology *Totem and Taboo*, *Civilization and Its Discontents*, and *Group Psychology and the Analysis of the Ego*, and more recently Joan Copjec, *Read My Desire* (1994) and *Imagine There's No Woman* (2002), Judith Butler, *The Psychic Life of Power* (1997), Eric Santner, *The Royal Remains* (2011), Julia Reinhard Lupton, *Citizen-Saints* (2005), and the entire enormous oeuvre of Slavoj Žižek.

4. Giorgio Agamben, *Homo Sacer: Sovereign Power and Bare Life*, trans. Daniel Heller-Roazen (Stanford: Stanford University Press, 1998), 59. Agamben belongs to an arc along which I would also situate not only Foucault and Judith Butler, but also Michael Hardt and Antonio Negri and David Graeber, and the so-called "new materialisms." For helpful overviews of aspects of these trends in critical theory, see Tim Brennan, *Wars of Position: The Cultural Politics of Left and Right* (New York: Columbia University Press, 2007); Jodi Dean, *Democracy and Other Neoliberal Fantasies* (Durham: Duke University Press, 2009); and Jord/ana Rosenberg, "The Molecularization of Sexuality: On Some Primitivisms of the Present," *Theory and Event* 17, no. 2 (2014).

5. For a recent, compelling argument in favor of the symbolic, see McNulty, *Wrestling with the Angel*.

6. Jacques Lacan, "Seminar on the Purloined Letter," in *Écrits*, trans. Bruce Fink (New York: W.W. Norton, 2006), 17.

7. Sigmund Freud, "The Question of Lay Analysis," in *The Standard Edition of the Complete Psychological Works of Sigmund Freud*, vol. 20 (1925–1926) (London: Hogarth, 1959), 245.

8. Freud, "The Question of Lay Analysis," 251.

9. Freud, "The Question of Lay Analysis," 194.

10. Freud, "The Question of Lay Analysis," 227.

11. Jacques Lacan, *The Four Fundamental Concepts: The Seminar of Jacques Lacan, Book XI*, ed. Jacques Alain-Miller, trans. Alan Sheridan (New York: W.W. Norton, 1998), 2.

12. Badiou, *The Concept of Model*, 54.

13. For a thorough discussion of the political promise of retroactive causality, see Molly Anne Rothenberg, *The Excessive Subject* (Cambridge: Polity Press, 2013).

14. Lacan, *On Feminine Sexuality*, 93.

15. Jacques Lacan, *The Other Side of Psychoanalysis: The Seminar of Jacques Lacan, Book XVII*, ed. Jacques Alain-Miller, trans. Russell Grigg (New York: W.W. Norton, 2007), 90.

16. Lacan, *The Other Side of Psychoanalysis*, 90. *Seminar XVII* is, not coincidentally, Lacan's most intensely formalist seminar *and* his most overtly political seminar.

17. Lacan, *Écrits*, 691. These 101 readings correlate as well to the numerous names Lacan gives to the letter as Real: *object a*, gaze, lamella, extimate kernel, etc.

18. Lacan, *The Other Side of Psychoanalysis*, 169.

19. "Just like psychoanalysis which, as I said one day, is done by psychoanalysts, this is its principal characteristic, you have to begin with the psychoanalyst." Lacan, *The Other Side of Psychoanalysis*, 82.

20. On formalization as a specific undertaking at the conjuncture of philosophy and science in postwar France, see Tom Eyers, *Post-Rationalism: Psychoanalysis, Epistemology, and Marxism in Postwar France* (London: Bloomsbury, 2015). The most detailed study of Lacan's relationship to Lévi-Strauss is Markos Zafiropoulos, *Lacan and Levi-Strauss* (London: Karnac Books, 2010).

21. This famous revision of Saussure directly followed Lévi-Strauss's interpretation of Saussure and Jakobson. Indeed, Lacan attests: "If I wanted to characterize the way in which Claude Levi Strauss's work has supported and carried me forward, I would say that it was in his emphasis on . . . what I would call the function of the signifier." *Bulletin de la Société française de philosophie* 18 (1956): 114; cited in Zafiropoulos, *Lacan and Levi-Strauss*, 166.

22. Lacan, *The Four Fundamental Concepts*, 149. Dany Nobus points out the crucial fact that Lacan would go on to lament the redundancy of "as a language" in his 1966 intervention at the much-feted Johns Hopkins conference on the sciences of man. See "Lacan's Science of the Subject: Between Linguistics and Topology," in *The Cambridge Companion to Lacan*, ed. Jean-Michel Rabaté (Cambridge: Cambridge University Press, 2003), 58.

23. Lacan, *The Other Side of Psychoanalysis*, 135.

24. Lacan, *The Four Fundamental Concepts*, 20.

25. Lacan, *The Four Fundamental Concepts*, 20.

26. Claude Lévi-Strauss, *Structural Anthropology* (New York: Basic Books, 1973), 159.

27. None more clearly than Derrida established this, in the seminal "Structure, Sign, and Play in the Discourse of the Human Sciences," in *The Structuralist Controversy*, ed. Richard Macksey (Baltimore: Johns Hopkins University Press, 2007), 247–64.

28. Lacan, *The Other Side of Psychoanalysis*, 66.

29. Lacan, *On Feminine Sexuality*, 119.

30. As he argued fervently at the same Hopkins conference where Derrida made his intervention, the letter is the gap between meaning and discourse, the place of loss, a surface of subtraction: "Analogy to what? 'S' designates something which can be written exactly as this S. And I have said that the 'S' which designates the subject is instrument, matter, to symbolize a loss. A loss that you experience as a subject (and myself also). In other words, this gap between one thing which has marked meanings and this other thing which is my actual discourse that I try to put in the place where you are, you as not another subject but as people that are able to understand me. Where is the analogon? Either this loss exists or it doesn't exist. If it exists it is only possible to designate the loss by a system of symbols. In any case, the loss does not exist before this symbolization indicates its place. It is not an analogy. It is really in some part of the realities, this sort of torus. This torus really exists and it is exactly the structure of the neurotic. It is not an analogon; it is not even an abstraction, because an abstraction is some sort of diminution of reality, and I think it is reality itself." Jacques Lacan, "Of Structure as an Inmixing of an Otherness Prerequisite to Any Subject Whatever," in Macksey, *The Structuralist Controversy*, 195–96.

31. This sense of the letter as the writing of structure, of the letter as structure, drives Lacan's late turn to the topological axis of formalization, studying the surfaces of geometrical figures, accessing "the letter" in the dimension of its surface and the paradoxical volume thereof. Where ego psychology and the detour from Freud had enshrined depth models, Lacan's topology contrastingly asserted the planarity of the unconscious: a plane of folds and twists, surely, but a plane vis-à-vis which it is not possible to take up a position elsewhere. Topology is not a study

of structure, "it is structure"; Lacan is "trying to show with topological formulas . . . that these surfaces are structures"; Jacques Lacan, "L'étourdit," in *Autres écrits* (Paris: Seuil, 2001), 240. The structure of loss, the structure of the subject, the structure of the torus, the structure of the letter *S*, these are so many indices of decompletion, so many occasions for navigating the gap, for negotiating relation across the nonimmanence of meaning.

32. Slavoj Žižek has similarly argued that the political core of psychoanalysis rests with identifying this nonidentity, the nonsensical kernel responsible for the discontent at the heart of any culture, a nonsense that his work on Hegel often probes as antagonism. See Slavoj Žižek, *Tarrying with the Negative* (Durham: Duke University Press, 1993), chap. 1, "Cogito: The Void Called Subject"; Žižek, *Less than Nothing: Hegel and the Shadow of Dialectical Materialism* (New York: Verso, 2012), especially interludes 1 and 3, "Marx as a Reader of Hegel, Hegel as a Reader of Marx" and "King, Rabble, War . . . and Sex." For a strong systematization of the place of antagonism in Žižek's thought, see Jodi Dean, *Zizek's Politics* (New York: Routledge, 2006), especially chap. 1, "Enjoyment as a Category of Political Theory."

33. Mladen Dolar, "Freud and the Political," *Theory & Event* 12, no. 3 (2009): 7.

34. Lacan, *The Other Side of Psychoanalysis*, 20–21.

35. This difference is the subject of the entire seminar.

36. Lacan, *The Other Side of Psychoanalysis*, 171.

37. Jacques Lacan, *The Psychoses: The Seminar of Jacques Lacan, Book III*, ed. Jacques Alain-Miller, trans. Russell Grigg (New York: W.W. Norton, 1997), 199.

38. Lacan, *The Psychoses*, 200.

39. Lacan, *The Psychoses*, 201.

40. On this point, of course, the canonical argument is Gilles Deleuze and Felix Guattari, *Anti-Oedipus: Capitalism and Schizophrenia* (Minneapolis: University of Minnesota Press, 1983).

41. Sigmund Freud, "Moses and Monotheism," in *The Standard Edition of the Complete Psychological Works of Sigmund Freud*, vol. 23 (1937–1939) (London: Hogarth, 1959), 105.

42. Kenneth Reinhard, "Lacan and Monotheism: Psychoanalysis and the Traversal of Cultural Fantasy," *Jouvert* 3, no. 12 (1999), 3–4, http://english.chass.ncsu.edu/jouvert/v3i12/reinha.htm http://english.chass.ncsu.edu/jouvert/v3i12/reinha.htm.

43. Sigmund Freud, "Constructions in Analysis," in *The Standard Edition*, 23:260.

44. Reinhard, "Lacan and Monotheism," 6 (emphasis original).

45. Lacan, *The Other Side of Psychoanalysis*, 176.

46. Lacking space for it here, it is nonetheless necessary to observe that the culmination of Lacan's seminars in the late 1970s pursues the possibility of constructions of a new signifier via literary language. By *Seminar XXIII*, Lacan arrives at the conclusion that formalization qua matheme is not the only formalization—that literary language may also well be understood as a practice of singularizing the materiality of the letter, subtracting (in and through multiplying) the significations from the signifier. In his commentary on the status of formalization in Lacan, Andrew Cutrofello points to this proximity of the literary signifier and the matheme: "If psychoanalysis aspires to the condition of mathematical formalization, we should not expect to be able to say whether the results will more closely resemble mathematics or poetry"; Andrew Cutrofello, "The Ontological Status of Lacan's Mathematical Paradigms," in *Reading Seminar XX: Lacan's Major Work on Love, Knowledge, and Feminine Sexuality*, ed. Suzanne Barnard and Bruce Fink (Albany: SUNY Press, 2002), 143. This is no doubt because formalization, as is so often charged, amounts to a production of nonsense—a production of the signifier subtracted of sense as well as full of too much sense. Formalization, like literary language, albeit

differently, endeavors to think the signifier as what Cutrofello calls a "textured surface" (164), a space across which intersubjectivity comes to exist: "The signifier as such refers to nothing if not to discourse, in other words, a mode of functioning or a utilization of language qua link. . . . The link . . . is a link between those who speak (Lacan, *On Feminine Sexuality*, 30). When literary language attunes us to the polyvocality, resonations, and materiality of the signifier, it activates this texturality, this substantiality in and across which the signifier weaves social links.

47. Lacan, *The Other Side of Psychoanalysis*, 43.

48. "There are not thirty six ways to make laws, whether motivated by good intentions, justice, or not, for there are perhaps laws of structure that make it the case that the law will always be the law located in this place that I am calling dominant in the master's discourse." Lacan, *The Other Side of Psychoanalysis*, 43.

49. Joan Copjec observes that the "preposterous" figure of the primal father is integral: "That he is unthinkable within this regime of brothers does not gainsay the fact that the *institution* of the regime is inexplicable without him. For if we did not posit his existence, we would be incapable, without resorting to psychologism, of explaining how the brothers came together in this fashion. What Freud accounts for in *Totem and Taboo* is the structure, the real structure, of a society of equals, which is thus shown to be irreducible to the labile relations of equality that never obtain absolutely. . . . Structures . . . are not to be located among the relations that constitute our everyday reality; they belong, instead, to the order of the real." Copjec, *Read My Desire*, 11–12.

50. For more on this negative, see Žižek, *Tarrying with the Negative*, chap. 1.

51. Todd McGowan, *Enjoying What We Don't Have* (Lincoln: University of Nebraska Press, 2013), 4.

52. McGowan, *Enjoying What We Don't Have*, 19.

53. McGowan, *Enjoying What We Don't Have*, 264.

54. McGowan, *Enjoying What We Don't Have*, 283.

55. McGowan, *Enjoying What We Don't Have*, 283.

Conclusion

1. Walter Benajmin, "Critique of Violence," in *Reflections: Essays, Aphorisms, Autobiographical Writings*, ed. Peter Demetz (New York: Harcourt Brace, 1978), 277–300.

2. Jodi Dean, *Crowds and Party* (New York: Verso, 2016); Fredric Jameson, *An American Utopia: Dual Power and the Universal Army*, ed. Slavoj Žižek (New York: Verso, 2016).

3. Dean, *Crowds and Party*, 5.

4. Dean, *Crowds and Party*, 25.

5. For more on this particular psychologism, see Anna Kornbluh, *Realizing Capital: Financial and Psychic Economies in Victorian Form* (New York: Fordham University Press, 2013).

6. For a sustained argument about the political theory that emerges across these texts, see Anna Kornbluh, "Freud's Return to Lacan," in *After Lacan*, ed. Ankhi Mukherjee (Cambridge: Cambridge University Press, 2018), 41–57. Alenka Zupančič's discussion of the intrinsically objective dimension of psychoanalysis comes in her book, *What IS Sex?* (Cambridge, MA: MIT Press, 2017).

7. Sigmund Freud, "Civilization and Its Discontents," in *The Standard Edition*, vol. 21 (1927–1931), 112.

Bibliography

Adorno, Theodor W. *Aesthetic Theory*. Edited by Robert Hullot-Kentor. Minneapolis: University of Minnesota Press, 1998.

Agamben, Giorgio. *Homo Sacer: Sovereign Power and Bare Life*. Translated by Daniel Heller-Roazen. Stanford: Stanford University Press, 1998.

———. *State of Exception*. Chicago: University of Chicago Press, 2005.

———. *The Time That Remains: A Commentary on the Letter to the Romans*. Stanford: Stanford University Press, 2007.

———. *The Use of Bodies*. Translated by Adam Kotsko. Stanford: Stanford University Press, 2016.

Allott, Miriam, ed. *The Brontes: The Critical Heritage*. New York: Routledge, 2010.

Althusser, Louis. *Lenin and Philosophy and Other Essays*. New York: Monthly Review Press, 2001.

———. *On the Reproduction of Capitalism*. New York: Verso, 2014.

Anderson, Amanda. *Bleak Liberalism*. Chicago: University of Chicago Press, 2016.

———. *The Way We Argue Now: A Study in the Cultures of Theory*. Princeton: Princeton University Press, 2006.

Arata, Stephen, et al., eds. *A Companion to the English Novel*. Hoboken: Wiley-Blackwell, 2015.

Arendt, Hannah. *The Human Condition*. Chicago: University of Chicago Press, 1998.

Aristotle. *The Politics*. New York: Penguin, 1981.

Armstrong, Isobel. *Victorian Glassworlds: Glass Culture and the Imagination, 1830–1880*. Oxford: Oxford University Press, 2008.

Armstrong, Nancy. *Desire and Domestic Fiction: A Political History of the Novel*. Oxford: Oxford University Press, 1990.

———. *Fiction in the Age of Photography: The Legacy of British Realism*. Cambridge, MA: Harvard University Press, 2002.

———. *How Novels Think: The Limits of Individualism from 1719–1900*. New York: Columbia University Press, 2006.

Arrighi, Giovanni. *The Long Twentieth Century: Money, Power, and the Origin of Our Times*. 1994. Reprint, New York: Verso, 2010.

Ashcroft, Bill, Gareth Griffiths, and Helen Tiffin, eds. *The Post-Colonial Studies Reader*. 1st ed. New York: Routledge, 1995.

Auerbach, Erich. *Mimesis: The Representation of Reality in Western Thought.* Princeton: Princeton University Press, 2003.

Badiou, Alain. *Being and Event.* Cambridge: Continuum, 2007.

———. *The Concept of Model: An Introduction to the Materialist Epistemology of Mathematics.* Translated by Zachary Luke Fraser and Tzuchien Tho. Melbourne: re.press, 2007.

Bakhtin, Mikhail. *The Dialogic Imagination.* Austin: University of Texas Press, 1981.

Banfield, Ann. *The Phantom Table: Woolf, Fry, Russell, and the Epistemology of Modernism.* Cambridge: Cambridge University Press, 2007.

Barthes, Roland. *Camera Lucida: Reflections on Photography.* Translated by Richard Howard. New York: Hill and Wang, 1982.

Baucom, Ian. "Hydrographies." *Geographical Review* 89, no. 2 (1999): 301–13.

———. *Specters of the Atlantic: Finance Capital, Slavery, and the Philosophy of History.* Durham: Duke University Press, 2005.

Baudrillard, Jean. *Selected Writings.* Edited by Mark Poster. Stanford: Stanford University Press, 1988.

Beaumont, Matthew. "Beginnings, Endings, Births, Deaths: Sterne, Dickens, and *Bleak House.*" *Textual Practice* 26, no. 5 (2012): 807–27.

Beer, Gillian. *Alice in Space: The Sideways Victorian World of Lewis Carroll.* Chicago: University of Chicago Press, 2016.

———. *Darwin's Plots: Evolutionary Narrative in Darwin, George Eliot, and Nineteenth-Century Fiction.* Cambridge: Cambridge University Press, 2009.

Bellofiore, R., and N. Taylor, eds. *The Constitution of Capital: Essays on Volume 1 of Marx's "Capital."* New York: Palgrave Macmillan, 2004.Benjamin, Walter. *Illuminations.* Edited by Hannah Arendt. Translated by Harry Zohn. 1968. New York: Harcourt Brace, 2007.

———. *Reflections: Essays, Aphorisms, Autobiographical Writings.* Edited by Peter Demetz. New York: Harcourt Brace, 1978.

Best, Stephen, and Sharon Marcus. "Surface Reading: An Introduction." *Representations* 108, no. 1 (2009): 1–21.

Bhabha, Homi K., ed. *Nation and Narration.* New York: Routledge, 1990.

Bishop, Alan. "Western Mathematics: The Secret Weapon Cultural Imperialism." In *The Postcolonial Studies Reader*, edited by Bill Ashcroft, Gareth Griffiths, and Helen Tiffin, 80–83. 2nd ed. New York: Routledge, 2006.

Bishop, Benjamin Joseph. "Metonymy and the Dense Cosmos of *Bleak House.*" *SEL Studies in English Literature 1500–1900* 54, no. 4 (2014): 793–813.

Bloch, Ernst. *The Utopian Function of Art and Literature: Selected Essays.* Translated by Jack Zipes and Frank Mecklenberg. Cambridge, MA: MIT Press, 1989.

Blonsky, Marshall, ed. *On Signs.* Baltimore: Johns Hopkins University Press, 1985.

Boole, George. *The Mathematical Analysis of Logic.* New York: Macmillan, 1847.

Bottomore, Tom, et al., eds. *A Dictionary of Marxist Thought.* Cambridge, MA: Harvard University Press, 1983.

Bourdieu, Pierre. *Outline of a Theory of Practice.* Translated by Richard Nice. 1977. Cambridge: Cambridge University Press, 2013.

Brantlinger, Patrick. *Fictions of State: Culture and Credit in Britain, 1694–1994.* Ithaca: Cornell University Press, 1996.

Brassai. "Carroll the Photographer." In *Lewis Carroll: Photos and Letters to His Child Friends*, translated by Warren Weaver, edited by Guido Almansi, 188–98. Parma, Italy: Franco Maria Ricci, 1975.

Brennan, Timothy. *Wars of Position: The Cultural Politics of Left and Right.* New York: Columbia University Press, 2007.

Brontë, Emily. *Wuthering Heights.* 1847. New York: Penguin Classics, 2002.

Brooks, Peter. *Reading for the Plot: Design and Intention in Narrative.* Cambridge, MA: Harvard University Press, 1992.

Brown, Bill. "The Dark Wood of Postmodernity (Space, Faith, Allegory)." *PMLA* 120, no. 3 (2005): 734–50.

Butler, Judith. *Excitable Speech: A Politics of the Performative.* New York: Routledge, 1997.

———. *The Psychic Life of Power: Theories in Subjection.* Stanford: Stanford University Press, 1997.

Buzard, James. "'Anywhere's Nowhere': *Bleak House* as Autoethnography." *Yale Journal of Criticism* 12, no. 1 (1999): 7–39.

Cameron, Sharon. *Thinking in Henry James.* Chicago: University of Chicago Press, 1989.

Carroll, Lewis. *Alice's Adventures in Wonderland and Through the Looking-Glass.* Edited by Hugh Haughton. New York: Penguin Classics, 2003.

———. *Sylvie and Bruno.* New York: Dover, 1988.

Certeau, Michel de. *The Practice of Everyday Life.* Berkeley: University of California Press, 1988.

Chatman, Seymour. *Later Style of Henry James.* Oxford: Blackwell Publishers, 1972.

Cheah, Pheng. *What Is a World? On Postcolonial Literature as World Literature.* Durham: Duke University Press, 2016.

Chute, Hillary. "Comics as Literature? Reading Graphic Narrative." *PMLA* 123, no. 2 (2008): 452–65.

Claybaugh, Amanda. *The Novel of Purpose: Literature and Social Reform in the Anglo-American World.* Ithaca: Cornell University Press, 2007.

Clover, Joshua. *Riot. Strike. Riot: The New Era of Uprisings.* New York: Verso, 2016.

Clune, Michael W. *Writing against Time.* Stanford: Stanford University Press, 2013.

Copjec, Joan. *Imagine There's No Woman: Ethics and Sublimation.* Cambridge, MA: MIT Press, 2002.

———. *Read My Desire: Lacan against the Historicists.* Cambridge, MA: MIT Press, 1994.

Culler, Jonathan. "The Most Interesting Thing in the World." *diacritics* 38, nos. 1–2 (2008): 7–16.

———. *Structuralist Poetics: Structuralism, Linguistics, and the Study of Literature.* 1975. New York: Routledge, 2002.

Cunningham, David. "Capitalist Epics: Abstraction, Totality and the Theory of the Novel." *Radical Philosophy* 163 (2010): 11–23.

Cutrofello, Andrew. "The Ontological Status of Lacan's Mathematical Paradigms." In *Reading Seminar XX: Lacan's Major Work on Love, Knowledge, and Feminine Sexuality*, edited by Suzanne Barnard and Bruce Fink, 141–70. Albany: SUNY Press, 2002.

Dames, Nicholas. "'The People v. O.J. Simpson' as Historical Fiction." *Public Books*, 1 April 2016. http://www.publicbooks.org/the-people-v-o-j-simpson-as-historical-fiction/.

David, Deirdre, ed. *The Cambridge Companion to the Victorian Novel.* 2nd ed. Cambridge: Cambridge University Press, 2012.

Davis, William A. *Thomas Hardy and the Law: Legal Presences in Hardy's Life and Fiction.* Newark: University of Delaware Press, 2003.

Dean, Jodi. *Crowds and Party.* New York: Verso, 2016.

———. *Democracy and Other Neoliberal Fantasies.* Durham: Duke University Press, 2009.

———. *Zizek's Politics.* New York: Routledge, 2006.

Deleuze, Gilles. *The Logic of Sense.* Edited by Constantin V. Boundas. Translated by Mark Lester and Charles Stivale. New York: Columbia University Press, 1990.

Deleuze, Gilles, and Felix Guattari. *Anti-Oedipus: Capitalism and Schizophrenia.* Minneapolis: University of Minnesota Press, 1983.

De Man, Paul. "Georg Lukacs' *The Theory of the Novel.*" In *Blindness and Insight,* 51–59. Minneapolis: University of Minnesota Press, 1983.

———. "Semiology and Rhetoric." In *Allegories of Reading: Figural Language in Rousseau, Nietzsche, Rilke, and Proust,* 3–19. New Haven: Yale University Press, 1979.

De Morgan, Augustus. *Formal Logic.* London: Taylor and Walton, 1847.

Derrida, Jacques. "Architecture: Where the Desire May Live." In *Rethinking Architecture: A Reader in Cultural Theory,* edited by Neil Leach, 300–328. London: Routledge, 1997.

———. *The Beast and the Sovereign.* Vol. 1. Chicago: University of Chicago Press, 2009.

———. *Chora L Works: Jacques Derrida and Peter Eisenman.* Edited by Jeffrey Kipnis and Thomas Leeser. New York: Monacelli Press, 1997.

———. *Dissemination.* Translated by Barbara Johnson. Chicago: University of Chicago Press, 1983.

———. *Positions.* Translated by Alan Bass. Chicago: University of Chicago Press, 1982.

———. "Structure, Sign, and Play in the Discourse of the Human Sciences." In *The Structuralist Controversy,* edited by Richard Macksey, 247–64. Baltimore: Johns Hopkins University Press, 2007.

Detlefsen, Michael. "Formalism." In *The Oxford Handbook of Philosophy of Mathematics and Logic,* edited by Steward Shapiro, 236–317. Oxford: Oxford University Press, 2007.

Dickens, Charles. *Bleak House.* 1853. New York: Penguin Classics, 2003.

Dimock, Wai Chee. *Through Other Continents: American Literature across Deep Time.* Princeton: Princeton University Press, 2008.

Dolar, Mladen. "Freud and the Political." *Theory & Event* 12, no. 3 (2009).

Eagleton, Terry. *Heathcliff and the Great Hunger: Studies in Irish Culture.* New York: Verso, 1996.

———. *Myths of Power: A Marxist Study of the Brontës.* New York: Palgrave Macmillan, 2005.

Edelman, Lee. *No Future: Queer Theory and the Death Drive.* Durham: Duke University Press, 2004.

Elwall, Robert. *Building with Light: An International History of Architectural Photography.* London: Merrell Publishers, 2004.

Eyers, Tom. *Post-Rationalism: Psychoanalysis, Epistemology, and Marxism in Postwar France.* London: Bloomsbury, 2015.

———. *Speculative Formalism.* Evanston: Northwestern University Press, 2017.

Felski, Rita. *The Limits of Critique.* Chicago: University of Chicago Press, 2015.

Foucault, Michel. *The Birth of Biopolitics: Lectures at the Collège de France, 1978–1979.* New York: Picador, 2008.

———. *Discipline and Punish: The Birth of the Prison.* Translated by Alan Sheridan. 1975. New York: Vintage Books, 1995.

———. *The History of Sexuality.* 1978. New York: Pantheon Books, 1986.

———. *The Order of Things: An Archaeology of the Human Sciences.* New York: Vintage Books, 1973.

Frank, Ellen. *Literary Architecture: Essays toward a Tradition; Walter Pater, Gerard Manley Hopkins, Marcel Proust, Henry James.* Berkeley: University of California Press, 1983.

Frank, Joseph. "Spatial Form in Modern Literature." *Sewanee Review* 53 (1945): 221–40.

Freedman, Jonathan. *Professions of Taste: Henry James, British Aestheticism, and Commodity Culture.* Stanford: Stanford University Press, 1993.

Freire, Paolo. *Pedagogy of the Oppressed.* London: Continuum, 2000.

Freud, Sigmund. "Civilization and Its Discontents." In *The Standard Edition of the Complete Psychological Works of Sigmund Freud,* vol. 21 (1927–1931), 59–148. London: Hogarth, 1959.

———. "Constructions in Analysis." In *The Standard Edition of the Complete Psychological Works of Sigmund Freud,* vol. 23 (1937–1939), 256–69. London: Hogarth, 1959.

———. "Moses and Monotheism." In *The Standard Edition of the Complete Psychological Works of Sigmund Freud,* vol. 23 (1937–1939), 7–140. London: Hogarth, 1959.

———. "The Question of Lay Analysis." In *The Standard Edition of the Complete Psychological Works of Sigmund Freud,* vol. 20 (1925–1926), 179–270. London: Hogarth, 1959.

Friedman, Susan Stanford. *Planetary Modernisms: Provocations on Modernity across Time.* New York: Columbia University Press, 2015.

Gagnier, Regenia. *The Insatiability of Human Wants: Economics and Aesthetics in Market Society.* Chicago: University of Chicago Press, 2000.

Gallagher, Catherine. *The Body Economic: Life, Death, and Sensation in Political Economy and the Victorian Novel.* Princeton: Princeton University Press, 2006.

———. *The Industrial Reformation of English Fiction: Social Discourse and Narrative from 1832–1867.* Chicago: University of Chicago Press, 1985.

Gallagher, Catherine, and Stephen Greenblatt. *Practicing New Historicism.* Chicago: University of Chicago Press, 2000.

Geertz, Clifford. "Religion as a Cultural System." In *The Interpretation of Cultures: Selected Essays,* 87–125. New York: Basic Books, 1973.

Genette, Gérard. "La littérature et l'espace." In *Figures 2,* 43–44. Paris: Seuil, 1969.

Ghent, Dorothy Van. *The English Novel: Form and Function.* New York: Harper, 1953.

Gillman, Susan. "Remembering Slavery, Again." *Los Angeles Review of Books,* 7 February 2016. https://lareviewofbooks.org/article/remembering-slavery-again/.

Glynos, Jason. *Lacan and Science.* London: Karnac Books, 2002.

Gold, Joseph. *Charles Dickens: Radical Moralist.* Minneapolis: University of Minnesota Press, 1972.

Gosse, Edmund. "Mr. Hardy's New Novel." *Cosmopolis* 1 (1896): 60–69.

Graff, Gerald. *Professing Literature: An Institutional History.* Chicago: University of Chicago Press, 1987.

Graves, Robert Perceval. *Life of Sir William Rowan Hamilton.* Vol. 3. London: Longmans, Green, 1889.

Gray, Jeremy. *Plato's Ghost: The Modernist Transformation of Mathematics.* Princeton: Princeton University Press, 2008.

Hägglund, Martin. *Dying for Time.* Cambridge, MA: Harvard University Press, 2012.

Hale, Dorothy. *Social Formalism: The Novel in Theory from Henry James to the Present.* Palo Alto: Stanford University Press, 1998.

Hallett, Michael. *Cantorian Set Theory and Limitation of Size.* Oxford: Oxford University Press, 1996.

Hallward, Peter. *Badiou: A Subject to Truth.* Minneapolis: University of Minnesota Press, 2003.

Hardt, Michael, and Antonio Negri. *Multitude: War and Democracy in the Age of Empire.* New York: Penguin Books, 2005.

Hardy, Barbara. *Moral Art of Dickens.* 2nd ed. London: Bloomsbury Academic, 2002.

Hardy, Florence. *The Early Life of Thomas Hardy, 1840–1891*. New York: Macmillan, 1928.

Hardy, Thomas. *The Collected Letters*. Vol. 1, *1840–1892*. Edited by Richard Little Purdy and Michael Millgate. Oxford: Clarendon Press, 1979.

———. *Jude the Obscure*. Edited by Dennis Taylor. New York: Penguin Classics, 1998.

———. "The Science of Fiction." *New Review* 4 (1891): 315–19.

———. "The Tree of Knowledge." *New Review* 10 (1894): 681.

Harvey, David. *A Brief History of Neoliberalism*. Oxford: Oxford University Press, 2007.

Hayot, Eric. *On Literary Worlds*. Oxford: Oxford University Press, 2012.

Hays, K. Michael, ed. *Architecture Theory since 1968*. Cambridge, MA: MIT Press, 2000.

Hegel, G. W. F. *Hegel's Aesthetics: Lectures on Fine Art*. Vol. 1. Translated by T. M. Knox. Reprint, Oxford: Oxford University Press, 1998.

———. *Phenomenology of Spirit*. Translated by A. V. Miller. Oxford: Oxford University Press, 1979.

Henderson, Andrea. "Math for Math's Sake: Non-Euclidean Geometry, Aestheticism, and *Flatland*." *PMLA* 124, no. 2 (2009): 455–71.

———. "Symbolic Logic and the Logic of Symbolism." *Critical Inquiry* 41, no. 1 (2014): 78–101.

Hensley, Nathan K. *Forms of Empire: The Poetics of Victorian Sovereignty*. Oxford: Oxford University Press, 2017.

Heuser, Ryan, and Long Le-Khac. "A Quantitative Literary History of 2,958 Nineteenth-Century British Novels: The Semantic Cohort Method." Stanford Literary Lab, Pamphlet Series #4. May 2012. http://litlab.stanford.edu/pamphlets/.

Hollingsworth, Cristopher, ed. *Alice beyond Wonderland: Essays for the Twenty-First Century*. Iowa City: University of Iowa Press, 2009.

Jaffe, Audrey. *The Affective Life of the Average Man: The Victorian Novel and the Stock-Market Graph*. Columbus: Ohio State University Press, 2010.

———. *Vanishing Points: Dickens, Narrative, and the Subject of Omniscience*. Berkeley: University of California Press, 1991.

Jagoda, Patrick. *Network Aesthetics*. Chicago: University of Chicago Press, 2016.

———. "Wired." *Critical Inquiry* 38, no. 1 (2011): 189–99.

James, Henry. *The Art of Fiction and Other Essays*. Edited by Morris Roberts. New York: Oxford University Press, 1948.

———. *The Art of the Novel*. Chicago: University of Chicago Press, 2011.

———. *Literary Criticism: French Writers, Other European Writers, the Prefaces to the New York Edition*. New York: Library of America, 1984.

Jameson, Fredric. *An American Utopia: Dual Power and the Universal Army*. Edited by Slavoj Žižek. New York: Verso, 2016.

———. *The Antinomies of Realism*. New York: Verso, 2013.

———. *Archaeologies of the Future: The Desire Called Utopia and Other Science Fictions*. New York: Verso, 2007.

———. "Architecture and the Critique of Ideology." In *Architecture, Criticism, and Ideology*, edited by Joan Ockmanm, 51–87. Princeton: Princeton Architectural Press, 1985.

———. *The Geopolitical Aesthetic: Cinema and Space in the World System*. Bloomington: Indiana University Press, 1995.

———. *Ideologies of Theory*. 1988. New York: Verso, 2009.

———. *The Political Unconscious: Narrative as a Socially Symbolic Act*. Ithaca: Cornell University Press, 1982.

———. "Postmodernism, or the Cultural Logic of Late Capitalism." *New Left Review* 146 (1984): 53–92.

———. *Postmodernism, or, the Cultural Logic of Late Capitalism*. Durham: Duke University Press, 1992.

———. "The Realist Floorplan." In *On Signs*, edited by Marshall Blonsky, 373–83. Baltimore: Johns Hopkins University Press, 1985.

———. *The Seeds of Time*. New York: Columbia University Press, 1996.

———. *Valences of the Dialectic*. New York: Verso, 2010.

Jameson, Fredric, and Michael Speaks. "Envelopes and Enclaves: The Space of Post-Civil Society (An Architectural Conversation)." *Assemblage* 17 (1992): 30–37.

Johnson, Barbara. "My Monster/My Self." In *A World of Difference*, 144–54. Baltimore: Johns Hopkins University Press, 1989.

Johnson, Edgar. *Charles Dickens: His Tragedy and Triumph*. New York: Simon and Schuster, 1952.

Kaufman, Robert. Review of *Formal Charges: The Shaping of Poetry in British Romanticism*, by Susan J. Wolfson. Romantic Circles. 15 January 2001. https://www.rc.umd.edu/reviews-blog/susan-j-wolfson-formal-charges-shaping-poetry-british-romanticism.

Kline, Morris. *Mathematical Thought from Ancient to Modern Times*. Oxford: Oxford University Press, 1972.

———. *Mathematics for the Nonmathematician*. New York: Dover, 1985.

Kornbluh, Anna. "Freud's Return to Lacan." In *After Lacan*, edited by Ankhi Mukherjee, 41–57. Cambridge: Cambridge University Press, 2018.

———. *Realizing Capital: Financial and Psychic Economies in Victorian Form*. New York: Fordham University Press, 2013.

———. "Thomas Hardy's End of Prose." In *BRANCH: Britain, Representation, and Nineteenth-Century History*, edited by Dino Franco Felluga. Extension of Romanticism and Victorianism on the Net. http://www.branchcollective.org/?ps_articles=anna-kornbluh-thomas-hardys-end-of-prose.

Kramnick, Jonathan, and Anahid Nersessian. "Form and Explanation." *Critical Inquiry* 43, no. 3 (2017): 650–69.

Kreilkamp, Ivan. "Petted Things: *Wuthering Heights* and the Animal." *Yale Journal of Criticism* 18, no. 1 (2005): 87–110.

Kurnick, David. *Empty Houses: Theatrical Failure and the Novel*. Princeton: Princeton University Press, 2012.

Lacan, Jacques. *Écrits: The First Complete Edition in English*. Translated by Bruce Fink. New York: W.W. Norton, 2006.

———. *The Four Fundamental Concepts: The Seminar of Jacques Lacan, Book XI*. Edited by Jacques Alain-Miller. Translated by Alan Sheridan. New York: W.W. Norton, 1998.

———. "L'étourdit." In *Autres écrits*. Paris: Seuil, 2001.

———. "Of Structure as an Inmixing of an Otherness Prerequisite to Any Subject Whatever." In *The Structuralist Controversy*, edited by Richard Macksey, 186–96. Baltimore: Johns Hopkins University Press, 2007.

———. *On Feminine Sexuality, the Limits of Love and Knowledge: The Seminar of Jacques Lacan, Book XX, Encore*. Edited by Jacques Alain-Miller. Translated by Bruce Fink. New York: W. W. Norton, 1999.

———. *The Other Side of Psychoanalysis: The Seminar of Jacques Lacan, Book XVII*. Edited by Jacques Alain-Miller. Translated by Russell Grigg. New York: W.W. Norton, 2007.

———. *The Psychoses: The Seminar of Jacques Lacan, Book III.* Edited by Jacques Alain-Miller. Translated by Russell Grigg. New York: W.W. Norton, 1997.

Laclau, Ernesto. "Bare Life or Social Indeterminacy?" In *Giorgio Agamben: Sovereignty and Life,* edited by Matthew Calarco and Steven DeCaroli, 11–22. Stanford: Stanford University Press, 2007.

Latour, Bruno. *We Have Never Been Modern.* Translated by Catherine Porter. Cambridge, MA: Harvard University Press, 1993.

Leach, Neil. *Rethinking Architecture: A Reader in Cultural Theory.* 1st ed. New York: Routledge, 2005.

Lefebvre, Henri. *The Production of Space.* Translated by Donald Nicholson-Smith. New York: Wiley-Blackwell, 1992.

———. *Toward an Architecture of Enjoyment.* Edited by Łukasz Stanek. Translated by Robert Bononno. Minneapolis: University of Minnesota Press, 2014.

Leiter, Brian. "Legal Formalism and Legal Realism: What Is the Issue?" *Legal Theory* 16, no. 2 (2010): 111–33.

Lesjak, Carolyn. "1750 to the Present: Acts of Enclosure and Their Afterlife." In *BRANCH: Britain, Representation, and Nineteenth-Century History,* edited by Dino Franco Felluga. Extension of Romanticism and Victorianism on the Net. http://www.branchcollective.org/?ps_articles=carolyn-lesjak-1750-to-the-present-acts-of-enclosure-and-their-afterlife.

Levine, Caroline. "The Enormity Effect." *Genre* 50, no. 1 (2017): 59–75.

———. *Forms: Whole, Rhythm, Hierarchy, Network.* Princeton: Princeton University Press, 2017.

———. "Narrative Networks: *Bleak House* and the Affordances of Form." *Novel: A Forum on Fiction* 42, no. 3 (2009): 517–23.

———. "Victorian Realism." In *The Cambridge Companion to the Victorian Novel,* edited by Deirdre David, 84–106. 2nd ed. Cambridge: Cambridge University Press, 2012.

Levine, George, ed. *Aesthetics and Ideology.* Newark: Rutgers University Press, 1994.

———. *The Realistic Imagination: English Fiction from Frankenstein to Lady Chatterley.* Chicago: University of Chicago Press, 1981.

Levinson, Marjorie. "Notes and Queries on Names and Numbers." Romantic Circles. 2013. http://www.rc.umd.edu/praxis/numbers/HTML/praxis.2013.levinson.html.

———. "What Is New Formalism?" *PMLA* 122, no. 2 (2007): 558–69.

Lévi-Strauss, Claude. *Structural Anthropology.* New York: Basic Books, 1973.

Lewis, Clarence Irving. *A Survey of Symbolic Logic.* Berkeley: University of California Press, 1918.

Livingston, Paul. *The Politics of Logic: Badiou, Wittgenstein, and the Consequences of Formalism.* New York: Routledge, 2014.

Loraux, Nicole. *The Divided City: On Memory and Forgetting in Ancient Athens.* New York: Zone Books, 2006.

Lukács, Georg. *The Historical Novel.* Translated by Hannah Mitchell and Stanley Mitchell. Lincoln: University of Nebraska Press, 1983.

———. *The Theory of the Novel.* Translated by Anna Bostock. Cambridge, MA: MIT Press, 1971.

———. *Writer and Critic, and Other Essays.* Translated by Arthur Kahn. Lincoln: iUniverse, 2005.

Lupton, Julia Reinhard. *Citizen-Saints: Shakespeare and Political Theology.* Chicago: University of Chicago Press, 2005.

Macpherson, Sandra. "A Little Formalism." *ELH* 82, no. 2 (2015): 385–405.

Malthus, Thomas. *An Essay on the Principle of Population.* New York: Oxford World Classics, 1999.

Marder, Elissa. *Dead Time: Temporal Disorders in the Wake of Modernity.* Stanford: Stanford University Press, 2002.

Marx, Karl. *Capital.* Vol. 1. New York: Penguin, 1992.

———. *The Communist Manifesto.* New York: Penguin, 2002.

———. *A Contribution to the Critique of Political Economy.* New York: International Publications, 1979.

———. *Critique of Hegel's Philosophy of Right.* Cambridge: Cambridge University Press, 1970.

———. *Grundrisse: Foundations of the Critique of Political Economy* (rough draft). New York: Penguin Books in association with New Left Review, 1993.

———. *Mathematical Manuscripts of Karl Marx.* London: New Park Publications, 1983.

Marx, Karl, and Friedrich Engels. *The German Ideology, including Theses on Feuerbach.* Amherst, NY: Prometheus Books, 1998.

Matz, Aaron. *Satire in an Age of Realism.* Cambridge: Cambridge University Press, 2010.

———. "Terminal Satire and Jude the Obscure." *ELH* 73 (2006): 519–47.

McCarty, Willard. "Modeling: A Study in Words and Meanings." In *A Companion to Digital Humanities,* edited by Susan Schreibman, Ray Siemens, and John Unsworth. Oxford: Blackwell, 2004. http://www.digitalhumanities.org/companion/.

McGowan, Todd. *Enjoying What We Don't Have.* Lincoln: University of Nebraska Press, 2013.

McGurl, Mark. *The Novel Art: Elevations of American Fiction after Henry James.* Princeton: Princeton University Press, 2001.

———. "The Posthuman Comedy." *Critical Inquiry* 38, no. 3 (2012): 533–53.

McNulty, Tracy. "The Commandment against the Law: Writing and Divine Justice in Walter Benjamin's 'Critique of Violence.'" *Diacritics* 37, nos. 2–3 (2007): 34–60.

———. "The Event of the Letter: Two Approaches to the Law and Its Real." *Cardozo Law Review* 29, no. 5 (2008): 2209–38.

———. *Wrestling with the Angel: Experiments in Symbolic Life.* New York: Columbia University Press, 2014.

Miller, D. A. *The Novel and the Police.* Berkeley: University of California Press, 1988.

Miller, J. Hillis. *Ariadne's Thread: Story Lines.* New Haven: Yale University Press, 1995.

———. *Charles Dickens: The World of His Novels.* Cambridge, MA: Harvard University Press, 1958.

———. *The Form of Victorian Fiction.* South Bend: University of Notre Dame Press, 1970.

Mitchell, W. J. T. *Iconology: Image, Text, Ideology.* Chicago: University of Chicago Press, 1986.

Montag, Warren. "Necro-Economics: Adam Smith and Death in the Life of the Universal." *Radical Philosophy* 134 (2005). https://www.radicalphilosophy.com/article/necro-economics.

Monterrey, Tomas. "Architecture in Hardy's Narrative Technique." In *Traditions and Innovations: Commemorating Forty Years of English Studies at ULL (1963–2003),* edited by Manuel Brito, 325–33. Tenerife: RCEI, 2004.

Moretti, Franco. *Graphs, Maps, Trees: Abstract Models for Literary History.* New York: Verso, 2007.

Morson, Gary, and Caryl Emerson. *Mikhail Bakhtin: Creation of a Prosaics.* Stanford: Stanford University Press, 1990.

Moten, Fred, and Stefano Harney. *The Undercommons: Fugitive Planning and Black Study.* New York: Autonomedia, 2013.

Mucignat, Rosa. *Realism and Space in the Novel, 1795–1869: Imagined Geographies.* New York: Routledge, 2016.

Murray, Patrick. "The Social and Material Transformation of Production by Capital." In *The Constitution of Capital*, edited by Riccardo Bellofiore and Nicola Taylor, 243–73. New York: Palgrave, 2004.

Nagle, D. Brendan. *The Household as the Foundation of Aristotle's Polis.* Cambridge: Cambridge University Press, 2006.

Ngai, Sianne. *Our Aesthetic Categories: Zany, Cute, Interesting.* Cambridge, MA: Harvard University Press, 2015.

Nobus, Dany. "Lacan's Science of the Subject: Between Linguistics and Topology." In *The Cambridge Companion to Lacan*, edited by Jean-Michel Rabaté, 50–68. Cambridge: Cambridge University Press, 2003.

North, Joseph. *Literary Criticism: A Concise Political History.* Cambridge, MA: Harvard University Press, 2017.

Novaes, Catarina Dutilh. *Formal Languages in Logic: A Philosophical and Cognitive Analysis.* Cambridge: Cambridge University Press, 2014.

Orlemanski, Julie. "Scales of Reading." *Exemplaria* 26, nos. 2–3 (2014): 215–33.

Pecora, Vincent. *Households of the Soul.* Baltimore: Johns Hopkins University Press, 1997.

Pinkard, Terry. *Hegel's Phenomenology: The Sociality of Reason.* Cambridge: Cambridge University Press, 1996.

Pluth, Ed. *Badiou: A Philosophy of the New.* Cambridge: Polity, 2010.

Poovey, Mary. *Making of a Social Body.* Chicago: University of Chicago Press, 1995.

Puckett, Kent. "Caucus-Racing." *Novel: A Forum on Fiction* 47, no. 1 (2014): 11–23.

Pycior, Helena M. "At the Intersection of Mathematics and Humor: Lewis Carroll's 'Alices' and Symbolical Algebra." *Victorian Studies* 28, no. 1 (1984): 149–70.

Ramazani, Jahan. *Poetry of Mourning: The Modern Elegy from Hardy to Heaney.* Chicago: University of Chicago Press, 1994.

Rancière, Jacques. *The Politics of Aesthetics.* London: Bloomsbury, 2006.

Ransom, John Crowe. "The Concrete Universal." *Kenyon Review* 16, no. 4 (1954): 554–64.

Read, Jason. *The Micro-Politics of Capital: Marx and the Prehistory of the Present.* Albany: SUNY Press, 2003.

Reinhard, Kenneth. "Lacan and Monotheism: Psychoanalysis and the Traversal of Cultural Fantasy." *Jouvert* 3, no. 12 (1999). http://english.chass.ncsu.edu/jouvert/v3i12/reinha.htm http://english.chass.ncsu.edu/jouvert/v3i12/reinha.htm.

Richards, Joan L. *Mathematical Visions: The Pursuit of Geometry in Victorian England.* New York: Academic Press, 1988.

Robbins, Bruce. "Telescopic Philanthropy: Professionalism and Responsibility in *Bleak House*." In *Nation and Narration*, edited by Homi K. Bhabha, 213–30. New York: Routledge, 1990.

———. *Upward Mobility and the Common Good: Toward a Literary History of the Welfare State.* Princeton: Princeton University Press, 2007.

Robinson, Cervin, and Joel Herschman. *Architecture Transformed: A History of the Photography of Buildings from 1839 to the Present.* Cambridge, MA: MIT Press/Architectural League of New York, 1987.

Rosenberg, Jord/ana. "The Molecularization of Sexuality: On Some Primitivisms of the Present." *Theory and Event* 17, no. 2 (2014). https://muse.jhu.edu/article/546470.

Ross, Kristin. *Communal Luxury: The Political Imaginary of the Paris Commune.* New York: Verso, 2015.

———. *The Emergence of Social Space: Rimbaud and the Paris Commune.* New York: Verso, 2008.

Rothenberg, Molly Anne. *The Excessive Subject.* Cambridge: Polity Press, 2013.

Said, Edward W. *Beginnings: Intention and Method.* New York: Basic Books, 1975.

Santner, Eric. *The Royal Remains: The People's Two Bodies and the Endgame of Sovereignty.* Chicago: University of Chicago Press, 2011.

Shklovsky, Victor. "Art as Device." *Poetics Today* 36, no. 3 (2015): 151–74.

———. *Theory of Prose.* Elmwood Park, IL: Dalkey Archive Press, 1990.

Shonkwiler, Alison, and Leigh Claire La Berge, eds. *Reading Capitalist Realism.* Iowa City: University of Iowa Press, 2014.

Steinlight, Emily. "Dickens's 'Supernumeraries' and the Biopolitical Imagination of Victorian Fiction." *Novel: A Forum on Fiction* 43, no. 2 (2010): 227–50.

Stevens, Ann H. *Literary Theory and Criticism: An Introduction.* Peterborough, ON: Broadview Press, 2015.

Talbot, William Henry Fox. "Some Account of the Art of Photogenic Drawing." In *Photography into Print*, edited by Vicki Goldberg, 36–48. New York: Simon and Schuster, 1981.

Thompson, Ewa M. *Russian Formalism and Anglo-American New Criticism: A Comparative Study.* Berlin: De Gruyter Mouton, 1971.

Throesch, Elizabeth. "Nonsense in the Fourth Dimension of Literature: Hyperspace Philosophy, the 'New' Mathematics, and the Alice Books." In *Alice beyond Wonderland: Essays for the Twenty-First Century*, edited by Cristopher Hollingsworth, 37–52. Iowa City: University of Iowa Press, 2009.

Toscano, Alberto, and Jeff Kinkle. *Cartographies of the Absolute.* London: Zero Books, 2015.

Trotsky, Leon. *Literature and Revolution.* Edited by William Keach. Chicago: Haymarket Books, 2005.

Tschumi, Bernard. *Architecture and Disjunction.* Cambridge, MA: MIT Press, 1996.

Tucker, Irene. *The Moment of Racial Sight: A History.* Chicago: University of Chicago Press, 2013.

Turner, Victor. "Liminal to Liminoid, in Play, Flow, and Ritual: An Essay in Comparative Symbology." *Rice University Studies* 60, no. 3 (1974): 53–92.

V21 Collective. "Forum on Strategic Presentism." *Victorian Studies* 59, no. 1 (2016): 87–116.

Watt, Ian. *The Rise of the Novel: Studies in Defoe, Richardson, and Fielding.* Berkeley: University of California Press, 2001.

Wegner, Phillip. "Things as They Were or Are: On Russell Banks's Global Realisms." In *Reading Capitalist Realism*, edited by Alison Shonkwiler and Leigh Claire La Berge, 89–112. Iowa City: University of Iowa Press, 2014.

Wellek, René. "The Concept of Realism in Literary Scholarship." *Neophilologus* 45, no. 1 (1961): 1–20.

Williams, Raymond. *Marxism and Literature.* Oxford: Oxford University Press, 1977.

Wilson, Robin. *Lewis Carroll in Numberland: His Fantastical Mathematical Logical Life.* New York: W. W. Norton, 2010.

Wolfson, Susan J. *Formal Charges: The Shaping of Poetry in British Romanticism.* Palo Alto: Stanford University Press, 1999.

———. "Reading for Form." *MLQ: Modern Language Quarterly* 61, no. 1 (2000): 1–16.

Woloch, Alex. "*Bleak House* 19, 20, 21." *boundary2online.* 4 October 2016. https://www.boundary2.org/2016/10/alex-woloch-bleak-house-19-20-21/.

———. *The One vs. the Many: Minor Characters and the Space of the Protagonist in the Novel.* Princeton: Princeton University Press, 2003.

———. *Or Orwell: Writing and Democratic Socialism.* Cambridge, MA: Harvard University Press, 2016.

Zafiropoulos, Markos. *Lacan and Levi-Strauss.* London: Karnac Books, 2010.

Žižek, Slavoj. *For They Know Not What They Do: Enjoyment as a Political Factor.* 1991. New York: Verso, 2007.

———. *Less than Nothing: Hegel and the Shadow of Dialectical Materialism.* New York: Verso, 2012.

———. *Living in the End Times.* New York: Verso, 2010.

———. *Tarrying with the Negative.* Durham: Duke University Press, 1993.

Zupančič, Alenka. *What IS Sex?* Cambridge, MA: MIT Press, 2017.

Index

Page numbers followed by *f* refer to figures.